The Garda Club

A History of Dublin Metropolitan
Garda Recreation Club

TAURANT
WALTER

The Garda Club

A History of Dublin Metropolitan Garda Recreation Club

Edited by Antoinette Walker

First published in 2011 by
The Dublin Metropolitan Garda Recreation Club
Westmanstown Sports & Conference Centre
Clonsilla, Dublin 15, Ireland

ISBN 978-0-9565713-0-4

Design and layout by Joseph Gervin
Additional photography by Arnold Bell
Printed in Dublin by Wood Printcraft

Contents

Foreword

THE Garda Recreation Club, more affectionately known as Harrington Street, has for many decades been important to members of An Garda Síochána, particularly those serving in the Dublin Metropolitan Region. Those individuals who went before us and had the vision to put such facilities in place were providing a platform on which members of An Garda Síochána, their friends and families could build personal and professional relationships. The idea to provide opportunities through the Garda Recreation Club for members to relax in comfortable surroundings or organise promotion, retirement or other functions was truly visionary.

Throughout its history, the club went from strength to strength and from these not too humble beginnings in Harrington Street grew first the concept and then the reality of what is now Westmanstown Sports and Conference Centre.

I had the privilege of being associated with Westmanstown Golf Club since its inception and in those embryonic days served on the first committee of the Golf Club and later as Captain in 1994 and President in 1997. There are many other sporting clubs associated with An Garda Síochána (GAA, soccer, tennis, bowling, rugby, etc.) who have made Westmanstown their home, providing the ideal opportunity for us to share with our friends the sporting and recreational activities ongoing there.

I consider myself fortunate to have played some small part in the overall development of the Garda Recreation Club, and I do hope the very proud tradition of supporting the club will continue well into the future, hard as I know it is for people to continue contributions to it with other competing demands.

This book provides an ideal opportunity for all who read it to capture the knowledge and early history, including those associated with it. I congratulate and commend all involved in its compilation and publication.

Martin Callinan

Martin Callinan
Commissioner of An Garda Síochána

Foreword

IT is a great privilege and honour for me as chairman of the Garda Recreation Club to preside over the launch of this book on the history of the club.

It is true that great achievements come from small beginnings and in this case the determination of the late Edmund Garvey, when as chairman he led his small committee towards the purchase of Harrington Street and later Stackstown Golf Club. This was the beginning of great dedication, hard work and foresight from the numerous committees throughout the past fifty years, which provided the excellent facilities that we enjoy today.

This book gives an insight into the numerous clubs that have developed along with the Garda Club on this great journey, and I have no doubt it will continue well into the future.

I would like to take this opportunity to thank all our members, both past and present, for their loyalty and support and to all the committees for their dedication, commitment and drive which has made the club what it is today.

My congratulations and thanks go out to all concerned with the publication of this book, which like the club itself is intended for posterity.

David Dowling
Chairman
Dublin Metropolitan Garda Recreation Club

Foreword

Henry Ford & Son Limited has been a strong supporter of the Garda Recreation Club and, in particular, the Westmanstown Sports and Leisure Centre for nearly twenty years. From the first days of our involvement, I quickly saw how the Garda Recreation Club was such an important element of An Garda Síochána. I was also very impressed with the organisational ability of the club and its members.

To achieve a facility of the high standard of Westmanstown requires a huge amount of work and commitment. On practically every page of *The Garda Club* you can see evidence of that sense of passion and commitment which permeates every section of the Garda Recreation Club.

The book does a great job in showing the many years of effort, both individual and collective, of members and office holders of the club that went into establishing and providing the excellent facilities that are at the disposal of not just Garda members but also the wider civilian society.

I am sure the Garda Recreation Club and its facilities will continue to be an important part of the lives of individual members of An Garda Síochána for many years to come. In this regard, I and the team at Ford Ireland look forward to maintaining our strong working relationship with the club executive.

Edward J Murphy
Chairman and Managing Director
Henry Ford & Son Limited

Feel the difference

Acknowledgements

THE idea to publish a book on the history of the Dublin Metropolitan Garda Recreation Club was born out of a recognition to celebrate the great achievements of its many committed members and to record the remarkable sporting traditions of An Garda Síochána. Compiling a book that drew on club records and the memories of so many individuals involved in the Garda Recreation Club was no easy task. In this effort, it relied on many contributions – penned, spoken or photographed – to capture the scale of the undertakings and the spirit of the times.

The Garda Club book committee – comprising Jim Murphy, Helen Corrigan and Christy McCarthy – and the editor wish to express their gratitude to the following for their invaluable contributions and to all who made this publication possible: Garda Commissioner Martin Callinan, Derek Byrne, Dave Dowling, Conor McGuinness, Enda McCabe, Fergus Healy, Tony Twomey, Dick McDonnell, Fachtna Murphy, Patrick McGee (Garda Museum), the National Library of Ireland, Angela Bergin (Garda College Library), Mary Walker, Stephen Rea *(Evening Herald)*, Liam Collins *(Irish Independent),* the late Cathal O'Shannon, the late Tom Ryan, the late Brian Prendergast, Tony Ruane, John Duffy, John Murphy, Oliver Nugent, Paddy Murray, Fr Joe Kennedy CP, Charlie Gaffney, Seán O'Mahoney, Mary Daly, Chris Garvey, Eddie Ryan, Noel Burke, Michael B Carroll, Bosco Muldoon, Majella Ryan, Jim Tymond, Cyril Doyle, Eddie MacBride, Gerry Byrne, Edward Doyle, Charlie O'Connor (FÁS), Ned Ryan, Eamonn Brady, Colm Mohan (Pontederia), Robbie Dolan (Crunch Fitness), Liam O'Brien (AIB), Paddy O'Reilly, PJ Gallagher, Richie Garvey, Teresa Murphy, Clare Murphy, George Kyne, Ray Campion, Gus Keating, Lucy Nugent, Carmel Synnott, Brendan Quinn, Dominic Power, John MacNamara, Jo O'Leary, Gabriel McIntyre, Liam Geraghty, John Doherty, Kate Curtin, Peter O'Connor, Jerome Twomey, Willie Cooper, and the staff at both Harrington Street and Westmanstown.

A special word of thanks to the late Brian Lenihan TD, who was a strong supporter of the Westmanstown Project and always available and willing to help in whatever way possible. He was proud of his connections to the Garda Club and of his father-in-law, Tom Ryan, one of the founder members of the club.

Heartfelt thanks are also accorded to the governing bodies down through the years and the many members, the unsung heroes, who gave freely of their time and energy in the development of the club in the early days. Finally, for the sponsorship of this book, the Garda Recreation Club gratefully acknowledges the assistance of Eddie Murphy of Ford Ireland, and also for its enduring support to the club over many years.

History is a guide to navigation in perilous times.
History is who we are and why we are the way we are.

David C McCullough

A Police Force is Born

Chapter

1

The Garda Síochána will succeed, not by force of arms or numbers, but by their moral authority as servants of the people.

Chapter 1
A Police Force is Born

THE story of Irish policing is a unique one. It is inextricably linked to the history and culture of Ireland in all its richness and upheavals. An Garda Síochána as we know it today as an organised body of police officers of various rank, responsible for maintaining and enforcing law, was set up in 1922 with the foundation of the Irish state. However, policing on the island of Ireland had various incarnations in the 700-year history of British rule. As the first colony in the British Empire, Ireland over seven centuries became a testing ground for the authorities to put down rebellion and uprising, while striving to maintain civil order. Responsibility for keeping law and order in the early days of colonial rule fell to the military, and later in the eighteenth century to baronial constabularies governed by the local aristocracy as well as a system of watchmen, who patrolled towns and cities and were paid for by the local authority, and revenue police. In the event of rebellion, the British army and local militia could be relied upon to quell any civil unrest and restore order.

Modern policing in Ireland dates from 1814, when the Chief Secretary for Ireland, Robert Peel, introduced the Peace Preservation Force. In so doing, he unwittingly gave the word 'Peelers' to the English language. These new policemen bridged the gap between the traditional idea of the old constabulary and watch systems and the modern concept of a civil police force. In 1822, a separate Irish Constabulary was formed to tackle rampant lawlessness, which in 1836 subsumed the Peace Preservation Force to become a national police force. Even so, separate municipal police had existed in some cities previously, notably Dublin, Belfast and Derry. While the origins of policing in Dublin city lay in the night watch system, an Act of Parliament in 1786 saw the establishment of the Dublin Metropolitan Division. It was the first de facto 'police force' in the British Isles. The district was divided into four divisions headed by a high constable. The headquarters for the district was Dublin Castle and its recruit training depot was located nearby at Kevin Street. Unlike the Irish Constabulary, the Dublin Metropolitan Police (DMP) as they became known in 1836, were unarmed.

In 1867, the constabulary was conferred with the title of Royal Irish Constabulary (RIC) by Queen Victoria in recognition of its efforts in suppressing the Fenian Rising. Indeed the RIC came to serve as a model for policing trouble spots in the British Empire largely drawn on classical colonial lines: an armed, well-disciplined and utterly reliable force. By 1900, the RIC had approximately 11,000 men stationed in nearly 1,600 barracks around the country and these policemen became increasingly integrated into society. In its heyday the RIC had a Catholic membership of 75 per cent drawn from the people, according to Gregory Allen in *The Garda Síochána: Policing Independent Ireland 1922–1982*. Despite the social integration, the decade leading up to independence saw the fortunes of the RIC diminish. It was one of the most turbulent periods in Irish history, beginning with the backlash against the execution of the leaders of the 1916 Easter Rising and the internment of thousands of Irishmen in Britain. It resulted in a fierce and bloody military campaign waged by the Irish Republican Army (IRA) against the British Crown forces.

The long drawn-out fight for freedom over the period 1918 to 1921 resulted in the decimation of the RIC. The strength of the force was sorely depleted by the resignations and early retirements as well as the murder of many of its members. Under constant attack, the force retreated to the relative safety of heavily garrisoned towns and cities. In 1920, in an effort to augment the strength of the RIC, militias in the shape of the ill-disciplined Black and Tans and Auxiliaries joined forces with them and established what could only be described as a reign of terror. Any attacks on the British forces were met with savage reprisals against republicans.

A New Dawn

The end of the War of Independence came on 11 July 1921 with the signing of the Truce between the Irish Republican Army and the Crown forces. Some three weeks later, General Michael Collins and the Chief Secretary for Ireland, Sir Hamar Greenwood, met to discuss future policing of the new Ireland. It was by now widely accepted that the days of the RIC were numbered. Nationwide there was neither support nor sympathy for the RIC men and, despite the Truce, they were still targets of attack. In the interests of a peaceful changeover it was decided to retain the Dublin Metropolitan Police, as it was then constituted, for a further period.

Efforts to put an interim police force in place had begun in June 1921, when a general order confirmed the organisation of a police force called the Irish Republican Police (IRP). Formed from IRA Volunteers, Simon Donnelly was its chief of police and a commandant in each brigade area was appointed to oversee the local police officers attached to battalions and companies. The duties of the police officers were confined solely to public order and the detection and punishment of offenders, according to Garda archivist Gregory Allen.

Once the Anglo-Irish Treaty was signed on 6 December 1921, the need to establish a police force became ever more pressing. During the War of Independence, the rule of law had broken down and civil policing was largely in abeyance in most parts of the country. Furthermore, the threat of civil war loomed large when Anti-Treaty forces voiced their opposition to the settlement terms with Britain, and resorted to taking up arms again to achieve a United Ireland. Under the terms of the Treaty, the

RIC was to be disbanded and control of the Dublin Metropolitan Police transferred to the new Irish government. From 1922 until 1925 it was officially known as Poilíní Átha Cliath (the Dublin Police). The remnants of the RIC continued to be targets of attack, however. The date of their disbandment was set for 20 February 1922 but this was delayed for some time. As Conor Brady notes in *Guardians of the Peace*, it took just under seven months, from February to August 1922, for the 10,000 men of the RIC to disappear from the towns and villages of Ireland. The Royal Ulster Constabulary replaced it in the North and the Civic Guard in the South. Remnants of the RIC officer corps subsequently went abroad to influence policing in Britain, Palestine, India, Canada, Australia, New Zealand and other colonial outposts.

Civic Guard established

Setting up the Civic Guard required considerable planning. After ratification of the Treaty by Dáil Éireann on 7 January 1922, General Michael Collins, both chairman of the Provisional Government and Minister for Finance, set up a meeting for the purpose of establishing the new police force. Gregory Allen notes that the Provisional Government had at one stage considered the IRP as the new force and had appointed Seán Lemass as its first training officer. But by 17 January, Eamonn Duggan, Minister for Home Affairs, had ordered the volunteers assigned to police duties to rejoin their units until a regular police force was formed. In the meantime the responsibility for law and order fell to each volunteer company in its own area.

The Gresham Hotel, Dublin, was the scene of the inaugural meeting of the Police Organising Committee on 9 February 1922, which was presided over by General Richard Mulcahy, Minister for Defence. Also in attendance were Eamonn

RIC legacy

The RIC left a legacy to An Garda Síochána and to the Royal Ulster Constabulary by providing trained officers and personnel as a foundation for both forces. In addition, it left a network of barracks, defined Divisions, Districts and Sub-districts throughout Ireland, together with an established system of policing which required little modification and which has stood the test of time. The Depot itself – as a fully equipped, centrally located, training establishment – was probably the greatest legacy left by the RIC to An Garda Síochána.

Donal J O'Sullivan, The Depot: A History of the Garda Síochána Depot at the Phoenix Park, Dublin

Right: RIC sergeant

Duggan, Minister for Home Affairs, General Eoin O'Duffy, Chief of Staff of the National Army, Dublin City Alderman Michael Staines TD and a small group of Volunteer officers: Michael Ring, Patrick Brennan and Jeremiah Maher. Another Volunteer, Commandant Martin Lynch, joined the committee later in February. Efforts to secure the help of RIC men sympathetic to the Provisional Government and willing to train the new police force were successful. Much-needed professional police experience was provided to the committee by Patrick Joseph Walsh, District Inspector of the RIC in Letterkenny, County Donegal and John Kearney, District Inspector of the RIC in Boyle, County Roscommon. The meeting elected Michael Staines as chairman and Patrick Walsh as vice chairman of the committee. Both men later went on to become commissioner and deputy commissioner of the new police force, respectively. Subcommittees were set up to look into various aspects of the new force, such as organisation, recruiting, training, and conditions of service.

The committee set to work in earnest and delivered their recommendations to the Provisional Government by 27 February. According to Gregory Allen, Staines presented a 'blueprint for a "People's Guard", 4,300 strong, organised in 21 divisions, compared with about 7,000 men who patrolled 29 divisions in the twenty-six counties, excluding the city of Dublin, based on deployments in 1914'. They recommended that the police force be centrally controlled and responsible to the Executive Government. Administered by a commissioner, the force would be non-political, unarmed and called the Civic Guard. The policing of Dublin was left under the control of the DMP for the time being.

Reports of the time indicate that the Government accepted most if not all of the recommendations put to it by this founding committee. Indeed, the influence of Michael Collins was evident, though he had delegated the task of establishing the

Strength in numbers

The maximum estimated strength required is 4,119 ordinary Guards; the statutory maximum is 4,400, leaving a margin of about 200, if it should be considered necessary. There will be a small Reserve Force maintained in the Depot, a Reserve Force of about 200.

The number of barracks in the occupation of the RIC on the 1st June, 1914, exclusive of those situated in the Six North-Eastern Counties, was 1,129; the proposed total establishment of the Civic Guard provides for 807 stations.

Kevin O'Higgins TD, Minister for Home Affairs, Dáil Debates, 31 July 1923, Vol. 4

DMP mounted police in Kevin Street training depot

new police force to Staines: his idea was to have a force lightly armed with revolvers and truncheons, something similar to the RIC but with its own distinguishing uniform, insignia and rank titles. The committee recommended that there should be recruiting stations at each county headquarters, as well as a Civic Guard officer aided by a local medical officer and a representative of the National Army. At first, training commenced at the Royal Dublin Society (RDS) Showgrounds in Ballsbridge and later at the artillery barracks in Kildare town. Much later in 1923, it was transferred to the Depot at the Phoenix Park, where it remained until 1964 when it moved to its final location at Templemore, County Tipperary.

The type of recruit also came in for deep scrutiny. Clearly, candidates having previous military or police experience were favoured by the committee. In the selection of recruits, serving IRA men were to be preferred, then constables of the Irish Republican Police, RIC men who had been dismissed or resigned from the RIC or DMP for conscientious or patriotic motives, the civilian population, and, finally, members of the disbanded RIC and DMP. Recruits were to be at least 5 feet 9 inches, unmarried and between the ages of 19 and 27. They would also be compelled to sit examinations in reading, spelling and arithmetic. As it turned out, recruits to the new force came mostly from rural backgrounds. The western seaboard counties in particular supplied the greatest numbers. In the six months the new policemen waited to be issued with their new uniforms, they wore plain clothes with armbands to distinguish rank.

Attractive pay rates were proposed for the various ranks of the new police force, beginning with £3 10*s* a week for ordinary guards and rising to £1,300 a year for the commissioner. In a sign that Ireland was throwing off the shackles of imperialism and the privileged class, the committee recommended an end to the RIC officer cadet system: all promotions would henceforth come from the ranks, except for ex-RIC men who could expect promotion given their previous experience. In the event, this exception was to cause considerable grievance. In May 1922, a mutiny took place

Reluctant recruits

Most of the [recruits] were totally unused to any great discipline and found it difficult to adjust to life in the depot. Infringements such as being slovenly in dress, smoking on parade, having hands in pockets, talking to lady friends in the vicinity of the depot, visiting the pubs in Ballsbridge during the day and breaking out at night were quite common.

Liam McNiffe, A History of the Garda Síochána, *p17*

Top: **Dublin Metropolitan Police**
Above: **Recruits in Newbridge, County Kildare, July 1922**

Above: **Commissioner O'Duffy addressing Civic Guard members at the depot**
Below: **The Civic Guard in Dublin Castle in 1922**

in the training camp in Kildare when anti-Treaty sympathisers of the Provisional Government among the recruits seized the armoury and rebelled at the appointment of RIC officers to senior rank. According to Liam McNiffe in *A History of the Garda Síochána*, 6.5 per cent of recruits were RIC men.

Commissioner Staines responded by isolating the mutineers and depriving them of their pay, and set up a rival training centre in Dublin. Collins, desperate for a resolution in the threat of imminent civil war, met the men and promised to hold an inquiry. The mutiny lasted six weeks and was finally resolved when President Arthur Griffith and Eamonn Duggan intervened. They arrived at the depot and proposed that all men be paid all monies due to them, an inquiry be held immediately, and all the men be suspended. The subsequent inquiry recommended that the Civic Guard be technically disbanded and reformed with selective re-enrolment to weed out undesirables, that the force should be unarmed, and that no politicians should serve in the force. As a sitting TD for Dublin North-Central, this signalled the end of Commissioner Staines' police career. He was subsequently replaced by General Eoin O'Duffy in September 1922. The new policemen were also obliged to take an oath in which they would swear not to join any political party or secret society, including the Freemasons.

Moral authority

The attempt to defy the authority of Commissioner Staines had served only to reinforce the absolute need for an unarmed force. Gone were the armed garrisons, the Martini-Henry carbines, the bayonet and the sword. Instead, there was the support of the community and a philosophy of moral authority for policing independent Ireland. The overriding creed of the new force was that it would operate as the servants of the people. In the execution of this role, there was to be a sharp focus on crime prevention and public order by maintaining close contact with the community and gaining its consent and approval.

The oft-quoted statement of Commissioner Staines on the formation of the Civic Guard that the 'Garda Síochána will succeed, not by force of arms or numbers, but by their moral authority as servants of the people' has endured to this day. In today's language, this could be interpreted as the original mission statement of An

Jump and roll

The energy and exuberance of such large numbers of [recruits] manifested itself in pranks on fellow recruits, as well as the occasional jump from a moving train in order to be back for roll-call.

Liam McNiffe, A History of the Garda Síochána, *p16*

General Eoin O'Duffy

Garda Síochána. The prophetic and far-seeing nature of this statement, mission or otherwise, has frequently been acknowledged and lauded. The force also had its own motto, according to Donal J O'Sullivan in *The Depot: A History of the Garda Síochána Depot at the Phoenix Park, Dublin*. He notes how recruits in training were constantly reminded of the guidelines of An Garda Síochána: 'Service, law, justice, duty.'

Some of the first new recruits were dispatched to police Dublin city and became members of the Poilíní Átha Cliath. This allocation resulted in large numbers of young men being attached to stations within their area of operation. The Civic Guard, as with its predecessor the RIC, was also set up along semi-military lines. The young single men attached to the various stations were obliged to live in the station or barracks and be in their allocated accommodation by 12 midnight when not on duty. This obligation prevailed until the late 1950s.

Naming the force

The name for the proposed new force was the subject of lengthy debate. The committee suggested that it be named 'The People's Guard'. However, the Provisional Government, not exactly enamoured with this rather banal title, thought otherwise and changed it to the 'Civic Guard'. It is believed this originated from Henry Grattan's unarmed Civic Guard that existed in Dublin in 1795, and which was supervised by the Lord Mayor and Dublin Corporation. By all accounts, this title became popular and was favoured by Michael Collins. The title Civic Guard endured until 31 July 1923, when at the end of a lengthy, controversial Dáil debate on the Civic Guard Miscellaneous Provisions Bill, it was proposed by the Labour TD Cathal O'Shannon that the title of the Bill before the House be changed to 'An Garda Síochána Miscellaneous Provisions Bill'. Cathal O'Shannon, a renowned

Right: An inspection during the 1940s

125B

Pay scales in the Civic Guard

Pay was better in all ranks than it had been in the RIC. The Commissioner, whose functions were exactly similar to those of the RIC Inspector-General, was to receive £1,300 a year plus a lodging allowance of £120; a Chief Superintendent was to receive £650 on appointment, rising to £800; a Superintendent was to receive £400 on appointment, rising to £600, and an Inspector was to start at £310, rising to £350. A sergeant was to draw £5 a week on appointment, rising to £5 12*s* and a guard £3 10*s*, rising to £4 10*s*.

Conor Brady, Guardians of the Peace, *pp44–45*

Above: **Directing traffic in Dublin in the 1940s**
Left: **Harry Feeney as a young guard in 1923**

politician, trade unionist and journalist, had a particular interest in policing, though admittedly of a force less centralised. His life and career was bound inextricably to the emerging nation state – a one-time member of the Irish Republic Brotherhood and Conradh na Gaeilge; a founding member of the Irish Volunteers in Belfast in 1913; he assisted James Connolly as a trade union organiser for the Irish Transport and General Workers Union in Belfast and was a member of the Socialist Party of Ireland; interned following the 1916 Easter Rising; served in the Irish Republican Army in 1920/21; and elected to Dáil Éireann in the 1922 general election as a Labour Party TD for Louth-Meath. O'Shannon's foresight was impressive. Changing the title of the Bill in effect was a further recognition of the words already inscribed on the crest and badges of the force: 'Gárda Síochána' (Guardians of the Peace).

O'Shannon's proposal appears to have been unanimously accepted and was carried by the Dáil. Sadly, this historic amendment went unnoticed by the general public and the media of the day. Nonetheless, the Garda Síochána Miscellaneous Provisions Act 1923 came into being and this has been the official title of the force ever since. Its add-on of Garda Síochána na hÉireann, translated as 'Guardians of the Peace of Ireland', was subsequently adopted into everyday usage. In some cases, variants of the title, such as 'the Guards' or the Gardaí, became the norm.

After the Civil War, it was clear that a national force of armed detectives was needed to tackle the emerging political crime and violence, especially from republican quarters. As a consequence, the detective division of the Dublin Metropolitan Police, the infamous 'G Division', was transferred to Garda Headquarters to form the Special Branch. The amalgamation of the Dublin Metropolitan Police and the Garda Síochána took place in 1925, though the absorption of the DMP did undermine morale in the national force for a time.

Nonetheless, out of bloodshed and conflict a modern police force was born that had preservation of peace and moral authority as a central plank in its mission and which would stand it in good stead for many a year.

The title

'An Act to establish in Saorstát Éireann, and regulate a Police Force to be called the Civic Guard.'

Cathal O'Shannon: I move to substitute Garda Síochána for the words 'Civic Guard', if that would be in order.
Agreed.

Dáil Debates, 31 July 1923, Vol. 4

Right: Cathal O'Shannon

'The Pulse of the Nation'

Sport and Recreation in the Irish Police Forces

Chapter

2

Participation in athletic exercises has moral value. The man who is training for some form of competition will be more likely to keep both mind and body under control than the man to whom such incentive is lacking.

Chapter 2
'The Pulse of the Nation'

THE twin pursuits of sport and recreation were part and parcel of police life from earliest times. Sport was naturally a necessary element of police training, arising from its semi-military nature. However, it became more than just maintaining health and fitness for the rigours of active police work. It represented an *esprit de corps* and way of life that would serve policemen well in demoralising times. In many ways the RIC embodied all that was positive about sport. Pictures of the time portray fine specimens of muscular manhood in well-fitting uniforms that enhanced their form. According to Donal J O'Sullivan in *The Depot*, they had the 'finest physique and appearance of manhood in Ireland'.

The story of sport and recreation in An Garda Síochána is a remarkable one. All the more so because sport played a crucial part in forging strong bonds with local communities and healing war-induced divisions. Through participation in sport, many Garda members achieved great renown and became household names, in particular in Gaelic football and hurling, boxing and rowing. On the international scene, Garda members represented Ireland at various Olympic Games, for example, in boxing, judo and rowing.

In 1922, the sporting traditions of the RIC and DMP were a welcome legacy to the police force of the fledgling state. From earliest times, there were impressive sporting traditions in the old police forces. Soon after the RIC Depot was established in the Phoenix Park in 1842, approximately nine acres were allocated as a recreational and athletic facility. According to O'Sullivan in *The Depot*, at that time a railing was erected around the sports ground and a small dressing-room/pavilion was constructed. The RIC became deeply involved in athletics and team sports and participated as individuals at the highest level in field and track events around the country. Various police sports clubs existed and an annual sports day was organised on a grand scale, which attracted the citizenry of Dublin. By all accounts, the RIC had an excellent cricket team, boasting its own cricket grounds in the Phoenix Park. Tug-of-war and boxing were two sports that also gained special prominence in the RIC and DMP. These sports in particular could be relied upon to tackle a demoralised force in time-honoured fashion.

The history of tug-of war in Ireland is associated with the DMP, who had made their debut in the sport in the 1870s. Restoring morale in the DMP in the 1890s fell to Chief Superintendent John Mallon, who trained the tug-of-war team. So successful

Above: **Garda Transport Gaelic football team in 1924**
Below: **Garda football team (date unknown)**

Garda tug-of-war team in 1927

were his efforts that in 1893 the DMP became world champions by defeating the Royal Scots Greys. Members of the RIC also took part in boxing championships and frequently competed with teams from the army and foreign police forces. RIC boxers could also avail of the gymnasium facilities at the Depot for physical training and body-building exercises.

One important link between the RIC and Gaelic games, though eclipsed over the years, is Thomas St George McCarthy. A district inspector of the RIC stationed at Templemore, County Tipperary, McCarthy was a founder member of the Gaelic Athletic Association (GAA). He attended its inaugural meeting at Hayes Hotel, Thurles, on that memorable day on 1 November 1884. An Ireland rugby international, capped in 1881, and a sporting enthusiast, McCarthy had a profound love for Gaelic games. But any hopes of the RIC fielding a team were dashed when the GAA instituted a ban on the British Crown forces participating in Gaelic games, much to the disappointment of fellow founder Michael Cusack. It took over a hundred years for McCarthy's participation to gain recognition. This came about after the signing of the Good Friday Agreement and when Rule 21 of the GAA, banning police forces in Northern Ireland from playing Gaelic games, was abolished in 2001. In McCarthy's honour in October 2002, the Thomas St George McCarthy Cup was instituted. This was to became an annual challenge match in Gaelic football between the Garda GAA and the Police Service of Northern Ireland (PSNI). History was further in the making on Friday, 25 November 2011, when the two teams met on the hallowed grounds of Croke Park for the first time ever. The memorable occasion was witnessed by 150 guests, including Garda Commissioner Martin Callinan, PSNI Chief Constable Matt Baggott, Northern Ireland's Minister of Justice David Ford MLA and Deputy First Minister Martin McGuinness MLA. The Garda team ran out the winners on a scoreline of 4-16 to 1-8, though a thoroughly enjoyable game was had by all.

Circumstances conspired to make sport a mainstay of police life in the early days of the Civic Guard. A unique set of circumstances existed. From the earliest days at the RDS training depot in 1922, sport was a feature. A scarcity of police training manuals and lecturers in the RDS forced sport and drilling higher up the agenda. The emphasis became wholly on physical training – marching, drilling, athletics, boxing and wrestling. So much so that internal sporting events were arranged as well as events where the public could take part. This continued with the move to Kildare in April 1922. According to McNiffe in *A History of the Garda Síochána*, training there consisted of drill, police duty classes and some instruction in the Irish language, and football matches became a regular occurrence. Indeed the first annual sports of the Civic Guard was held in Kildare in September 1922. On that occasion, James Mulroy of Straide, County Mayo won the heavyweight boxing title and would later go on to receive the first Scott Medal for Valour in 1924. The following year, 1923, the annual Civic Guards sports day was held on 15 August in Croke Park. Again, such was its appeal that special train services from each division area were laid on for the occasion, as noted by McNiffe.

The second major influence was Commissioner O'Duffy who succeeded Commissioner Staines in September 1922. His dominant personality and love of games ensured that sports would play a prominent role in the new police force. O'Duffy's promotion of sport was born not just from a deep love but a moral philosophy. A healthy body in a healthy mind made a good policeman. Moreover, sport not only built characters but could restore morale as well. By bringing guards and people together, it was also a way to build communities on trust and friendship. Furthermore, it could heal divisions that existed in a country still licking the wounds of civil war. Sport was, in O'Duffy's words, 'the pulse of the nation'. Through his efforts, Garda clubs were established on a firm footing. A true nationalist, O'Duffy was highly enthusiastic about the guards participating in Gaelic sports. In February 1923, he issued a general circular to all stations urging the Civic Guards to join local hurling, football and athletic clubs. Through his encouragement, they could take part in any sport of their choice. In 1923–4, hurling, football, boxing, athletics, cycling and handball teams were formed at the Depot. Gradually over the years other sports emerged within the force such as rugby, soccer, tennis, pitch and putt, basketball and badminton.

The Civic Guard GAA Club was set up in 1922 in Dublin. A year later they took part in the Dublin Championships and the hurling team took the county title and dominated the scene for the remainder of the decade. Clearly, there was a certain interest in GAA games among the DMP as well. Mick Dunne, in *Playing with the Guards: The Story of the Garda GAA Club*, notes that a club representing the DMP had also applied to the Dublin County Board for club affiliation and had been accepted. This was in 1925, the year of amalgamation with An Garda Síochána, which may explain why nothing more was heard of the club in subsequent years. Dunne reflects that perhaps it was an attempt by those who served in the DMP to 'make some sort of mark' on the football history of the county before the DMP went out of existence. For a brief time, they fielded a football team in the city. They played a senior league match on 20 March 1925 against O'Dwyers, beating them, after which they met Kickhams, whom they also beat, as they did Keatings, but they were finally knocked out by O'Tooles on a score of 2-1 to 0-3.

O'Duffy's powers of persuasion and encouragement meant that about 7,000 young energetic, highly motivated men actively participated in sports in the 1920s. Such was his regard for the character of sportsmen that he trawled the country with indefatigable energy to recruit the best young sportsmen he could find. Many were renowned sportsmen in the national games, like Paddy Perry, a national handball champion. Many came from counties that were bastions of hurling, Gaelic football and handball such as Cork, Kerry, Tipperary, Galway, Clare and Mayo. O'Duffy was

Mother knows best

Sometime after winning the handball championship [in 1931], there was a banquet in Boyle at which the cup and medal were to be presented [to me before I headed off to work in America] and Eoin O'Duffy ... came down to make the presentation. He was a wonderful organiser and at the time very great emphasis was placed on sport in the Garda, much more than in the force nowadays, and O'Duffy was encouraging young sportsmen to join the force.

What I didn't know was that he'd met my mother the night he came to Boyle and asked how she felt about me going to America. Naturally, she said she'd prefer to have me stay at home. I didn't know Eoin O'Duffy at all at the time, but when I met him in the hotel he asked if I'd like to stay in Ireland. I answered: 'I would if I had a job, but it would have to be a fairly good job because I am going out to an uncle who has plans for me and I don't want to let him down.'

I told him I'd leave the decision to my mother – not knowing he'd already been talking to her. So that year I was brought into the Guards, but of course I didn't get special privileges because I was a handballer: I had to go through the same training – six months in the Depot – as everyone else.

Paddy Perry, Irish Handball Golden Jubilee Yearbook, *1974*

also surrounded by like-minded individuals when it came to sport. On amalgamation of the DMP and An Garda Síochána in 1925, he was greatly aided in his endeavours by the DMP Commissioner William Murphy, a boxing and tug-of-war enthusiast. Right up to his retirement in 1955, Commissioner Murphy was still active in promoting sports and held a meeting in June 1954 at Brugh An Gharda, Islandbridge, to revive rowing on a competitive basis in An Garda Síochána.

On taking possession of the Phoenix Park Depot in December 1922, O'Duffy put sport on a firmer foundation. A general purposes committee was set up in February 1923 to deal with the welfare of the recruits, notably in relation to sport and recreation. Over the next few years certain changes were instituted. The old RIC cavalry riding hall was converted into a recreation hall for indoor sports and used for boxing tournaments in particular. The RIC sports grounds in the Phoenix Park were acquired in 1923 from the Office of Public Works for the exclusive use of An Garda Síochána as football and hurling grounds. This also included the old RIC sports pavilion. Subsequently, the playing pitches were approved and the pavilion rebuilt. O'Sullivan in *The Depot* notes how a cinder running track of 130 yards was constructed and a gymnasium was fitted with boxing equipment. Two tennis courts were also provided at the Depot, and viewing galleries added to the ball alleys. Almost 75 per cent of the cost of these facilities came from members of the force themselves through a sports fund, at a subscription of a shilling a year. In the divisions, some recreation facilities such as ball alleys were also provided by the men. In later years a new Garda boathouse at Islandbridge and a new handball alley at the Depot were constructed. Throughout the country, O'Duffy also encouraged the construction of handball alleys against the back walls of suitable Garda stations.

Influence of Coiste Siamsa

The genesis for promoting sport at an official level in the force was initially Conradh Gaelach an Gharda. This was a small group of Garda members that came together in 1923 with a view to promoting the Irish language and national pastimes in An Garda Síochána. Led by O'Duffy, it also included Chief Superintendent Mathias McCarthy, Superintendent JA O'Shea, Cadet John McNulty, Sergeant Sheahan, Sergeant Gardiner and Captain Denis O'Kelly. O'Kelly as editor of *Iris an Gharda*, later titled the *Garda Review*, ensured that sports featured widely in its pages.

Out of Conradh Gaelach an Gharda, O'Duffy formed Coiste Siamsa in 1926 to organise and control all indoor and outdoor recreational activities within a central body. Coiste Siamsa was effectively the Garda Síochána Athletic Association. An Ard Comhairle was established as well as subordinate bodies called Coiste Roinne in each division and district. O'Duffy, writing in the *Garda Review* in October 1929, claimed the fundamental aim of Coiste Siamsa was:

> *Not the perfection of champion athletes, but to ensure that the Garda as a body should contain a high proportion of men who would hold their own with the average athletes in every form of sport.*
>
> *From such participation would, in due course, spring champion athletes. Participation in athletic exercises has moral value. The man who is training for some form of competition will be more likely to keep both mind and body under control than the man to whom such incentive is lacking. Such participation in games leads to character building and the formation of good habits. The Gardaí owe it to the reputation of the force to keep fit in mind and body.*

Coiste Siamsa ushered in a glorious age of sport in An Garda Síochána. It organised a vast array of activities such as football, hurling, handball, boxing, cycling, gymnastics, athletics, swimming, rowing, tug-of-war, tennis, golf, billiards, chess and card tournaments.

Ireland too benefited immeasurably from the contributions of the new guards. O'Duffy's attempt to spread the gospel of sport reached every parish of the country.

Young guards stationed from Belmullet to Ballybunion became involved in organising Gaelic clubs and boxing teams. Just as O'Duffy had predicted, the guards did help to heal civil war divisions and in time became part of the social fabric of the towns and villages. With their sporting prowess, they were able to 'play their hearts into the hearts of the people'. As time went on, Garda sportsmen, in Gaelic games and boxing in particular, were in popular demand as coaches and trainers both at local level and nationally. Hundreds of teams throughout the towns and villages of Ireland were raised on the strength of the coaching of Garda sportsmen. By 1929, major Garda athletic meetings were held annually at seventeen different venues in various parts of the country, according to McNiffe in *A History of the Garda Síochána*. The Garda band frequently travelled from the Depot to play at these meetings, considered important local social events. If not participating in sport, guards were actively promoting it. O'Duffy and Commissioner Murphy in particular were elected to the governing bodies of several national sporting organisations. Murphy became president of the Irish Amateur Boxing Association in the 1920s and was instrumental in building the National Stadium on South Circular Road, Dublin. Much later Commissioner Broy, who succeeded O'Duffy in 1933, was made president of the National Cycling and Athletic Association and in 1935 president of the Olympic Council of Ireland.

With an eye for publicity, O'Duffy decided to showcase Garda sporting prowess on an annual basis. In Dublin, the annual sports drew crowds of up to 10,000 people. During the time of the Civic Guard, many of the divisions throughout the country organised their own annual sports day, in addition to sending participants to the annual sports in Croke Park in July. In July 1926, O'Duffy and Coiste Siamsa put events on a formal footing with his annual summer festival called Aonach an Gharda, an event that lasted five days. It was a throwback to RIC times with a formal garden party in the Phoenix Park Depot, attended by President Cosgrave and his ministers, the Governor General, TDs and senators, as well as senior army officers, the judiciary and leading figures from the cultural, sporting and social life of the nation. The occasion was also the perfect medium to present the annual Scott Medal awards. In addition to athletic events, there was a chess tournament as well as competitions in Irish dancing, drama, singing, Irish language conversation, and arts and crafts displays. Other sports like tennis, golf, handball, swimming and badminton also featured. The field events were dominated by the guards and the public were treated to the sights of hammer-throwing, javelin, discus, pole vault, high jump and long jump. Boxing was one of the most popular events and ensured good attendances; the punters were guaranteed to witness the finest boxers from Northern Ireland, the UK, Germany and many European countries spar with Garda boxers. Photographs from 1926 show a boxing ring erected in the middle of the Depot square, surrounded by

Above: Garda boxing team, 1924

chairs and seats, while hundreds of people watched the spectacle. These sports days were not entirely for entertainment and publicity, however. They also had an altruistic function: the proceeds of the sports day helped to establish a benevolent fund.

In the first decade of the force's existence, 1922–32, Garda members won an astonishing number of sporting titles. It was truly the sporting heyday of the force. They had their greatest successes by far in athletics, boxing and tug-of-war. In athletics, gardaí won forty-four Irish, six British and fifty-four Irish provincial titles. In Gaelic football, they captured two Dublin senior championships and two senior leagues. In hurling, they won five Dublin senior championships, two provincial championships, while gardaí representing Dublin won the All-Ireland title in 1927. Some gardaí were also part of All-Ireland football and hurling teams, winning for their native or adopted counties. In handball, gardaí won eleven national senior, six provincial, and fourteen county titles. The Garda tug-of-war team had a string of successes and won the Tug-of-War World Championship at Wembley in May 1924. They also competed admirably against the army and the famous Guinness teams on many an occasion.

Boxing clever

The history of boxing in the force deserves special mention. The club had an extraordinary record of success at provincial, national and international level. As mentioned earlier, Commissioner William Murphy helped to establish the Garda Boxing Club in 1924 and hired Tommy Maloney as trainer with monies secured from

Boxing clever

Shortly after [beating the Ulster Champion], Dick Hearns was called to the Garda in January 1929. He didn't intend to take up boxing in his new career but one day while training in the gym, General Murphy saw him and said:

'Did you ever box before, Hearns?'

'No, sir.'

'If you take it up, I'll get you off the Square for two hours.'

Like Jim [Branigan], this 'carrot' was enough to swing it and Dick Hearns took up boxing, becoming Light Heavyweight Champion of Ireland in 1933, 1934, 1936, 1937, and 1938. In 1935 he became British Open Amateur Boxing Association Light Heavyweight Champion, having been beaten in the final of the same competition the previous year.

Bernard Neary, Lugs: The Life and Times of Jim Branigan

Dick Hearnes

a Garda sports fund. Maloney, from the Liberties in Dublin, was a former British army boxer and raised the Garda team to international stature. Membership of the Garda Boxing Club grew rapidly: their members were akin to a protected species and their police duties extended to sentry duty at the Depot only. Garda boxers, often in the heavier weights, formed the backbone of many Irish international boxing teams. They fought in Northern Ireland, sometimes against the RUC, throughout England and Scotland, in European countries such as Italy, Poland, Germany, Norway and France, and further afield in Chicago. By 1932, Garda boxers had won fifteen national titles and two Amateur Boxing Association championships. The Irish teams at the Olympics Games in Amsterdam in 1928 and in Los Angeles in 1932 were heavily represented by Garda boxers.

Though Coiste Siamsa recognised only the amateur status of its sportsmen, the Garda boxers, capturing Irish, British and European titles, were, in effect, semi-professional. They were precluded, however, from accepting prize money but to circumvent this, McNiffe notes, victorious Garda boxers sometimes received vouchers

Going down in history

He was never knocked out in his career in the ring and his title of 'The Battler' was well earned in ... what was perhaps one of Jim's greatest nights in the ring, a night in which he will never forget, in Leipzig in pre-war Germany on 10th January 1938. On that occasion Jim Branigan did Ireland proud in a Germany–Ireland International Tournament. Jim was to meet a German named Pietch, who had a great reputation as a KO merchant, in a three three-minute round contest. Before the fight a German friend told Jim to steer well clear of Pietch's right hook. In the opening seconds of the fight, with the bold Jim keeping a wary eye on the famous right hook, the German put him down with a left hook. As Jim got to his feet he came to the conclusion that he had misunderstood the advice he had received and that it was the left hook that he should have watched.

That was where Jim made his biggest mistake for as soon as Pietch saw an opening for his right, he put Jim down for nine. It is a proud boast of Jim Branigan today that nobody ever knocked him out, but if he ever came near it, it must certainly have been in this fight. That first right hook put the German in command – and others were to follow. Altogether, Jim was put on the floor nine times during the course of that fight. Five of the counts he took were of nine. Yet he did not know the meaning of surrender. At the end of the contest Jim was still on his feet, without a hope of victory yet without a notion of giving in. And when the bell rang the cheers were all for the loser whose exhibition of courage was still, in the mid-fifties, being talked about by German officials whenever Irish teams visited the country.

The tournament took place in the Leipzig Zoo and was watched by both Field Marshall Goering of white-suit fame and that famous propangandist, Josef Goebbels.... One of Jim's souvenirs of the trip [was] a large poster [of a German newspaper] which announced to the populace of Leipzig: 'IRELANDER BOBBYS BOXEN IM ZOO'. You don't have to be a linguist or an expert on the German language to fathom that one out.

Jim's performance was all the more remarkable for three days previously, on 7th January 1938, at Berlin, before a capacity audience that included Albert Speer and Rudolf Hess, he had battled against Niesen from Denmark in a gruelling three three-minute round contest, losing the contest on a technical knockout.

Bernard Neary, Lugs: The Life and Times of Jim Branigan

that could be cashed in a city store. The first wave of prominent Garda boxers at this time were heavyweights Matt Flanagan and Jack O'Driscoll, light-heavyweight Jim Murphy, middleweights Jack Chase and Jack Forde, and welterweight Frank Cooper. A second wave produced such boxing legends as Dick Hearns, Larry Flood, Gerry Mulligan, Paddy Hennelly, Billy Blackwell, Dom Lydon, Jim 'Lugs' Branigan and Ernie Smith. Lugs Branigan, synonymous with the Riot Squad, later became a living legend in Dublin city during the 1950s and 60s for his fair-minded, no-nonsense style of policing.

Beginning of decline

The era of great sportsmanship declined somewhat in the late 1930s. A sea change occurred when O'Duffy was dismissed from office by the incoming Fianna Fáil government in 1933. O'Duffy's successor was Eamon Broy, whose interest in sport sadly extended to athletics only. Fianna Fáil, under the leadership of Éamon de Valera, devoted their energies more to reviving the Irish language than to sport. In 1939, Aonach an Gharda had to be abandoned due to lack of interest. During the 1940s and 1950s, Coiste Siamsa fell into abeyance and there was no halting its slow inexorable decline. However, the greatest factor for the decline was the age profile of the members. Gone were the huge numbers of single, healthy, energetic young men. The 7,000 members had reached middle age and most were married, now juggling the demands of family life and work. It comes as no surprise that golf grew in popularity at this time.

A short-lived sports revival did occur with the arrival of new recruits in the mid-1940s. The Garda football team won the 1948 County Dublin senior championship but it was beaten in the replayed final in 1949. Luckily, the force got out of the sporting doldrums within a decade or so. The 1960s, epitomising all that was new, radical and exciting, saw a resurgence of sport in the Garda body. As in previous times, it was aided by the influx of 3,000 new recruits to the force. The scale of

Above and right: Garda boxing team

Jarda Conroy
Trainer Maloney
Jarda J. Keily
Jarda Chase
Jarda Cooper
Jarda J. Forde
Jarda J. O'Brien
Jarda Murphy

change in An Garda Síochána in this decade was something not witnessed since its foundation. The Dublin Metropolitan Division amalgamated with parts of the Dublin/Wicklow Division to create the Dublin Metropolitan Area, and new districts were formed. Not just sport but the welfare of members took centre stage: new Representative Bodies came into existence, the Garda Pensioners' Association was set up, St Raphael's Garda Credit Union was founded in Dublin in 1964 and St Paul's Garda Credit Union in Cork in 1967, and, crucially, the Dublin Metropolitan Garda Recreation Club at Harrington Street, Dublin in 1963.

One club that enjoyed a particular resurgence was the Garda Boat Club. The club, spearheaded by Commissioner William Murphy, was established on the banks of the Liffey in 1954. However, its establishment and development became in truth the personal project of one man – Tim O'Brien. O'Brien was a genial Kerryman who was a chief superintendent attached to the Dublin Metropolitan Headquarters during the 1950s. From early on, O'Brien became club president and took a keen interest in the day-to-day running of the club. It was widely accepted at the time that the club was the only project to have been funded to some degree by the original Dublin Metropolitan Garda Recreation Club. O'Brien's ever-presence and hands-on approach resulted in full participation by all involved in club activities. Largely through his efforts, all rowers were facilitated by 'rowing friendly' working times within the Garda service. Oarsmen were all attached to the same units, which meant they all had similar off-duty time and were thus able to train together. As the rowers began to prove themselves nationally, they were facilitated to an even-greater degree. This in turn drew remarks from envious colleagues who would jokingly refer to them as 'Tim O'Brien's Navy'. Nonetheless, O'Brien's policy proved correct, as the following generation of oarsmen competed at the highest level of their sport, including the Olympic Games and World Championship finals. In 1960, a new boathouse was constructed beside the pavilion and went some way towards contributing to the outstanding success of the club abroad.

The renaissance in sport continued apace. Coiste Siamsa was revived in 1962 with the same structures as before. However, it was on a strictly amateur basis this time. Later in 1972, it was awarded an annual grant by the then Minister for Justice, Des O'Malley TD, to assist in promoting sport in the force. Certainly by the 1970s there were at least eleven sports under its umbrella.

Aonach an Gharda was revived and held on 22 September 1962 at the Iveagh Grounds. The first 'Garda Week' of the new age took place in 1963, hosting competitions in hurling, Gaelic football, soccer, rugby, handball, golf, pitch and putt and tennis. The sports of angling, clay pigeon shooting and judo were added in 1965. When the organisation came to celebrate fifty years of existence in 1975, it could look back on a proud record. In the foreword of *Coiste Siamsa: Golden Jubilee* 1922–1972, the secretary of Coiste Siamsa during the 1960s, Edmund Garvey – and also chairman of the Garda Recreation Club – paid tribute to the vision of its founders:

Garda Boat Club

Over the years the club won seventeen national championships titles in eights, fours, pairs and sculls at senior level, plus all the other major events in Irish rowing including novice and international championships. In 1975, after winning the Thames Cup (for eights) at Henley Royal Regatta, four members of the crew and cox went on to represent Ireland in the World Championships at Nottingham in the coxed fours event. This four went on to the Olympic Games in Montreal in 1976, where they finished seventh. Garda oarsmen also competed in the World Championships at Amsterdam in 1977, New Zealand in 1978, Yugoslavia in 1979 and Switzerland in 1982, as well as the Olympic Games in Moscow in 1980.

DMA Coiste Roinne Yearbook 1996

In those early formative years, men of vision saw that the potential of an organisation of disciplined, mentally alert, and able-bodied young men might be so exercised as to afford an enrichment of the quality of life for all our people, and especially for the youth.

The domain of sports and athletics held a special attraction. Here was an area of activity where physical fitness, prized for its own sake by the Gardaí, could be harnessed to the worthy purpose of promoting an ever-widening active interest in track and field events, and in games generally.

Since example is better than precept and nothing succeeds like success, no effort was spared to foster the highest standards of performance within the Garda body itself. Little wonder, then, if, in the passage of fifty historic years, this sustained dedication resulted in a series of achievements of which the Garda Force may well be proud.

In the *DMA Coiste Roinne Yearbook 1996*, Brian Prendergast paid tribute to Edmund Garvey. Garvey's contribution to every activity, he claimed, just could not be quantified: 'His drive and leadership were primarily responsible for the development and recreation, along with station improvements and the establishment of "Garda Week" as an annual feature of sport in the Garda.'

By 2007, Coiste Siamsa promoted, encouraged and financially supported thirty-three sports at district, divisional, regional, national and international level. These included such diverse sports as sea angling, trout and salmon angling, athletics, badminton, basketball, lawn bowling, boxing, cricket, cycling, Gaelic football, golf, hurling, judo, motor sport, mountaineering and canoeing, pitch and putt, rowing,

Below: Garda competing at Henley in 1958 for the first time in the Thames Cup against Emmanuel College, Cambridge *(right)*. Garda crew included John Cuffe (bow), Joe Callinan, Gerry McDonagh, Jim Murphy, Ned O'Dea, Jim Maguire, Tom Casey, Tom Brennan (stroke) and Paddy Hoare (cox)

Above: First Garda rowing crew, 1955

Heyday of Garda sports

During those hectic years of the first decade, members of the force won the following titles: *Athletics:* 44 Irish, 6 British AAA and 54 Irish provincial titles. *Boxing:* 13 international team events contests, 15 national titles, 2 ABA championships and 2 European titles. *Gaelic football:* 2 County Dublin senior championships, 2 Dublin senior leagues, and they beat the army in 1926, '27 and '28. *Hurling:* 5 County Dublin senior championships and the All-Ireland title for Dublin in 1927. They beat the army in the President's Cup in 1926, '27 and '28. *Handball:* 14 county, 6 provincial and 11 senior titles.

Donal J O'Sullivan, The Depot: A History of the Garda Síochána Depot at the Phoenix Park, Dublin

Left: Garda Cycling Club

rugby, sailing, shooting (clay pigeon), skiing, snooker, soccer, squash, sub aqua, swimming, tennis, taekwondo, and volleyball. The sports are wide and varied, some more leisurely than others, and cater for all ages, golf being particularly popular. In 1983, the Annual Garda Sportstar Awards were set up to recognise the men and women of An Garda Síochána for their sporting feats. In the late 1980s and 1990s, sport was to enter a new golden age with the advent of the Garda-owned Stackstown Golf Club and the building of Westmanstown Sports Complex.

Recreation in the early years

The emphasis on recreation in the force in the early years was not as pronounced as it is today. In fact, in 1928 O'Duffy claimed that recreation was not a right but a privilege. It is difficult to realise now that many of the Dublin Metropolitan stations, or barracks as they were once called, were homes for unmarried men serving in these stations. In the 1920s, the vast majority of gardaí were single and obliged to live in barracks. They spent eight hours a day on duty, seven days a week, with just one day off a month. When off duty, they were required to remain in the barracks, though entitled to two hours of recreation each day. The men slept in dormitories and ate their meals in the kitchen. It fell to the mess man in each

'Patrols of the imagination'

In a place like Cootehall hardly any crime happened, so the guards spent their time in useless exercise writing reports and patrolling roads on which nothing happened ... As I grew older in the barracks I used to help the guards write their reports and they used to jokingly call them 'patrols of the imagination'. In a way they were the first fictions I took part in.

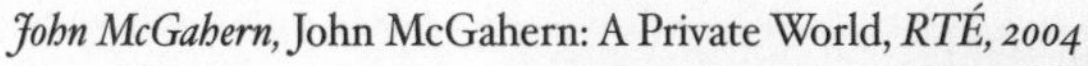

John McGahern, John McGahern: A Private World, *RTÉ, 2004*

Right: Playing cards in barracks

Below: Dublin Metropolitan Police Band pre-1922

station to organise meals, a position rotated among the men. Conditions in many of the barracks were often detrimental to health and morale. Marriage was seen as the only escape from the constraints of this way of life, although married members were forced to live in the married quarters of the barracks, if such existed. Edmund Garvey, in an interview with Henry Kelly in *The Irish Times* on 13 September 1975, recalled the lengths gardaí stationed at Pearse Street Station in the 1940s went to in order to get married:

> *To get married you had to show the superintendent £60 in cash. Sure where in the name of God would any of us at the time get £60. So what you did getting married was nip around to a local publican or a shopkeeper, get £60 in notes for a few minutes, show it to the super and then give it back. £60 was out of our wildest dreams, sure without help from home those days you could die, nearly.*

Many guards had just too much time on their hands. Criminal activity was nowhere as prevalent as it is today and life in the barracks was often slow and leisurely. Recreation took the form of card playing, draughts and rings to while away the time. It was not unusual for young men of the local area to pay social visits to the local guards in the evenings. In some instances, according to McNiffe, Garda barracks of the 1920s and 1930s were nothing short of a local club or meeting place at night-time. Guards, no different to many of their peers, when off duty enjoyed typical pastimes of going to the local cinema, dancehall or pub, visiting friends and relatives and courting young women.

Recreation at a formal level involved annual Garda dances. In fact, these were to become a regular feature of Garda social life. In the early years of the force, the converted riding hall in the Depot became a venue for such dances and fundraising concerts, though they occurred infrequently. Recitals by the Garda Band added greatly to the gaiety of the occasions. Based in the Depot since 1922, the Garda Band had replaced the RIC band, though the DMP band in existence since 1873 was allowed

Ban on beards

From the beginning, DMP band members were under strict instructions on how to look and dress. 'In future the bandsmen of the DMP are not to wear beards, as it is not becoming in men who wear caps. They may wear small whiskers, but the Commissioner would rather they wore none, as nothing looks so neat as a moustache only. The bass drummer may wear all his beard if he chooses. Anyone not complying will be reported.'

James MacCafferty, 'Band of Brothers', Garda Review, *February 2007*

to remain. Daniel J Delaney was hired as a civilian bandmaster and the cost of his employment was borne by a special band fund, through subscriptions from the force. The band was highly sought after and in 1923 played forty-three engagements as well as twelve free recitals in the Phoenix Park for the general public. So successful was the Garda Band that a studio was set up in the Depot to facilitate the broadcast of recitals on the State's new radio station, Radio 2RN (a forerunner to RTÉ Radio 1). In 1926, the committees of the DMP and Garda bands were amalgamated, pooling their funds but remaining as distinct bands.

The decision to run fundraisers, particularly during the 1920s, was taken by certain members of the Dublin Metropolitan Division. Garda dances were therefore organised to raise money for various charitable causes around the city. The Garda Band waived its performance fee if a particular event was for charity. As the 1930s progressed, annual Garda dances were held in each division and the proceeds donated to charity. The Garda representative bodies also got on board and helped to raise funds for Garda charities such as the Garda Benevolent Trust Fund. The events were many and ranged from dances to whist drives to sporting events. There were some developments in the 1940s, partly in response to the temporary recruitment drive, which boosted social events. In May 1945, Brugh an Gharda, a new social and sports club, was opened at the Garda Boat Club premises in Islandbridge. In addition, a Garda Boys' Club was established as well as a committee to co-ordinate Garda social functions in the Dublin Metropolitan Area.

Recreational needs at an informal level were also catered for, albeit modestly. Mindful of the living-in arrangements, architects of some of the older DMP barracks had allowed for the needs of the men by providing recreation rooms in the buildings themselves. The facilities were in most cases designed to facilitate card players and billiard enthusiasts: radios and televisions were unknown until the 1960s and dartboards, too, would come later. In the Dublin Metropolitan Division, the upkeep of these facilities was funded by voluntary contributions from the members themselves:

Long on time

Guards on barrack orderly duty were not engaged in clerical work all the time. They frequently played cards, read the newspaper, talked to the sergeant's family or listened to the radio from the kitchen of the married quarters. In the 1922–52 period the actual amount of work to be done was frequently insufficient to occupy a guard's time totally during his long hours of duty.

Liam McNiffe, A History of the Garda Síochána, *p112*

Gardaí cutting turf in the Dublin Mountains in 1941.
Front row, left to right: Tom Moore, Alex Finn and Thomas Keelan
Back row, left to right: Michael Murphy, Frank (JF) Moran and Patrick Farrell

a nominal sum of sixpence for members living in the stations and threepence for married men and members not living in the stations. The fund was administered from the Divisional Office, Dublin Castle, and, according to Tom Ryan, first honorary assistant secretary of the Garda Recreation Club in 1961, no one ever knew what amount was realised from these subscriptions, or what amount was in the fund itself, and no one ever asked.

With the influx of young men into the force during the 1940s and 1950s, a new interest in pastimes in general was generated. For example, inter-district billiard competitions were often held during this period. While sports of a specialised nature like football and rowing were being encouraged, the application of the recreation fund to the general body of members was haphazard, staid and unimaginative, according to Tom Ryan. When presentations were made – for transfers, marriage or promotion – the venue for such a function was very often a local licensed premises. When the last customer left, the gardaí would file in through the back door and proceedings would commence in 'hushed tones and continue that way in deference to the entreaties and blandishments of the proprietor'. As the 1950s drew to a close, this very unsatisfactory state of affairs did not go unnoticed. A groundswell of popular opinion was growing that the gardaí should have a club of their own.

Allied to this was the question of Garda members enjoying a social drink. In the early years of the force, while the Garda Síochána Code did not expressly prohibit members from socialising with friends in a local pub over a few drinks, it was not encouraged either. As a result, a wet canteen was often set up where drinks were on sale to members in the barracks, a practice also common to the RIC and British military. A wet canteen existed in the Depot and in some Dublin stations up to the late 1930s. However, the Garda authorities were always wary and watchful that a guard's job as a law enforcement officer was not undermined by his drinking habits. As McNiffe notes: 'A Garda who drank while on duty, was known to drink after closing hours, drank to excess, or was in debt to a publican was regarded as a serious liability to the force.' The welfare of members as regards handling drink and posing a threat to themselves or others was to the forefront of Edmund Garvey's mind when he founded the Garda Recreation Club in Harrington Street in 1963.

The Beginnings

Dublin Metropolitan Garda Recreation Club

Chapter

3

It is now abundantly clear that if the Garda are to have a club premises catering for their recreational needs then they must provide it themselves.

Chapter 3
The Beginnings

THE 1960s as a time of civil rights and revolution rippled right around the globe. At home in Ireland, An Garda Síochána was not immune to the turbulence of the period. The decade witnessed substantial changes in their pay and conditions, greater power wielded by the various Garda representative bodies and not least the advent of the Garda Recreation Club. The origins lay in the 1950s and early 1960s when the founding members of the force began to retire en masse. This led to a massive recruitment campaign that saw a huge influx of young men to stations in the Dublin area. These thoroughly modern young men were not prepared to accept the military-style discipline and conditions endured by previous generations. Not least was the requirement that gardaí living in stations should be in their rooms by midnight each night. The basic wage for a guard was about £10 a week, he worked unlimited hours with no compensation and had about two days' leave each month. The outcome of protracted pay talks, however, was not in their favour. Gardaí serving five years or less were refused a pay award, including a rent allowance given to their older colleagues. In Dublin the disaffected gardaí revolted at delays in addressing these grievances and forced the government of the day to negotiate directly with rank-and-file representatives. Their frustration culminated in what became known as 'The Macushla'. This name derived from a meeting of 815 gardaí that took place in the Macushla Ballroom, off Amiens Street, on 4 November 1961. Denied the right of assembly in their code of practice, the men boldly flouted the direct order of Commissioner Quinn and met in public. The meeting resulted in the dismissal of twelve young members identified by the authorities and the Government as the ringleaders. The campaign was eventually brought to a swift end by the intervention of the all-powerful Catholic Archbishop of Dublin, Dr John Charles McQuaid. The then Minister for Justice, Charles J Haughey TD, sealed its conclusion by granting the gardaí a much overdue pay rise and sanctioned the reinstatement of the twelve dismissed members.

Regenerating the Garda Recreation Club

One man well placed to observe the effects of poor pay and substandard accommodation on the welfare of guards was Edmund (Ned) Garvey. His efforts to improve their lot had quite a bearing on the actions of the disaffected members. In the late 1950s and early 1960s, Garvey, later to rise to Garda Commissioner, was

Above: Last passing-out parade at the Depot in 1963
Below: Macushla Ballroom, Dublin

the detective inspector stationed at College Street, subsequently named Pearse Street Station. Hailing from Ballinlough, County Roscommon, Garvey had spent all his Garda service in the Dublin area since joining the force in 1939. A humanitarian at heart, he displayed a keen interest in improving living arrangements in the local stations to which he was attached, notably College Street, Harcourt Terrace and Kevin Street.

Within the Dublin Metropolitan Division (DMD) as it was then called, unmarried members of the force were obliged to live in Garda stations in deplorable accommodation with inadequate catering facilities. Catering in particular was a bone of contention between members who resided at home and members living in stations. Kitchens were manned by outside staff who looked after members living in – which posed problems with increasing regularity. It was not unusual for dinners prepared for members on night duty to disappear from where they were left by staff. There was also the problem of members who resided at home seeking to have their breakfasts cooked by kitchen staff exclusively paid for by the members living in through their elected mess man. Mess men are now a thing of past, a throwback to the semi-military days of the RIC when they were responsible for catering arrangements in the barracks. According to the personal reminiscences of a former chairman of the Dublin Recreation Club, the late Brian Prendergast, mess men were renowned for their first-class management of the Christmas canteen. Indeed Garda stations in the

A Garda's lot in the 1960s

The 1960s introduced some new aspects to Garda work especially in the cities and larger towns. The increased volume of traffic on Irish roads occupied a great deal of the force's time. Juvenile delinquency and vandalism were on the increase and street fights between rival gangs, armed with knives, were becoming more common. There was a marked increase in indictable offences, with the Dublin Metropolitan Area accounting for over 60 per cent of the country's crime.

Hundreds of Gardaí were posted along the border with Northern Ireland in early 1968 to prevent the spread of 'foot and mouth' cattle disease.

Influenced by events in the US, Europe and Northern Ireland, some Irish citizens later in that year took to the streets of Dublin to register their disapproval of events at home and abroad, including the Vietnam War. Such protests sometimes resulted in baton charges by the Gardaí.

A number of administrative changes were implemented during the decade. In 1964 the Dublin Metropolitan Area was reorganised and extended to include the newly built-up suburban areas.

Liam McNiffe, A History of the Garda Síochána, *p163*

DMD were the only places in Dublin where drink was available for social purposes on Christmas Day.

The structure and decor of many stations were unchanged from their DMP days. Little had been done to maintain or improve the buildings over time. Appointed housing officer in 1961 under Commissioner Costigan, Ned Garvey had worked tirelessly to improve the level of accommodation throughout the country. He put pressure on the Board of Works to improve conditions in College Station in particular; he acquired proper chairs and carpets in the recreation room, but most of all he organised a canteen shared by all members, both living in and residing at home. Improvements were also made at Harcourt Terrace Station. To his credit, this was achieved through sheer commitment, energy and drive at a time when money, both public and personal, was very scarce indeed.

When the success of his work in the B District of College Street and Harcourt Terrace became generally known, Garvey was asked – or maybe he suggested himself, as Tom Ryan surmised – that a new Dublin Metropolitan Recreation Club should be formed. Either way the seed for what was to follow was sown. The matter was discussed at a Divisional weekly conference where it was agreed that a new recreation committee representing all the DMD districts should be formed.

A committee referred to as the Dublin Metropolitan Recreation Committee had existed in the force since its early days. It was controlled from Dublin Castle and semi-official in nature. Not much is known of its activities, other than it administrated a fund to supply stations with cards and billiards, and organised games in different stations and the occasional dance in Kevin Street. Some perceived it to be interested only in the promotion of the Garda Boat Club. Monthly committee meetings were held in Dublin Castle yet little exists in the way of club records except correspondence to the Leinster & Munster Bank on Dame Street from 1948 to 1960. These letters either informed the bank of resolutions to set up a bank account or of changes in committee personnel, detailing those now entitled to sign cheques on the club's behalf – with sample signatures enclosed. Though the records shed little light on the committee's activities, they give us an indication of the individuals involved. On 8 February 1948, the chairman Michael Gill requested the bank to set up an account and to honour cheques signed by Bernard Rafferty and Daniel O'Connor. In March 1949, writing from Dublin Castle, Bernard Rafferty, the then honorary secretary, informed the bank that Andrew McDyer had been appointed honorary treasurer in place of Daniel O'Connor who had retired. Some months later in July 1949, Michael Gill, writing from Rathmines Garda Station, informed the bank that Edmond Flaherty had been appointed secretary in place of Bernard Rafferty. In 1953, the bank was duly informed that Bernard Rafferty had resigned as secretary and that Cornelius Flannery now held the post. In 1960, R Baxter was honorary secretary and wrote to the bank with news that the position of treasurer was no longer held by JV Chatten.

An Garda Siochana
Dublin Metropolitan Division
Recreation Committee
Dublin Castle.

The Manager,
Munster & Leinster Bank
Dame Street
Dublin

26th March 1949.

Appointment of Garda Andrew Mc Dyer, College Station as Hon. Tres. to above Committee.

Dear Sir,

Herewith please find copy of the minute of Dublin Metropolitan Division Recreation Committee meeting held at Dublin Castle on Wednesday 15th December 1948 concerning above appointment

"It was proposed by S/O James Ginnity and seconded by Garda Edward Flaherty that Garda Andrew Mc Dyer be appointed to the position of Hon. Tres. to the Committee in place of Garda Daniel O Connor, who has retired from that position"

The above motion was carried and Gd. McDyer is now Hon. Tres. to our Committee.

Bernard Rafferty Hon. Sec.

Garda Siochana.

Recreation Club,
Dublin Castle.
13/1/59 60.

Manager,
Munster & Leinster Bank,
Dame St., Dublin.

Dear Sir,

I wish to inform you that Mr. J. V. Chatten is no longer Treasurer of the above Club as he has resigned from An Garda Siochana as and from the 14th inst., and therefore Mr. Chatten is not now entitled to sign any cheques.

Signed,

R. Baxter
(S.R. Baxter)

Hon. Secretary.

In case of any further communication on this subject, please quote the following reference and address—
The Superintendent,
Detective Branch
(Special Sect.) Dublin Castle

GÁRDA SÍOCHÁNA
DUBLIN METROPOLITAN DIVISION
SUPERINTENDENT,
DETECTIVE BRANCH,
SPECIAL SECTION,
DUBLIN CASTLE.

26th February, 1953.

Dear Sir, Garda Metro Div Recreation Committee

I am to inform you that Gárda Edmond Flaherty has resigned from the post of Secretary to the D.M.D. Recreation Committee. At a meeting of the Committee held at Dublin Castle on Wednesday, 11th February, 1953, Gárda Cornelius Flannery was duly appointed Secretary in place of Gárda Flaherty.

I enclose herewith specimen of Gárda Flannery's signature.

Yours faithfully,

Michael Gill

SUPERINTENDENT, and
COMMITTEE CHAIRMAN.

The Manager,
Munster & Leinster Bank,
Dame Street,
DUBLIN.

Cornelius Flannery

It was clear to Ned Garvey that the time had arrived to radically revive the club, such as it was. In 1961, he saw an opportunity to extend the scope of its activities. Armed with the tacit approval of his colleagues, he did not delay matters further. A meeting was called for 13 April 1961 and notices to that effect sent to each Dublin station. The meeting took place at Kevin Street Station, where Garvey was now the district officer. It was well attended and from the general enthusiasm and the views expressed, it was clear there was an appetite to overhaul and regenerate the existing committee with a view to improving recreational facilities and establish a Garda Social Club. This would essentially be a private members' club to cater for retirements and presentations, with provision for catering and a bar licence. It would also allow for the families of members to meet and socialise, and for wives and girlfriends to attend functions if they wished. Garvey was forthright in his views and called for residing in stations to cease, Christmas canteens be abolished as they created a bad image, and retirement functions in Garda stations with barrels supplied from local publicans to stop. Establishing a club of their own could fill the void.

The meeting was presided over by Chief Supt Denis Connolly in charge of the Dublin Metropolitan Division at the time and thus lending an air of authority. The club committee was duly reborn and elected Ned Garvey as chairman and Denis Connolly as president. Jim Daly became honorary secretary and Tom Ryan the assistant secretary with special responsibility for drafting club rules. Charlie Gaffney was elected to the position of honorary treasurer. The various districts in what was then called the DMD, along with the detective branch of SDU (Special Detective Unit) and CDU (Central Detective Unit) as well as Headquarters, were represented on the committee. Members included Tommy O'Grady, Ned Lafferty, Harry Thynne, John O'Gara, Gerry Erskine, Johnny McEvoy, Sean O'Mahoney, Bill Byrne, Peter Kelly and Frank Kiernan. The new committee set out on its venture with the princely sum of £37 in the hands of its treasurer, Charlie Gaffney. One of its main objectives, to provide recreational facilities for its members, was difficult to achieve on such meagre funds. Nonetheless, in its first year the club made a grant of £125 towards the cost of repairing two billiard tables and easy chairs as well as supplying twenty-three radio sets to Dublin stations. Despite how modest these grants were, the immediate needs of members were catered for and not sacrificed for the greater goal of providing a club premises.

All feet to the floor

A move towards financial independence was made when two separate accounts in the club's name were opened in the then Munster & Leinster Bank on Dublin's Dame Street. This move in May 1961 began a long and fruitful relationship with the Munster & Leinster and its successor Allied Irish Bank, which remains the club's banker to the present day. The committee then embarked on a venture that was to be of major significance in terms of its future. It started to run Sunday night dances in the old recreation hall in Kevin Street Station. Not an easy thing to have done at the time, but it can be supposed that they had the consent of the local district officer, one Ned Garvey. The venture had the dual objective of providing entertainment and raising funds. It could not have come at a better time. Dancing was truly the craze of the day. All around Ireland large dancehalls had started to sprout in the countryside. The showband era had arrived; it was fun time in sixties style. Towns and cities swung to the sounds of the Miami, the Royal and many more showbands, and spawned legends like Brendan Bowyer, Earl Gill, Dickie Rock and Sonny Knowles. This trend was not lost on a number of farsighted gardaí in the Dublin area, adamant that they and their colleagues would not be left behind. They yearned

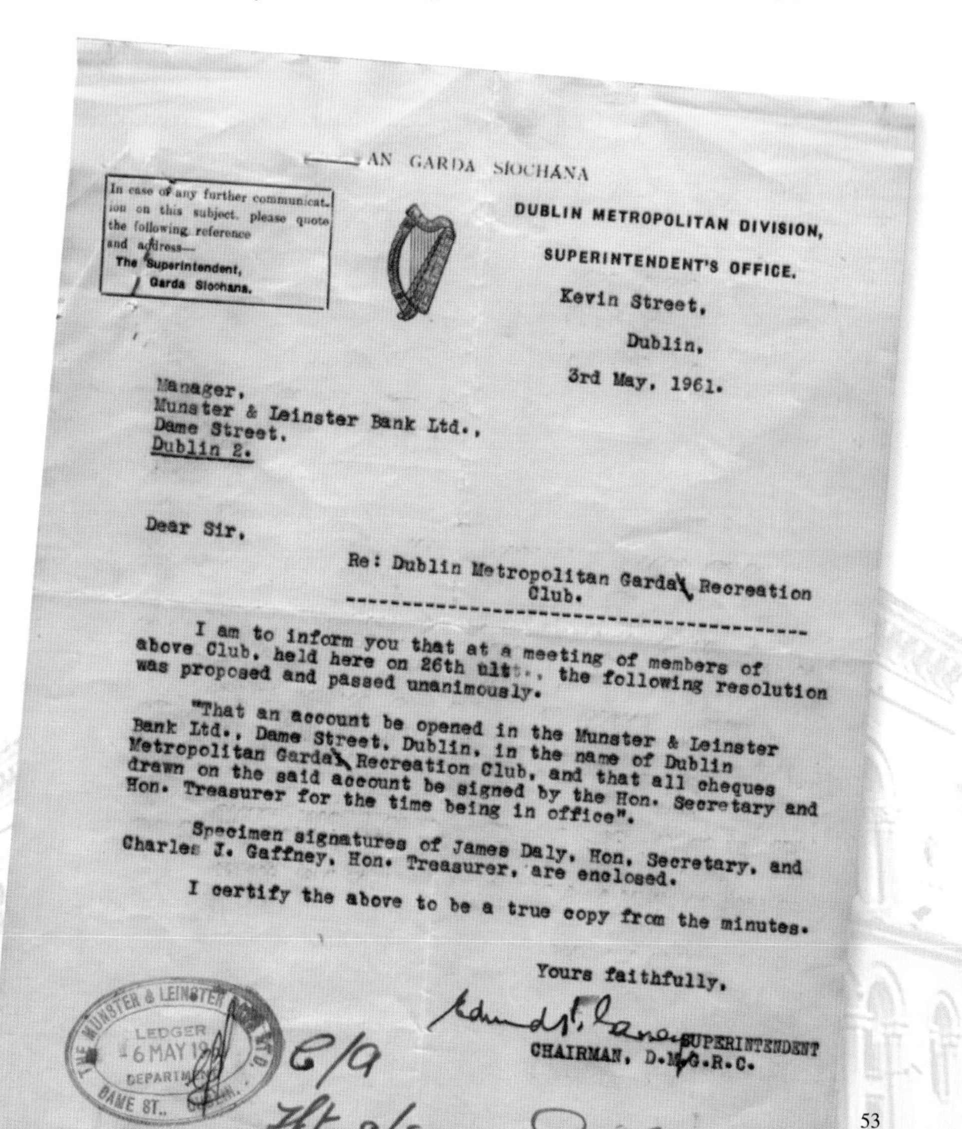

AN GARDA SIOCHÁNA

In case of any further communication on this subject, please quote the following reference and address—
The Superintendent,
Garda Siochana.

DUBLIN METROPOLITAN DIVISION,
SUPERINTENDENT'S OFFICE.
Kevin Street,
Dublin,
3rd May, 1961.

Manager,
Munster & Leinster Bank Ltd.,
Dame Street,
Dublin 2.

Dear Sir,

Re: Dublin Metropolitan Garda Recreation Club.

I am to inform you that at a meeting of members of above Club, held here on 26th ult., the following resolution was proposed and passed unanimously.

"That an account be opened in the Munster & Leinster Bank Ltd., Dame Street, Dublin, in the name of Dublin Metropolitan Garda Recreation Club, and that all cheques drawn on the said account be signed by the Hon. Secretary and Hon. Treasurer for the time being in office".

Specimen signatures of James Daly, Hon. Secretary, and Charles J. Gaffney, Hon. Treasurer, are enclosed.

I certify the above to be a true copy from the minutes.

Yours faithfully,

SUPERINTENDENT
CHAIRMAN, D.M.G.R.C.

THE MUNSTER & LEINSTER BANK LTD.
LEDGER
6 MAY 19
DEPARTMENT
DAME ST.

to compete with entertainment hotspots like the National Ballroom, the Irish Club, the Teachers' Club, Barry's Hotel, Clery's Ballroom and the Metropole.

The recreation hall had seen many changes of use during its lifetime. It was part of the Kevin Street complex that had served as the old training depot for the Dublin Metropolitan Police for almost ninety years until its amalgamation with An Garda Síochána in 1925. In his personal reminiscences, Tom Ryan, assistant secretary of the club at the time, recalls that the hall was old but structurally sound. He remembers on one occasion having to accompany an officer from Dublin Corporation on a fire hazard inspection of the building. After looking into every nook and cranny, the officer expressed concern at the divisions between some of the floorboards and was fearful that a lighted cigarette end or match could fall between one of these fissures and a fire would inevitably result. His concerns were heeded in double-quick time: the 1962/63 balance sheet records a sum of £220 having been spent 'By repair to recreation hall'.

Far from sumptuous, the hall lacked the requisite maple floor for seasoned dancers to glide their partners along. Efforts to improve the surface of the uneven wooden floor often had the reverse effect and made dancing a hazardous experience instead. But what the hall lacked in style, the resident band, The Altonaires, made up for immeasurably as the crowds kept coming back in droves each week. Members of the club committee supervised the dances with such diligence that no complaints were ever received. The dances were an obvious success and proved to be a welcome money earner with the proceeds being ploughed back into the club.

Dancing days

In the days before the Garda Recreation Club was established at Harrington Street in the 1960s, Kevin Street Garda Station was the social centre for gardaí serving in that area. Dances were held in the recreation hall situated to the rear of Kevin Street Station and the public, as well as gardaí, were allowed access to these dances on payment of a small admission fee. Nurses from the local Meath and other hospitals used it as their ballroom too and many flames of romance were ignited there. Lifelong partnerships were established and many still prevail to this day.

The Olympic Ballroom too, in Pleasant Street, was also a popular venue for gardaí, nurses, teachers and civil servants resident in the nearby flatlands of Rathmines and Ranelagh. The Garda Boat Club in particular held regular dances in that ballroom on Sunday nights. Yes, those were the days!

Tony Ruane, Garda Male Voice Choir

Financial success

Tom Ryan notes that the first bank account, a thrift account, had £624 credit by the end of August 1961. The second, a current account, at the end of the same period, stood at £285 and consisted of members' subscriptions. The subscription was sixpence a week for members living in barracks and threepence for married men and men not residing in barracks, as it had been since 1953 in the years of the previous club.

After a few months of trading, the club stepped up a gear to maximise profits. It decided to publicise the reconstituted club more widely, target young members to support the Sunday night dances, and organise a weekly draw. A circular was sent to all members stationed in the Dublin area outlining the club objectives, what had been achieved, and what was likely to be achieved in the future, as well as a request for a small weekly subscription in return for membership. The response to this appeal was excellent and enabled the committee to make considerable progress. The club started the financial year 1962/63 with a balance of £1,946, whereby £100 was invested in prize bonds. (The winds of fortune were certainly blowing their way – the club won £200 the following year.) At the time the membership stood at 846. Together with the members' subscriptions and a members' weekly draw, the receipts for the year ending 31 March 1963 began to look even healthier. Annual receipts from dances were £3,200.16.20 (with £1,602.10.5 in expenses), from membership subscriptions £1,214, and the weekly draw £624.4.7. The sum of £911 was given out in prizes. By 1964, a total of £7,000 had accumulated, which represented a substantial sum in those days. It was no mean measure of success for the committee and they could now set their sights even higher.

Ballroom of Romance

I think memories of these Sunday night dances [in Kevin Street] are firmly etched in the memories of many of those who attended. The unpretentious appearance of the hall itself, the difficulty experienced by dancers trying to glide over the rough, knotty wooden floor gave the occasion a rural Ballroom of Romance atmosphere. We often tried improving the surface of the wooden floor for dancing with liberal applications of a substance called 'Glido' but to no avail; it made the knots more slippery, and turned part of the hall into an ice skating rink.

We had our own resident band, called The Altonaires, and even now when I hear once again the Jim Reeves' song *Put Your Sweet Lips a Little Closer to the Phone* and other numbers such as *North to Alaska*, I am once again back at the door of the hall, collecting the small entrance fee and assuring patrons that the spot prizes on the night were really good!

Tom Ryan, 'Personal Reminiscences', c1997

Going it alone

I would like to thank the club chairman [Ned Garvey] for his interest in matters affecting members' welfare during the year, and also members of the committee without those assistance we would be unable to carry on. A word of special appreciation for the devoted few whose wholehearted endeavors at a time of great inconvenience to themselves has produced such results.

The volume of work in Recreation Club matters is growing... It is now abundantly clear that if the Garda are to have a club premises catering for their recreational needs then they must provide it themselves. The provision of such a club was the chief aim of this committee when it was re-organised two years ago. The substantial progress made since then is indicative of the fact that this ideal has not been lost sight of but much work remains to be done before its attainment becomes an established fact. Progress must be maintained and I trust that the progress made during the year will continue and that success will breed success in the months ahead.

Tom Ryan, Assistant Honorary Secretary, Annual Report, AGM 1963

Below: Founding fathers, *left to right:* Jim Daly, Ned Garvey, Tom Ryan and Brian Prendergast in the 1980s

Harrington Street

Chapter

4

The Garda Club in Harrington Street always provided a home from home for all the exiles from country areas and became an institution in its own right.

Chapter 4
Harrington Street

THE success of the dances and other fundraising activities inspired the Garda Club committee to forge ahead with its ambitious plans. With every passing week, the idea of their own premises and a private members' club gathered greater momentum. The necessity of having to pay for repairs to the hall in Kevin Street, a building the club would never own and which was also used for official Garda purposes, began to rankle with the committee. It certainly concentrated their minds on finding a venue of their own. The chief driver of the idea was Ned Garvey.

With his experience as housing officer, Garvey was also acutely aware of the welfare of gardaí, especially recruits to the force. For over forty years, rural Ireland had supplied the force with recruits while only a tiny minority came from the Dublin city area. Many recruits were farmers' sons who experienced something of a culture shock on arriving in the capital. Mindful of the dangers of drink, Garvey wanted a place 'for the lads', a home from home, where they could enjoy a drink in comfort and safety. A place, not unlike a country hotel, where they could bring their families when visiting from the country. The 'Teddy boy' problem of the 1950s had seen the city engulfed in gang warfare. Violence was not uncommon on the streets after dark and necessitated the formation of the Riot Squad in the early 1960s. At heart, Garvey believed that a guard had to maintain certain standards as an upholder of the law, which impinged on his social life. He did not want guards to compromise themselves in that environment. When asked years later in 1985, on the twenty-first anniversary of the Harrington Street Club, why he had set it up, Garvey told Liam Collins of the *Evening Herald:* 'Young members of the force were drinking and going into dirty old pubs. We thought if they were going to do anything wrong, they might as well do it among their own.'

Ned Garvey's duty of care also extended to the other end of the age spectrum, the retired members of the force, now considerable in number. To this end, the idea of a club was publicised in *An Síothadóir*, the official organ of the then Garda Síochána Pensioners Association, in its very first issue in January 1962. According to John Duffy, deputy general secretary of the now Garda Síochána Retired Members Association (GSRMA), the article appeared to sow the seeds for what became known as the Garda Club. It outlined how both serving and retired members of the force could develop a facility to cater for their many social and recreational needs outside their primary career activity. It proposed a three-way membership for all members serving and retired, both within and outside the DMA. Essentially, it proposed a life membership for those within the DMA of £8 8*s* and for those outside of £4 4*s*. An ongoing annual membership fee of £2 2*s* was proposed for those within the DMA and Dublin County and of £1 1*s* for those outside. The proposal was accompanied by a sign-up slip whereby an interested member could provide his name and address and indicate which option he wished to avail of.

Adequate premises for the proposed Garda Social Club became the preoccupation of Ned Garvey and his colleagues. Always on the lookout, their main criteria were a building of suitable size and a good location. As the adage says, good things come to those who wait, and it certainly proved so for the committee. In Harrington Street on Dublin's South Circular Road at Nos 9, 10 and 11 stood premises collectively known as the CYMS Hall. It soon came to Garvey's attention that it was up for sale and at last success was in sight.

The CYMS Hall was a facility operated since 1912 by the Saint Laurence Branch of the Catholic Young Men's Society (CYMS), later known as the St Laurence O'Toole Branch. The building was spacious and had a number of rooms as well as two large dance halls. According to its title deeds, it was a premises situated on lands called the Farm of Saint Pulchre, otherwise known as Saint Sepulchre, in the Barony of Upper Cross, on the south side of the part of the Circular Road known as Harrington Street. Indeed few of those who subsequently socialised in the Garda Recreation Club would associate the place with either Saint Sepulchre or the Barony of Upper Cross! The oldest traceable owners of the Georgian premises date from 1840 when ownership was transferred from Sophia Henry to Thomas Benjamin Middleton. It is believed that the latter or his estate possibly sold the premises to the CYMS in 1912. *Shaw's Dublin City Directory 1850* lists the occupants of No 8 Harrington Street as Charles J Meara and of No 10 as Rev James Wilson. Over a decade later, the Dublin Street Directory from *Thom's Irish Almanac 1862* lists the occupants of No 8 as Henry Brett, Esq CE, county surveyor for Wicklow; No 9 as the residence of Mrs Jane Stuart; No 10 as that of John Hayes, a merchant; and No 11 of George F Shaw, Esq, a fellow of Trinity College, Dublin. In the year before the CYMS purchased the premises, the 1911 Census reveals that a Russian-born Jewish dental surgeon, Bernard Jackson, lived at No 8 with his family and servants. No 9 was occupied by Frederick Eastham Birckley, a ship's chief steward, and his wife Caroline as well as her elderly mother and her younger brother and sister. No 10 was a boarding house run by a Miss Mary Kelly and housed two boarders at the time, a widowed Englishwoman, Mrs Maryann Reynolds, and a young civil engineer from Mayo called Michael Gallagher. No 11 was unoccupied.

During 1963, the governing body of the CYMS decided to sell the premises. The reason for their decision is not clear, but believed to be due to the premises falling into disrepair with little or no funds available for renovation. According to former

Garda Club chairman, Brian Prendergast, the reason also stemmed from the failure by the CYMS to obtain a club licence for the sale of liquor. The parish priest at St Kevin's Church on Harrington Street, Monsignor Hurley, had hitherto strenuously objected to the efforts of the committee to put a bar in the CYMS Hall.

The auctioneering firm of James H North & Co of 110 Grafton Street was instructed to conduct the sale on behalf of the vendors. An advertising campaign was mounted and notice of a public auction posted. Full particulars of the three Georgian houses were supplied by North: they were three-storey over-basement buildings fronting Harrington Street with a rear entrance at Synge Lane. Numbers 9/10 had a total floor area of approximately 15,000 square feet and were equipped with solid fuel central heating. The ground floor boasted a large ballroom with three offices, ladies and gents toilets, a cloakroom and a double staircase to the first floor. The first floor was dominated by a large billiard room and included four rooms with storage accommodation and toilets. The entire second floor had been converted into a 1,500-square-feet flat, comprising a sittingroom, three bedrooms, kitchen and bathroom. The basement of the same dimensions consisted of four rooms and a boiler room. As for No 11, the building had four sitting tenants at the time, mainly office accommodation for local businesses.

The auction was scheduled to take place at the Grafton Street premises of the auctioneers on 5 November 1963. In the meantime, Ned Garvey was not idle. It was a mark of the man – as indeed of many a great visionary – that he did not wait for his actions to be sanctioned first by the committee or the members at large. According to Tom Ryan, procedure was not always adhered to: 'We had, as a committee, an unusual procedural method of making decisions. In most committees, committee meetings are held, decisions made and authority given to proceed with certain transactions. We, however, took action first and then went back to the committee for retrospective approval, which, in fairness to the committee, was invariably granted.' On balance, Ned Garvey did discuss the intended sale with a small coterie of club officers and it was decided that the premises met their dual-suitability criteria of location and size. Inspections of the property followed and the intention to purchase solidified.

A visit was swiftly made to their local bank, the Munster & Leinster on Dame Street. After discussions with the manager, the board of the bank approved funding for the club's intended venture to purchase the CYMS Hall. This was later confirmed by letter from the sub-manager, Mr J Slattery, dated 24 September 1963, and again on 21 November. It authorised the amount of £25,000 on overdraft, to 'outstand at the pleasure of the bank pending review in twelve months'. It also stated that the bank would expect clearance to be effected gradually over a period of seven to eight years. These were helpful and generous terms at the time, bearing in mind the average gross Garda salary was in the region of £800 per year. Indeed in the context of Irish banking history, the club had approached the bank at a rather opportune time.

TELEGRAMS: NORTH, DUBLIN

TELEPHONE: 74721·3

Established 1829

James H. **NORTH** & Co. Ltd.

D. F. STEPHENSON, P.C., F.V.I., M.I.A.A. WILLIAM SPILLANE, M.I.A.A. RICHARD F. MELDON, M.I.A.A. R. B. CREGAN, M.I.A.A. J. D. KELLY, M.I.A.A. B. E. DE LA TORRE, M.I.A.A.

ESTATE AGENTS - AUCTIONEERS - VALUERS

110 GRAFTON STREET
DUBLIN·2

ALSO AT
20, PICCADILLY · LONDON, W.1
TELEPHONE: REGENT 3759
7, VICTORIA TERRACE, HOVE 3
TELEPHONE: HOVE 32538

WHEN REPLYING IT IS IMPORTANT TO QUOTE THIS REFERENCE

YOUR REF.

RC/CRE

2?th September, 1963.

Superintendent Garvey,
Garda Headquarters,
Kilmainham,
Dublin.

re: 9/10/11 Harrington Street

Dear Sir/Madam,

Some time ago you enquired about the above premises, and we have now been instructed to offer the property for sale by public auction on Tuesday 5th November and we enclose herewith full particulars.

Yours faithfully,

James H. North & Co.

Above: **Auctioneer's letter from 1963**

Below: **Munster & Leinster Bank letter from 1963**

PRIVATE

The Munster & Leinster Bank Limited

(G.P.O. BOX 96.)

TELEGRAPHIC ADDRESS: "MUNLIN, DUBLIN"
TELEPHONE 56731

ALL COMMUNICATIONS TO BE ADDRESSED TO THE MANAGER

JJS/NMcG

Dame Street,
Dublin, 2 21st November, 1963.

Chief Superintendent Garvey,
Garda Siochana,
A Branch and Technical Bureau,
St. John's Road,
Kingsbridge,
DUBLIN.

Garda Siochana.
Metropolitan Recreation Club.
Overdraft - £7,006.18.11.
Thrift Deposit
Credit - £ 578. 0. 0.

Dear Sir,

With reference to our recent interview, it is desired to notify that our Directors have authorised the required advance on the above-mentioned account as follows -

AMOUNT: £25,000 on overdraft.

REPAYMENT: To outstand at pleasure of the Bank pending review in twelve months, it being noted that clearance will be effected gradually over a maximum period of five years.

SECURITY: To be provided -
Registered Deposit of property, Nos. 9 & 10, Harrington Street, Dublin, which has been purchased for £24,200.

The advance is, of course, a substitution for that authorised by the Board on the 23rd September last.

We think it well to mention that we have not received the Solicitor's Letter of Undertaking regarding the deeds of the property purchased and we shall be obliged if you will arrange with Mr. O'Clery to forward the Undertaking required without delay. Messrs. Hickey & O'Reilly, Solicitors, are acting for the Bank in the matter and they will be in touch with Mr. O'Clery in due course.

We confirm that we have arranged provisional Fire Cover on the properties to the extent of £50,000 as requested and we are retaining the Cover Note at this Office.

Yours faithfully,

Sub-Manager.

Some years earlier it might not have been quite so favourable. Major changes to the structure of Irish banking occurred in the 1960s in the wake of a new pro-business government. Architects of the change, Taoiseach Seán Lemass and economist and public servant TK Whittaker published their second Programme for Economic Expansion in 1963. It heralded a new era in the economy of the Irish state. Smaller banks merged to form four main players and began to offer mass banking services to the general public hitherto considered the preserve of traders and the rich. There was an unprecedented willingness to support ventures that might have seemed risky by the standards of the day – such as the Garda Club. Interestingly, the main method of providing finance – as evidenced in the Garda Club case – was by overdraft or by discounting of bills. This practice continued until 1972 when term lending was introduced and overdrafts discouraged, as evidenced too by later Garda Club bank records.

The day of the auction of Nos 9/10/11 Harrington Street finally dawned on 5 November 1963. Ned Garvey and his team, which included Tom Ryan, Jim Daly and Charlie Gaffney, promptly went to the auction rooms of North & Co on Grafton Street at the appointed hour of 2.30 pm. As is customary, the auctioneer outlined the terms of the sale – the premises known as the CYMS Hall, located at Nos 9, 10 and 11 Harrington Street. He also outlined the procedures under which he would conduct the auction. What he did not tell the assembled bidders, however, was that there was a reserve of £29,000 on the property. This, of course, was information he was under no obligation to disclose in advance. Being a substantial property, there were a number of interested parties present with the intention of making a purchase.

Below: Solicitor's receipt from 1963

Ref. No. 758

MICHEAL B. O'CLEIRIGH & CO.,
SOLICITORS.
TELEPHONE: 61211.

16, MOLESWORTH STREET,
DUBLIN, 18 Nov 1963

re: C.Y.M.S. Hall.

Received from Supt. E. Garvey
the sum of Seven Thousand two hundred sixty Pounds ——— shillings
and ——— pence, Stg., being Deposit & auctioneers fees on 9/10 Harrington Street (purchase price £24,200 plus fees)

£7260-0-0

Micheál B. O'Cleirigh

In addition to Ned Garvey and those acting on behalf of the Garda Club, the well-known Dónall Ó Moráin, acting on behalf of Gael Linn, was also present. Mr Ó Moráin was the Ard Stiúrthóir of Gael Linn at the time and like Ned Garvey had similar objectives in seeking a permanent home for his organisation.

After the preliminary opening of the auction, the first bid of £10,000 was made by Ned Garvey. The bids rapidly increased in £1,000-jumps until the highest bid was £17,000. Thereafter, the bids continued upwards in £500-jumps until Ned Garvey's final bid of £26,000. As no higher bid was tendered, the property, not having reached its reserve price, was withdrawn from sale by the auctioneer. Post-auction negotiations continued over the next couple of weeks between the auctioneer and the highest bidder, Ned Garvey and his team. As a result of these talks, No 11 Harrington Street was excluded from the sale as it had sitting tenants and it did not appear to the Garvey team that vacant possession would be achieved in the immediate future. Following on from this consideration, the team proceeded to negotiate for the purchase of Nos 9 and 10. A deal on these two properties, which included the halls, was agreed with Ned Garvey at a price of £24,200. No 11 with its sitting tenants was sold subsequently to another purchaser at a price of £3,500. The total price of the properties amounted to £27,700, some £1,300 short of its reserve price on auction day.

A banner headline in the *Evening Press* of 12 December 1963 announced the news of the purchase: 'NEW LUXURY CENTRE FOR CITY GARDAI'. Citing it as the first of its kind in the country, the newspaper reported that the new recreation centre would have bar facilities, a restaurant service and eventually sleeping accommodation for visiting foreign police and gardaí from the provinces at a nominal charge. Indeed, it would be some time before members would consider the venue in any way luxurious. However, they could bask in the luxury of knowing the club was unique among police forces the world over – its creation was made solely through the voluntary efforts of its members without any outside assistance.

Drafting club rules

Now having to contend with post-sale legalities, the Garda Club committee engaged the legal services of Michael B O'Cleirigh & Co of 16 Molesworth Street to act on its behalf. Naturally a number of formalities consequent on the sale or purchase of any property had to be gone through. Title deeds had to be checked and their legality established. Finance had to be approved and the bank's interest protected. All legal and financial formalities were completed and the deeds of sale were finally signed on 22 July 1964. Given the historic nature of the acquisition and the character of Ned Garvey, it was perhaps inevitable that a certain mythology would develop. A tale surfaced in subsequent years that Ned Garvey and Tom Ryan had taken out a loan against their own homes to purchase the club premises. It was broadcast far and wide

THURSDAY, DECEMBER 12, 1963

EVENING PRESS

Vol. 10 (No. 296) (50th Week) Price 3d.

New luxury centre for city gardai

Evening Press reporter

THE C.Y.M.S. Hall, Harrington Street, Dublin, has been bought for £27,000 by the Dublin Metropolitan Garda Recreation Club, as a recreation centre for the members of the force attached to the Metropolitan Division.

When the centre is furnished and equipped the project will have cost more than £40,000 and it will be the first of its kind in the country.

The centre will have bar facilities, restaurant service and eventually sleeping accommodation for visiting foreign police and Gardai from the provinces who can have bed and breakfast at a nominal charge.

The hall consists of ... square feet and th... billiard room a ... There are abo... besides.

Soci...

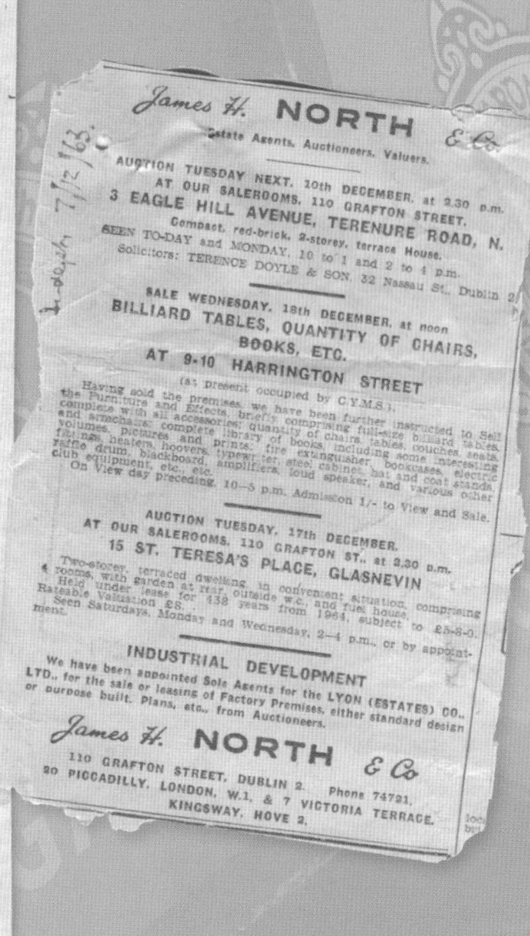

James H. NORTH & Co

Estate Agents, Auctioneers, Valuers.

AUCTION TUESDAY NEXT, 10th DECEMBER, at 2.30 p.m.
AT OUR SALEROOMS, 110 GRAFTON STREET.
3 EAGLE HILL AVENUE, TERENURE ROAD, N.
Compact, red-brick, 2-storey, terrace House.
SEEN TO-DAY and MONDAY, 10 to 1 and 2 to 4 p.m.
Solicitors: TERENCE DOYLE & SON, 32 Nassau St., Dublin 2.

SALE WEDNESDAY, 18th DECEMBER, at noon
BILLIARD TABLES, QUANTITY OF CHAIRS, BOOKS, ETC.
AT 9-10 HARRINGTON STREET
(at present occupied by C.Y.M.S.).

Having sold the premises, we have been further instructed to Sell the Furniture and Effects, briefly comprising full-size billiard tables complete with all accessories; quantity of chairs, tables, couches, seats and armchairs; complete library of books, including some interesting volumes, pictures and prints; fire extinguisher, bookcases, electric fittings, heaters, hoovers, typewriter, steel cabinet, hat and coat stands, raffle drum, blackboard, amplifiers, loud speaker, and various other club equipment, etc., etc.

On View day preceding, 10—5 p.m. Admission 1/- to View and Sale.

AUCTION TUESDAY, 17th DECEMBER,
AT OUR SALEROOMS, 110 GRAFTON ST., at 2.30 p.m.
15 ST. TERESA'S PLACE, GLASNEVIN

Two-storey, terraced dwelling in convenient situation, comprising 4 rooms, with garden at rear, outside w.c., and fuel house.

Held under lease for 438 years from 1964, subject to £5-8-0. Rateable Valuation £8.

Seen Saturdays, Monday and Wednesday, 2—4 p.m., or by appointment.

INDUSTRIAL DEVELOPMENT

We have been appointed Sole Agents for the LYON (ESTATES) CO., LTD., for the sale or leasing of Factory Premises, either standard design or purpose built. Plans, etc., from Auctioneers.

James H. NORTH & Co

110 GRAFTON STREET, DUBLIN 2. Phone 74721,
20 PICCADILLY, LONDON, W.1, & 7 VICTORIA TERRACE, KINGSWAY, HOVE 2.

Above: Notice of auction of contents of Harrington Street

Left: News of the new Garda Club reaches the *Evening Press* on 12 December 1963

yet no records, banking or legal, were ever found to support this claim. It was clear that that club's overdraft arrangement had secured the purchase of the premises. Nonetheless, the matter certainly went down in the annals of the club.

While waiting for the legalities to be completed, the committee in 1963 was busy preparing for things to come. On realising that they were now the owners of substantial premises whose value could greatly increase over the coming years, the committee felt it necessary to establish the club as a legal entity. This could only be achieved by having a set of rules drafted professionally that would serve the club and protect the interests of its members. The proposed rules would have to be such that they would satisfy the Circuit Court when the club applied for registration under the Registration of Clubs Act 1904–1962. A successful application would enable the club to sell alcoholic drinks legally to its members. To achieve this in a legal and proper manner, Michael O'Cleirigh engaged the services of Mr Colm Condon SC. The set of rules that Mr Condon drafted were adopted by the club at a special general meeting held in Kevin Street Station on 31 December 1963. These are still in force to this day, except for a few minor amendments necessitated by the passage of time and changes in the Liquor Licensing Acts.

The rules stated that the official title of the club was the Dublin Metropolitan Garda Recreation Club and its objectives were:

> *(a) the provision of social and recreational facilities of every nature and kind; (b) the provision and maintenance of a club house in Dublin and the provision and maintenance therein of social, recreational and catering facilities of such nature and kind as from time to time may be thought fit; (c) the making of a grant or grants for the purpose of supplying any article or articles of a recreational nature for the use of members at places other than in the said club house in the event of application being made for a grant or grants for such purposes and provided that it is clearly shown that the article or articles is or are for collective and not individual use; (d) the arrangement for and provision of social and recreational events of every nature and kind.*

Eligibility to join was extended to members of the previous club of the same name; all members of An Garda Síochána, including Ban Gardaí, serving in the Dublin Metropolitan Division (DMD) or residing there; retired members of the force who had at any time served in the DMD; wives or husbands or widows and widowers of any of the above classes of members; and any persons the governing body saw fit to admit as honorary members. The governing body of the club was to be known as the Divisional Committee and consist of a president, of chief superintendent rank in the DMD; a chairman; a vice chairman; an honorary secretary; an assistant honorary secretary and an honorary treasurer; and a member from each District and Detective

Branch in the DMD. In keeping with the democratic nature of the organisation, the executive committee would be elected by the members at the annual general meeting (AGM). The district representatives were elected in their respective districts and the elections subsequently ratified at the AGM. For the purpose of transacting Divisional Committee business, a quorum of five members was required and fifty for an AGM. In addition, trustees were to be appointed by the Divisional Committee for the purpose of acquiring, holding or disposing of property on behalf of the club. The number of trustees was set at three and any ordinary or honorary member of the club could be appointed by the Divisional Committee to hold the position. In practice, it became two officers of the club and the assistant commissioner of the DMA.

The rules also laid down the subscription rates for ordinary membership of the club. In 1963, it was set at £2.60 per annum for serving members and £1.30 per annum for retired members. For members outside the DMD who wished to avail of certain facilities of the club, a 'country member' rate was fixed at 50p per annum. After that it was at the discretion of the Divisional Committee to fix the rates from time to time. In subsequent years various rule changes came into force, such as relating to the president of the club, honorary membership, extending membership to gardaí attached to Headquarters, the quorum of the Divisional Committee, and so forth.

Preparation for the proposed registration of the club under the relevant Act continued apace. For this purpose the club solicitor engaged the services of Mr Anthony Hederman BL, a young and up-and-coming lawyer with an excellent reputation in the legal area of licensing. Without further ado, a legally required notice appeared in the *Irish Press* on 3 July 1964. This notice was to inform the public of the club's intention to apply to the Circuit Court, Chancery Street, Dublin, on the forenoon of 27 July 1964 for a certificate of registration under the Registration of Clubs Act 1908. The application was duly heard and granted by the presiding judge. The hearing gave rise to a few unexpected chuckles on the day. In the course of the proceedings, Judge Conroy asked the assistant chief state solicitor Walter Carroll if the gardaí had any objection to the granting of the licence, as is customary in liquor licensing applications. 'The Gardaí have no objection,' Mr Carroll duly replied, amid much laughter in the court. This legal imprimatur allowed the gardaí to become freemen in the world of drinking in their own club.

Right: Registration notice in the *Irish Press*, 3 July 1964

REGISTRATION OF CLUBS ACTS 1904 - 1962

TAKE NOTICE that on the 2nd day of July 1964 we lodged with the Registrar of Clubs, Dublin Metropolitan District, an application for a Certificate of Registration of the Dublin Metropolitan Garda Recreation Club in respect of premises at 9/10 Harrington Street in the City of Dublin in the Dublin Metropolitan District.

AND FURTHER TAKE NOTICE that said application will be heard at the Dublin Circuit Court, Chancery Place on the 27th day of July 1964 or on the first available opportunity thereafter.

MICHEAL B. O'CLEIRIGH & CO.,
Solicitors for the Applicants,
16 Molesworth Street,
Dublin 2.

It is ironic that both the late Mr Condon and Mr Hederman went on to become Attorneys General. The former served in that office from March 1965 to 1973 when there was a change of government, while the latter served from 1977 until 1981, vacating it too on a change of government. Mr Hederman was later appointed to the bench of the High Court, where he served with distinction for many years before being appointed to the Supreme Court. Older club members noted with a sense of ironic glee the subsequent success of the first two legal experts to render professional assistance to the fledgling club. Some members of the club would jokingly say their success was because of their work with the club. Others would say their success was in spite of their association with the club! Either way all members of the club, past and present, wished them both well on many an occasion.

Clerk of works

The euphoria of being the proud owners of a fine building subsided somewhat when the committee actually took possession. You could say it was in a less than desirable condition. This was hardly unexpectected as several inspections had been carried out prior to purchase. When the magnitude of the renovation task became apparent, Tom Ryan recalls that it was decided to seek help from the membership of the divisional force, especially from those who had a background in any of the trades. To this end, Ned Garvey sought out Brian Prendergast, who was attached to the Divisional Office in Dublin Castle.

'You worked in that builders' place in Lincoln Place, and your father tells me you were involved in the supply of building materials for big jobs in Dublin,' Mr Garvey enquired. 'I want someone who has some idea of that type of thing to help us get our premises into proper shape after we take it into our possession … after Christmas, in January.'

Clerk of works

Before I joined the force, I was an architectural ironmonger and maybe it was for that reason that I was asked by the late Edmund Garvey to join the committee on January 1, 1964, with himself, ex-Supt Tom Ryan, Supt Sean O'Mahoney and Station Sergeant John O'Gara. From my time in the Divisional Office I knew all kinds of useful people – plumbers, painters, bricklayers, etc. – and Garvey, who was a superintendent then, went out and got them while I acted as clerk of works.

Brian Prendergast, Garda News, *July/August 1990*

Little did Brian Prendergast think that his answer to Garvey's question, 'What do you call the person in a building site that organises the workforce and the supply of materials?' would cast him in the role of 'a clerk of works'. As the newly charged clerk of works, Prendergast was promptly co-opted on to the committee by Garvey. Indeed the management of the workforce was to prove as big a task as the actual work itself.

The scale of the task soon became evident. At the beginning of January 1964, Ned Garvey, Tom Ryan and John O'Gara met Brian Prendergast outside the CYMS Hall at 10 am as prearranged, according to Prendergast:

> *We entered the premises, the top floor rooms in total disrepair. The top hall had been a billiard room with central heating piping on each side of the hall and about three feet out from each wall. There was a number of rooms on the first floor in reasonable shape, but in need of decoration. The lower hall was reasonable; the floor very dirty and full of walked-in chewing gum. The basement was partly flooded and totally unusable.*

Unfazed, Ned Garvey then outlined what he wanted to happen. The priority lay with rooms that could be quickly prepared for functions that could give an income to the club. There was no doubt as to what the first venture would be. Bingo. It had at that time become very popular and was firmly established as a major recreational outlet – highly addictive too – for many people of advanced years. In fact, it was nothing short of a national sport. Hence, Ned Garvey wanted the top and lower halls decorated and made suitable to hold bingo sessions once more; he wanted the card tables found in the basement repaired in order to restart the whist drives, which had been held in the CYMS every Sunday night for many years. There were other reasons too that prompted Garvey to embrace bingo and whist. Keeping the local community involved and on side was no mean consideration when running a club and applying for a club licence. That said, it also appealed to his sense of community and inclusiveness. A deadline for April 1964 was then set to have the bingo and whist up and running.

It was decided that the rooms on the top floor were to be left until money to renovate them became available. The four rooms on the first floor were to be decorated. The central heating pipes in the top hall were to be tidied into the wall and covered with wooden seating. This in reality entailed a good deal of modernisation. Walls and iron/steel girders holding up the roof had to be cleaned and painted. Stairs and walls likewise needed cleaning and painting as did the entrance hallway. In the downstairs hall the remains of a chimney stack had to be removed, the wall plastered and all walls cleaned down and painted. In addition, wooden seating had to be fitted around the wall, similar to the top hall. The whist tables in the basement had to be repaired and covered in green baize.

Above: Ray McEneaney clearing up after a bingo session and overseen by the clerk of works, Brian Prendergast, in 1964

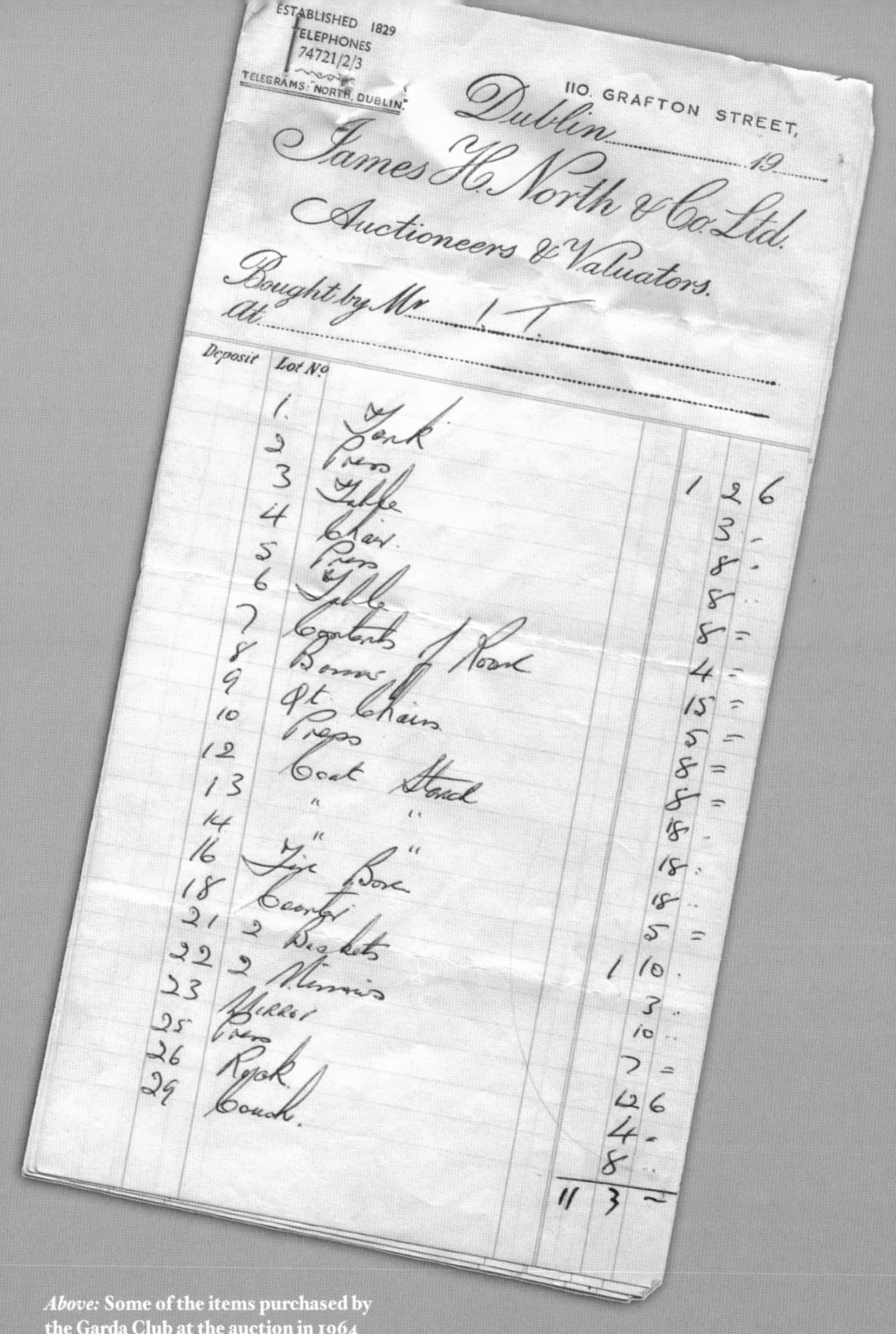

ESTABLISHED 1829
TELEPHONES
74721/2/3
TELEGRAMS: "NORTH, DUBLIN."

110. GRAFTON STREET,
Dublin .... 19 ....

James H. North & Co. Ltd.
Auctioneers & Valuators.

Bought by Mr ...... I. T. ......
At ....

Deposit	Lot No		£	s	d
	1.	Tank	1	2	6
	2	Press		3	-
	3	Table		8	-
	4	Chair.		8	-
	5	Press		8	-
	6	Table		4	-
	7	Contents of Room		15	-
	8	[illegible]		5	-
	9	[illegible] Chairs		8	-
	10	Press		8	-
	12	Coat Stand		18	-
	13	" "		18	-
	14	" "		18	-
	16	Fire Box		5	-
	18	Counter	1	10	-
	21	2 Baskets		3	-
	22	2 Mirrors		10	-
	23	Mirror		7	-
	25	Press		2	6
	26	Rack.		4	-
	29	Couch.		8	-
			11	3	-

Above: **Some of the items purchased by the Garda Club at the auction in 1964**

With lightning speed the men set to work, purchasing a dozen galvanised buckets, two dozen paint scrapers, two reams of cleaning cloths, two dozen packets of sugar soap from Dockeralls of George's Street, as well as several industrial-strength rubber gloves. Once the call had gone out for help, the response from the membership far exceeded the committee's expectations. In the following weeks and months, about fifty interested members came forward – plasterers, plumbers, electricians, carpenters, bricklayers and others – with a willingness to help. This was in an era when prospective Garda applicants had spent their preparatory time working on building sites in England, rather than in the third-level colleges of today. As a result, most of the younger members had some basic skills in the common trades. The recruitment of women to the force, which had begun in 1959, was also a welcome boon. Though small in number, these Ban Gardaí, as they were then called, contributed to the decor in various ways.

The contents of the CYMS Hall had been auctioned off around the same time as the sale of the property. The auction presented the club with an opportunity to purchase a range of items required for running a private club and functions – from seating and other furniture to floor coverings, furnishings, and electrical, whist and billiard equipment. The more substantial pieces of furniture included five presses, various chairs, three coat stands, eight couches, four tables, four glass cases, ten armchairs and a counter. With a view to future ventures, the club bought two whist drive blackboards for 10 shillings, about eighty whist tables and twenty-seven chairs, a whist sign for 6 shillings, a spotlight for 12/6p, a bandstand for £4 10*s*, an easel and board for 4 shillings, and a dummy door for 2 shillings. A quantity of books was bought for 5 shillings; housed in glass cases these were placed in the room that became known as the library but that had previously been the billiard room.

Though it is impossible to remember every member who was pressed into service, some come to mind: Frank Kieran, Michael Vaughan and Tom Keenan, who did the painting along with Brian Prendergast; the Mulcahy brothers who did the internal plastering; Bill Cloney and Paddy Prendergast who covered the whist tables repaired by Michael Prendergast; the general workforce responsible for the major clean-up of the premises included Sean O'Mahony, Charles Gaffney, Oliver Nugent, Paddy Wallace, Frank Barry, Harry Feeney, John Shields, Tom Ryan, John O'Gara and Finbarr Kelly. The seating around the walls of both halls was constructed by Tim Farrell. Repairs to the roof were effected by John Murphy and Peter O'Connor. The brickwork at the front of the premises was repointed by Tom Lohan and Leo Fayne. Sarah McGuinness and Phyllis Nolan amongst others were involved in organising the curtains fronting the premises and advising on colour schemes and furnishings.

The tradesmen, as Tom Ryan recalled, were the important people in this effort but the work of the unskilled labourers was also crucial. Tom, putting himself amongst the latter, remembers when it was decided that the dance hall floor needed

Slated

In the early sixties, I was a young recruit stationed at Harcourt Street Garda Station. I can recall finishing duty at 2 pm on a very wet day and having my meal break when I got a telephone call from Det Insp Ned Garvey of Pearse Street Garda Station, whom I had never met before. He informed me who he was and that he had signed a contract to purchase the CYMS Hall in Harrington Street earlier that day.

'Slates are missing from the roof and you can see what sort of a day we're having,' he then said. 'A birdie told me you've the reputation of being able to drive a nail straight.'

'I've been known to be able to do that,' said I.

He then asked if I could meet at the CYMS in an hour, which I did. There I also met John Murphy for the first time along with Ned Garvey.

The rain was just pouring in. John and myself went onto the roof for a closer look and we decided that about twelve Blue Bangor slates would do the job. We told Ned of our findings and he said: 'Come on.' We got into his cream Beetle car and headed off for McGovern's place in Islandbridge. Now, part of McGovern's business was knocking down old houses and selling off old slates and stuff. We went into the yard and Ned went to Mr McGovern, whom he seemed to have known before. Ned told Mr McGovern of the purchase he had made and that the roof was leaking and that he needed some slates and had no feckin' money.

After some discussion, Mr McGovern told us that we could have any slate in the yard bar a full one. I proceeded around the yard picking up some slates that had a little damage to the corners but were still perfect for the job. I continued collecting until we had enough. Next morning, John and myself did the repairs to the roof and the leak was soon gone!

Peter O'Connor

sanding. He was given the unenviable task of scraping hardened chewing gum off the floor before sanding could commence. On another occasion he was entrusted with the job of removing an old stage from the end of the bottom hall. By his own admission, he approached the job with caution and cunning. It would, he reasoned, simplify matters if he could find a main support for the structure and commence work at that point. He was, unfortunately, correct in his prognosis. When he pushed the support, the entire structure collapsed on top of him in a mass of hardboard sheets and plastic fittings, while a huge cloud of thick black dust, in residence since the turn of the century, descended on him!

As work and effort continued the committee knew that the services of a professional were needed for the dream to be fully realised. The architect James O'Toole of Lynch O'Toole Walsh, based in Rathfarnham, was employed to give professional assistance to what was, in fact, a huge undertaking. He progressed with his work and employed the building firm of James Nolan & Sons of Drumcondra to carry out a full refurbishment of the entire building. This involved both halls and the inclusion of bars and kitchen and restaurant facilities. The cost of this work amounted to £13,528. In addition, the firm of mechanical engineers, PJ O'Reilly &

'Will you do the bar?'

In mid-1964 the bar and lounge were finally open for business. After all the cleaning and refurbishment, all that remained was to find a barman. True to form, Mr Garvey had received intelligence that I had some bar experience as a young man growing up in Clonmel, County Tipperary.

'Will you do the bar?' Mr Garvey asked in his gentlemanly way, more a request than a question.

'I will,' said I, thinking I had little choice but wanting to help out all the same.

And with that I became the first barman in the Garda Club. The first person I had the honour of serving was no other than Mr Garvey himself in the company of a professor friend from Trinity College. They lifted up the shutter while I got behind the bar and served them. A glass of Britvic orange juice for Mr Garvey, a lifelong pioneer, and a pint of stout for his friend. Then together they sat at the bar counter and, like old friends, had a good chinwag.

Oliver Nugent, former Divisional Committee member and former president and captain, Stackstown Golf Club

Sons, based in Rathmines, was engaged to install a full heating and air extraction system. The cost of this work came to about £1,710. A total of £15,238 was spent on refurbishment, which represents 63 per cent of the purchase price of the building. This cost, of course, did not include furnishings and fittings.

As work on the bingo and the whist got underway, Ned Garvey focused his attention elsewhere – the club bar and lounge. The most difficult job in the modernisation of the club premises was, as agreed by all who can remember it, the clearing out and rebuilding of the basement for the said club bar and lounge. The basement had been unused for many years by the previous owner. It was pitch dark, damp and musty, and rainwater from the street percolated through the roof. A place hardly fit for a convivial drink. Nonetheless, the architects drew up a plan in which the available space was maximised to full advantage and at the same time created a decor and ambience in keeping with the structural detail of the building. Most of this work was handled by Ned Garvey with the assistance of John Murphy and his brother Mike who was well experienced in bar design. The cost of this reconstruction was estimated to be £12,000. At the time it was an excellent investment in that it increased the earning potential of the club considerably, boding well for the future. Former committee member Oliver Nugent recalls that the bar was ready some six to eight months after the premises were purchased.

Once the bottom hall was modernised, all that remained to be acquired were chairs, amplification and a machine capable of being operated for the random selection of bingo balls! It was discovered that the best value in these machines could be found in Cork. Needing no encouragement, Tom Ryan, Jim Daly and John Fleming drove to the city by the Lee and duly bought the machine. It was a basic well-constructed model, manually operated, and served its purpose for many years in the Garda Club. Before the bingo could start up, however, the room to the right of the entrance hall had to be developed as a 'sweetshop' to cater for the bingo patrons before the session and at the interval. This was no trivial consideration. A bingo without a sweetshop was like a dance hall without drink. Bingo patrons knew only too well how wine gums or bon-bons or bulleyes could ease the anticipation and excitement of watching their numbers being called out. At this stage, John Murphy came to the rescue and built the counter and shelving for the sweetshop. Indeed John's capacity for construction knew no bounds; he also made fifty-six tables with ten seats each for the hall. The room to the left of the entrance hall was designated as the office, in which the controls for the amplification system for the bingo and public announcements were to be installed.

Bang on schedule, the hall was ready for bingo and whist by April 1964. At first the bingo was held on Tuesday and Friday nights and then on Sunday afternoons as well, such was its popularity. On Garda duty by day, on bingo duty by night, notable members in this regard were John Fagan, caller, John Fleming, top hall caller, and

AN CHUIRT DUICHE
(THE DISTRICT COURT)

THE DUBLIN METROPOLITAN AREA

THE GAMING AND LOTTERIES ACT 1956

LICENCE PURSUANT TO SECTION 28

WHEREAS John Murphy, Honorary Secretary of the Dublin Metropolitan Garda Recreation Club has made application to me on the 31st day of August 1977 for a licence for the promotion of periodical lotteries on the Sunday of each week during the period from the 28th day of August 1977 to the 27th day of August 1978 AND WHEREAS I am satisfied that the applicant has duly served on the proper Officer of the Garda Siochana the notice required under the provisions of the said Act.

Now I the Justice having heard the application and considered same do grant to the said applicant the said licence under Section 28 of the Gaming and Lotteries Act 1956 (No. 2 of 1956) for the promotion of periodical lotteries on Sunday of each week during the period from the 28th August 1977 to the 27th August 1978 subject to the following hereinafter contained conditions:

1. The kind of lottery to be carried out is Bingo and same is to be carried out at the Garda Club Premises 8/10 Harrington Street in the City of Dublin.

2. The purpose of the lottery is to provide higher education for children of Garda Siochana in the Dublin Metropolitan area.

3. Not more than 40% of the gross proceeds shall be utilised for the expenses of the promotion including commission.

4. Prizes shall be awarded as follows:-

10 Prizes of £6.00 each	£ 60.00
8 Prizes of £10.00 each	£ 80.00
2 Prizes of £15.00 each	£ 30.00
1 Prize of £25.00	£ 25.00
1 Prize of £100.00	£100.00
	£295.00
Pool Prize	£100.00
Snowball	£100.00

making a total of £495.00 not a sum in excess of £500.00 weekly.

5. The value of each prize shall be stated on every ticket or coupon declared.

DATED THIS 24 DAY OF August 1977.

Signed [signature]

One of the Justices of the said District Court assigned to the said District

Left and below:
Bingo licence issued to Garda Club

Brian Prendergast, floor and auxiliary caller. Paddy Wallace and Finbarr Kelly sold the books, while Phyllis Nolan served in the sweetshop. Other members involved at the time were John Murphy, Joe Campbell, Tom Noone and Oliver Nugent. Bingo proved then and over the following years to be the club's best money earner. It is true to say that the money generated by the twice- and the later three-times weekly bingo sessions helped in no small way to clear the outstanding debt and generate enough for the future development of the club.

When both halls were ready, the dances at the recreation hall in Kevin Street were discontinued and effectively transferred to the Garda Club. To the delight of the committee, the transfer of dancers from one venue to the other was as smooth as could be desired. These dances continued for many years and again were a source of great revenue for the club and a wonderful social venue for the myriads who attended.

The club could now offer members the use of two large halls, a number of meeting rooms, a bar and lounge, a TV room and a private lounge. Records show the

Home from home

The establishment of the Garda Recreation Club in Harrington Street in 1964 provided a welcome social centre for the youth who resided in its vicinity. At that time there were no worries about 'pay and display' parking, or drink driving regulations, for the simple reason that very few patrons owned any kind of motor vehicle and, anyhow, intoxicating liquor was not served at these gatherings. Only soft drinks, tea or coffee could be obtained in the 'mineral bars' of these dance halls.

But everyone seemed to be happy and joyful: 'public order offences', as defined in much later legislation, were rare occurrences, as throngs of these youngsters filled the footways of Lower Rathmines Road as they made their way homeward to their bedsits. Taxis were out of the question for these pedestrian travellers because of a simple funding issue. If a girl happened to 'get off' with a fellow who owned some kind of a motor car, she would tell all her friends, who would avail of a lift home in a very crowded vehicle!

But the Garda Club in Harrington Street always provided a home from home for all the exiles from country areas and became an institution in its own right. Sports and other organisations used the venue for their functions and a 'céad míle fáilte' was extended to all.

Tony Ruane, Garda Male Voice Choir

Overleaf: Balance sheet from 1964

DUBLIN METROPOLITAN

Superintendent E.P. Garvey,
CHAIRMAN,
Dublin Metropolitan Garda Recreation Club.

Hereunder is General Balance S
Metropolitan Gárda Recreatio

To cash on hands at 1/4/63. Current A/C.	£ 652. 7. 2.	
" " " " " Thrift A/C.	£2,823. 6. 9.	
" Prize Bonds	£1,100. 0. 0.	£4
" Receipt Dances (nett)...................	£2,819. 5. 6.	
" Subscriptions	£1,811. 6. 3.	
" Weekly Draw £1,610. 5. 0.		
" Less Prizes £ 930. 0. 0.	£. 680. 5. 0.	£5
" Bank Interest		
" Win in Prize Bonds		
" Advertisement in Membership Card.		
" Bank Balance O/D at 31/3/64.	£2,195. 9. 0.	
" Less Thrift Account in credit	181. 13. 0.	£2
		£12

I certify that the receipts and expenses outlined in the abo
and correct.

M.O'6.

REATION CLUB.

9/10 Harrington St.,
6th. June, 1964.

ing Receipts and Expenses of Dublin
r the period 1/4/63 to 31/3/64.

	By Repairs, Hall & Furniture.	£	32.	0.	0.
	" Grants.	£	235.	0.	0.
	" Billiards..................	£	105.	14.	9.
	" Footballs & Sports Goods...	£	106.	10.	10.
10.	" Cheques to G.A.A. (Half Proceeds Dance		44.	8.	9.
	" Radio Repairs & T.V. licences ..		51.	7.	0.
	" Printing & Advertising	£	83.	13.	0.
	" Loan to Sub Aqua Club	£	264.	0.	0.
. 9.	" Insurance	£	10.	18.	4.
	" Performing Rights Society ..	£	6.	10.	0.
. 10	" Bank Fee. Cheques Int......	£	53.	13.	6.
. 0.	" Compensation	£	15.	10.	0.
. 0.	" Deposit on new hall & repairs	£	8853.	1.	6.
	" Wages	£	107.	2.	4.
	" Architect's Fees	£	3.	3.	3.
. 0.	" Heating	£	47.	10.	8.
	" Canteen	£	103.	8.	9.
	" Prize Bonds on Hands, 31/3/64		2,000.	0.	0.
. 5.			12, 123.	2.	5.

Sheet, are to the best of my knowledge and belief tru

Signed ______________________ Gárda, Hon Treasurer
CHARLES GAFFNEY, D/Gárda.

club in a healthy state after trading for a few years. The balance sheet on 31 March 1965 showed a net profit of £17,864 on the year's working. Bingo receipts were £14,961, dance receipts £2,250, whist drives £278. Members' subscriptions and the weekly draw amounted to £3,121, while a new entry in the 'Revenue' column read: bar and shop – £845. Total assets were £47,495. In that year the overdraft was reduced by £18,148. The following year's balance sheet – 31 March 1966 – showed a net profit of £22,199. Bingo provided £16,326, members' subscriptions and the weekly draw drew in £3,380, bar and shop £4,825, and the overdraft was reduced by just £4,973 to £13,174. So after three years the club was starting to go into overdrive. Members' enthusiasm and wholehearted determination to make the venture a success was beginning to pay dividends.

No 8 Harrington Street

Fifteen months after the purchase of the premises, 31 March 1965, the Harrington Street building itself was valued at £43,500. Within four years the debt was well under control and further expansion was possible. The opportunity for this presented itself when the house next door, 8 Harrington Street, came on the market, owned by Miss Maud Atkin Gill. Tom Ryan recalls the 'horse trading in a subtle and persuasive way' that formed much of the offer and counter-offer negotiations engaged in by both parties. A price of £11,000 was settled on and the deed of sale finally signed on 14 October 1968. Again the signatories on behalf of the club were, as in the previous purchase, its three trustees: Ned Garvey, Tom Ryan and Jim Daly.

Plans were drawn up to extend the existing club into this new acquisition; it involved extending the kitchen and catering facilities and above all the basement bar and lounge. It would also give extra space to the two halls. This proved most welcome and was much needed to cater for the growing business in the Garda Club. By now the club members were supporting their club on a large scale. The club was also equipped to cater for many social functions of an official and private nature.

Before refurbishment could commence, however, the not insignificant matter of a number of sitting tenants had to be dealt with. As the tenants showed no inclination to vacate their accommodation in the immediate future, the committee was forced into measures to ease their departure from No 8. It was decided to purchase another house nearby and relocate the tenants from No 8 there. After some negotiations and searching, a property about a quarter of a mile away at Longwood Avenue in Portobello was purchased. With the tenants safely relocated, redevelopment work on No 8 could go ahead.

A major renovation and extension plan got under way without delay. It increased the floor area of the premises by approximately one-third. The existing bar and lounge were extended and a bed and breakfast facility was provided for members resident outside the DMA and also for members of visiting police forces. The kitchen area

Opposite: No 8 Harrington Street by Don Donohoe

was extended and a restaurant with seating accommodation for seventy-five diners was constructed. When this facility was fully operational, over 1,000 meals a week were served, in addition to parties and dinner dances at weekends. The cost of the renovation and extension work resulting from the purchase of No 8 amounted to a figure in the region of £175,000. Admittedly, it was a lot of money for its time, but a capital investment that substantially increased the value of the property as a whole. On 13 November 1974, the new extension was officially opened by Mr Patrick Cooney TD, Minister for Justice. As Mr Cooney turned the key in the door of No 8, flanked by a delighted Ned Garvey, former Garda Commissioner Patrick Malone, architect James O'Toole and Mrs O'Toole, he was met with cheers and loud applause by the assembled guests. At the event, Mr Cooney paid tribute to the chairman, Ned Garvey, and all concerned for their achievements in having the most modern and up-to-date club premises of its kind anywhere in the world.

In light of the Garda Club's acquisition of land at Stackstown for a golf club earlier in 1973, more revenue had to be generated. To this end, the club started up bimonthly draws in 1973 with attractive prizes. Tickets cost £1 each and were confined to members of the force only. First prize was a new Opel Kadett car, which the club assured any sceptical patrons was a new model; second prize was a Philips TV set, while third prize was a transistor radio. Later the draws become monthly with attractive prize money. Profits for the year ending March 1975 showed the bar brought in £25,604; catering £8,571; bingo £20,812; whist £1,735; raffle 4,926. The net profit for the year was £32,103. Indeed the weekly income from bingo, bar and whist allowed the club to clear many of its debts again.

With the increased floor area in 1974 and exceptional facilities, business grew brisk and continued unabated in succeeding years. Given the scale of the functions, it was tough work and great credit goes to the organisers and the members who voluntarily manned the cloakroom and entrance door and saw that nothing untoward occurred.

Above: Opening of extension in November 1974 *(left to right):* architect James O'Toole, former Garda Commissioner Patrick Malone, Minister for Justice Mr Patrick Cooney TD, Mrs O'Toole and Garda Commissioner Ned Garvey

Timing is everything

Brian Prendergast, honorary secretary, outlined details of a TV screen 6' × 4' that could take all channels and could be used to screen the World Cup for the convenience of members at a cost of £4,500. After discussion it was decided that the cost was too much, and the Committee gave the go ahead to install an additional TV and to bring the hired TV to the lounge.

Minutes of Special Divisional Committee meeting, 25 May 1978

The chairman [Brian Prendergast] spoke of the club's purchase of a large TV screen which would be operational in the club to cover the World Cup and other events as the occasion demanded.

Minutes of Divisional Committee meeting, 28 May 1986

Entertainment at the club

The excellent facilities meant the club could keep pace with music trends and demands down through the decades. Be it for cabaret, disco, céilí, country and western or indeed classes in line dancing, salsa, swing and ballroom, all were accommodated. In the 1960s and 1970s, the Saturday night dances at the Garda Club were among the most popular in town. The Altonaires showband, which had entertained members so memorably in the Kevin Street hall, made the transition to Harrington Street to become the resident band. Keyboard player Seán Young was the leader of The Altonaires, and with David McDermott, Billy Byrne on guitar, Michael Young on bass, Liam Heffernan on trombone and Jimmy McGivern, they thrilled audiences with their vast repertoire of songs.

The 1970s saw the emergence of cabaret shows in Ireland. These shows, whose most famous exponent was Jury's Irish Cabaret, put the best of Irish traditional and contemporary music, song, dance, drama and comedy on display. As this became the rage throughout the land, the Divisional Committee got in on the act. By the mid-1970s, the Saturday night cabaret and dancing had joined the ranks of bingo and whist as top entertainment in the club. The night began with dancing from 8 pm to 10 pm followed by the one-hour cabaret, after which dancing resumed until 1 am. With high attendances, the show was hosted from 1974 to 1978 by the genial Paddy Murray, then a member of the fledgling Garda Press and Public Relations Office. Paddy, a master of chat and charm, was as entertaining as the featured artists, who ranged from Sonny Knowles to Eithne Dunne. The cabaret also had its own musical director, Tommy Delaney, with his band Duovox. With Tommy on vocals and accordion, his daughter Anne on drums, Mick Delahunty on vocals and Michael McEvoy on vocals and guitar, the dance floor never suffered the embarrassment of being empty. Garda talent was not in short supply either. Baritone John Roche featured regularly, opening his act with *Blaze Away*, the song made famous by Josef Locke, and thereafter enthralling the audience with favourites such as *Granada*, *Some Enchanted Evening* and *The Boys of Wexford*. Tenor Michael Lang, a native of Sligo, equally charmed the audience with numbers such as *Love Thee Dearest* and *Bring Flowers of the Rarest*.

A brief fall-off in support for the cabaret in 1977 was due to the loud amplification in the hall and the late starting time – both of which were rectified – but its halcyon days were over by the late 1970s. Nonetheless, it continued sporadically until 1983, augmented by spot prizes and 'sing along'. It still proved popular at the Christmas and New Year season but efforts to revive it on a regular basis in 1987 were unsuccessful.

Talent competitions were particularly in fashion in the 1970s and An Garda Síochána proved to be an Aladdin's cave of talent. The final of the first Garda All-Ireland Talent Competition took place in Harrington Street in 1976 in the downstairs ballroom. The conviviality and atmosphere of the Garda Club made for a successful night's entertainment. Such were the crowds that the event was relayed upstairs on a screen to cater for the overflow – with patrons readily agreeing to the £5 entrance charge. The Bureaucats was just one act that regularly appeared in the talent competitions. It comprised ten gardaí with lead singers Michael Lang and John Roche, all drawn from the Garda Technical Bureau, who sang only Scottish songs in flamboyant Scottish dress. Out of the talent competitions emerged the Garda Variety Group, often performing for charity, and who enjoyed considerable success in the competitions it entered. Later in the 1980s the group put on cabaret-style talent competitions in the Garda Club for the New Year season. A seven-week run in 1987 attracted sponsorship from Smithwicks, who generously gave £1,000 in prizes.

In the 1980s 'Big Band' dancing was a Thursday night feature. Many of the 1960s showbands still on the scene, such as the new Miami showband, appeared in the club to rapturous crowds. Divisional Committee member Jim Murphy was a veritable impresario, hiring bands to play at the club each week and often giving rural bands an entrée into the Dublin scene. The Johnny Flynn Band, in particular, was in high demand in the Garda Club. Hailing from the one-time showband capital of Ireland, Tuam, the Flynn Band had travelled the length and breadth of the country and toured the US on many an occasion. Their varied dancing programme of pop, Dixieland, country and ballads was guaranteed to set feet in motion. A measure of the 'Big Band' success in the Garda Club was that crowds would clamber to get into the dance by ten o'clock when doors would close. Each week queues would curl their way down Harrington Street as far as Camden Street and South Richmond Street, anxious not to be turned away.

Equally important on the dancing calendar in the 1980s were the Friday night discos run by the Garda GAA Club and overseen by Jim Murphy. The days of disco with DJs, loud music and flashing lights had reached Irish shores after the success of the 1977 movie *Saturday Night Fever*, featuring John Travolta. Young people flocked to the Garda Club and throbbed to the beat of the new phenomenon. The age of video disco also advanced on Harrington Street. Giant screens installed in the stage area sent dancers spinning and gyrating to the music and attracted even more patrons. The video disco enjoyed a short reign, however. It became a victim of its own success, like the Big Band nights, with problems of crowd control on the streets outside the club and parking in the residential neighbourhood. When the Big Band nights were discontinued in the mid-1980s, the GAA disco moved to the Thursday night slot. Such was the success of the discos that they netted £53,000 for the Garda Club for the year 1983/4 alone. The added revenue paved the way for new sound systems and disco lighting systems to be installed in both halls in the late 1980s and 1990s, as well as extensive hall renovations, to boost the disco experience even further.

The 1980s were perhaps the heyday of the club, with entertainment of one sort or another available several nights a week. At one point dances were run on Monday nights by Stackstown Golf Club for fundraising. There were also certain annual events guaranteed to draw the crowds, particularly in the 1970s and 1980s. The eves of All-Ireland hurling and football finals, when thousands of people descended on the capital – 'up for the match' – and rugby internationals witnessed many beating a hasty path to Harrington Street, where a good night's entertainment was decidedly assured. St Patrick's Day was another opportunity for an exceptional night's cabaret and dancing. The influx of visitors from abroad, often police forces from the USA, made for a night of assured gaiety and craic, still vividly recalled by patrons to this day. For three consecutive years in the mid-1970s the Boston Police Emerald Society paraded in uniform in the St Patrick's Day parade and was given a warm welcome in the Garda Club each time.

Throughout the 1980s the revenue raised from the dances and discos was substantial. Not only did this permit improvements to Harrington Street but more crucially was responsible for getting the Westmanstown project off the ground, which would cater for sport and recreation on a grand scale. And while the club appeared to enter a quieter period in the 1990s and 2000s, it was no quiescent period for the committee. The scale of the Westmanstown project, overseen by Jim Murphy, was truly colossal and would consume much of their time and energies.

Above: **Brian Prendergast, John Kearney, Jim Daly, Harry Thynne, Charlie Gaffney and Ned Lafferty socialising at the club in the 1970s**

Above: **Tommy Delaney, musical director**

Left: **Paddy Murray MC**

Above: **The Bureaucats**

G BAND NIGHT !
ARDA CLUB, HARRINGTON STREET
THURSDAY NIGHT
JOHNNY FLYNN'S BIG BAND
Strictly reserved * Neat dress essential
ancing 10 p.m. to 1-30 a.m.
– COMPLIMENTARY

Above: **Mick Lang and John Roche entertaining the guests at a function for Ned Garvey in 1983**

Doormen in the doghouse

The chairman again spoke re the disco on the Friday night previous and stated that three members had complained to him about the overcrowding and that skinheads had entered the disco and were not stopped, that the doormen were standing in the hallway, chatting up some ladies and were not interested in their job. The members stated they would not be back again.

Minutes of Divisional Committee meeting, 3 September 1980

Being a hive of activity for young people, the Garda Club inevitably bred romance. And many a lifelong union started on the dance floor under the mirror ball. The legendary coupling of guards and nurses and guards and teachers had special resonance in Dublin, aided somewhat by issuing nurses and teachers with complimentary tickets to dances in the Garda Club and publicising these events in the local hospitals and the Teachers' Club on Parnell Square. In later years, as the nightclub scene exploded in Dublin during the Celtic Tiger period and youngsters displayed an insatiable appetite for new and novel clubs, disco attendances waned at the Garda Club. As a result, student discos and supervised underage discos were avenues explored to increase revenue in the club. Over the years, céilí and traditional Irish music nights drew crowds to a lesser extent than discos, but remained a firm favourite.

Love in the Club

Ah yes! The Garda Club! Where many a love story began! They used to say that about Zhivago's. Well, I can assure you that the Garda Club was where many a couple met and fell in love and then got married and raised a family. People talk about how important the Metropole Ballroom was, and how special Clery's Ballroom was, and how many a courting couple met at the Pillar in the heart of O'Connell Street. Yes, but many a young garda met his or her life's partner in the Garda Club. I know for sure, because I celebrated many a Garda wedding when Fr Clarence was down the country giving missions. In fact, early in 2007 I met Mick Fortune and Edel O'Halloran (from Tipperary). They got married in 1990 and Fr Ralph celebrated their wedding. And where did they meet? Yes, you've got it in one! They met in the Garda Club just a year before that. I rest my case!

Fr Joe Kennedy CP, Garda Chaplain, Mount Argus

Bingo at the club

The twice- and later thrice-weekly bingo sessions played to full houses in the 1960s and 1970s. Harrington Street became a bingo mecca drawing crowds from near and far, often stretching to North County Dublin. It was the highlight of the week for many a bingo devotee. Several members can recall selling the books and calling out the numbers, and, despite the hard work, it was pure entertainment. Indeed it was not unusual to see Ned Garvey himself helping out on many a night.

Like all entertainment events from cabaret to bingo, heydays are followed by inevitable declines. Dwindling crowds and falling revenue were the death knell for bingo in the late-1970s. Even so, its passing drew the ire of some of its most faithful followers. Irate letter-writers contacted the *Gay Byrne Show* on RTÉ Radio 1 to express their deep disappointment and anger at the decision of the Garda Club to call time on bingo. The renowned broadcaster also received a petition to have the bingo retained, containing many signatures. However, as Gay Byrne pointed out, it was a private club and its members were entitled to run it as they wished. The significance of ending bingo was not lost on the committee members. It was with a heavy heart they made the decision to cease the bingo nights, greatly saddened at ending what had been key to the success of the Garda Club since it opened its doors in 1964.

Lights out

One night when we had a power failure during a bingo session all sorts of lights, lamps and candles were pressed into service to enable the caller identify the numbers called and the patrons to mark their cards. With lights flashing all over the place, the halls used for bingo sessions resembled a disco dance hall gone mad. Many suggestions were made as to how the position could be rectified, all sadly of an impractical nature. Despite how hilarious it was while the darkness was upon us, we were very relieved when the lights came back on again.

Tom Ryan, 'Personal Reminiscences', c1997

Functions at the club

The club got busier with every passing year and was widely used by its members. Following the extension programme in the early 1970s, the bar and lounge got going in earnest. Like any private club, the bar and lounge were sacrosanct to its members: a welcome retreat from the cares of the day; a place to unwind and relax; to encounter colleagues new and old; to catch up on news of recent retirements, promotions and transfers. The cosy environment allowed members' families and friends to meet and partake in refreshments in comfort. It also catered for small functions of between fifty and one hundred guests. Members could host their station or district functions, such as farewell parties on transfer or promotion, book a room for a meeting or host police and guests from other parts of the country or abroad. Visiting gardaí to the club and police personnel from other jurisdictions were always astounded by the size of the club and the social facilities it had to offer. Wear and tear in the downstairs bar and lounge forced the committee to renovate the entire area in 1988 and in later years. The burgeoning bar business in the club as a whole necessitated the purchase of the rere of No 12 Harrington Street in 1988 for use as a storage facility at a cost of £11,500. In 1991/92, a new bar and cold room were installed in the bottom hall at a total cost of £25,000.

Aside from its regular entertainment nights, the Garda Club catered for a considerable range of functions over the years. These included twenty-first and other birthday parties, wedding receptions, retirement parties, Irish classes, dance classes, Garda promotion exams, Garda Síochána Tidy Stations prize nights, stag nights and various fundraisers. Quiz nights, the perennial favourite of fundraisers, were popular with non-Garda fundraisers and proved to be a decided asset to the club's business. Book launches were a feature of the many functions. Notable nights out in this regard were Bernard Neary's book on the legendary Garda boxer and Riot Squad supremo, *Lugs: The Life and Times of Jim Branigan*, launched in the Garda Club in 1985; and, more recently in October 2003, RTÉ crime correspondent Paul Reynolds' book *Sex in the City*, which lifted the lid on prostitution rackets in the capital.

With its spacious ballrooms and central location, the club was also a sought-after venue for dinner dances. It was and still is particularly popular for Christmas parties and indeed many local hospitals, businesses and government departments and units, from the then named Posts and Telegraphs to Customs and Excise, availed of the facilities. A VIP Room had existed since the early days of the club and was something of a moveable feast. It had been relocated within the building on a number of occasions but was always suitable for private meetings. Local businesses could conduct AGMs there from time to time, such as Player Wills. Over the years, the Garda Club became a hub for organisations to discuss topical issues or grievances in private. Wide and varied were these organisations, many long since disbanded. They included the Married Persons' Tax Reform Association, the North Leitrim Development Group, the National University of Ireland, the Bread Salesman's Association, the National Union of Vehicle Builders, and the Garda Representative Body, to name but a few.

Catering and accommodation in the club

Catering in the Garda Club brought mixed success in the early years. Once the kitchens were in order in 1965, catering for functions began on a small scale. Brian Prendergast recalls that one of the first functions was for Garda Week in 1965, when there was a presentation of trophies and a reception upstairs. For the occasion, Sgt Patsy Murray was the MC, while Frank Kiernan and Brian Prendergast ran a makeshift bar in the kitchen corner in the top hall. In later years with the purchase of No 8 Harrington Street, the kitchens and restaurant were extended and modernised. Catering on a large scale was certainly a new departure when the club's new restaurant opened on 25 November 1974. This was a much-needed facility for members and their friends. Meals were initially served during the day and later, upon hiring additional staff, it was extended to evening hours.

By 1977 the restaurant was supplying midday lunches that were reasonably well-patronised. For the first two decades the club employed catering staff to cook and serve meals on the premises. High staff and food costs as well as falling patronage, however, meant that opening times had to be curtailed. In 1986, the kitchen and catering service were closed down during the daytime and staff made redundant. Changing times and customer trends, beyond the control of management, contributed to this situation. The catering function was then contracted out to various franchises over subsequent years, such as Frank Redmond in 1987, Eddie Saul in 1988, Larry Kiernan in 1994, and Eddie Saul returned later for a time.

A fall-off in business prompted the committee to cease providing a restaurant service in the late 1990s. The daytime service was discontinued but catering at functions was provided by Eddie Saul. The kitchen and restaurant were extensively upgraded over the years, but the committee had other plans for the restaurant.

Garda steak-out

Miss Griffin [the club manageress] attended the meeting and stated that the restaurant was to open on 10 March 1981. Hours of opening were from 6.30 pm and last orders at 10.30 pm, Tuesday to Saturday inclusive. The menu was discussed in full and after a long discussion it was decided that an 8 oz steak with one vegetable and chips would cost £4.80. A 10 oz steak and one vegetable and chips would cost £5.50. It was also decided on a proposal by D Buggy and seconded by B Prendergast that all items on the menu would be priced separately.

Minutes of Divisional Committee meeting, 4 March 1981

It was finally converted into upmarket office accommodation, with its first tenant being Media One, a computer software company. Current catering at the club is provided by caterers in Westmanstown.

Another departure for the club was its well-appointed accommodation. After the extension programme in 1974, the club possessed five bedrooms – two single rooms, two double rooms and one treble room – all for the use of members, visiting or otherwise. The chairman's wife, Mrs Bridget Garvey, contributed to the effort in no small way. Her interior decorating skills ensured the curtains and furnishings were of the highest standards. It was a particular pleasure to Ned Garvey that this venture was in operation. His lifelong creed made the care of the membership and their everyday needs a priority. Young gardaí coming from Templemore to Dublin were now assured of a bed and good meal at the club until they acquired more permanent accommodation. In the 1980s the accommodation was further extended to twenty-two bedrooms of various sizes to cater for members and visiting policemen from all over the world. For example, members of the RUC were occasionally guests of the club and availed of the facilities following an enjoyable day's golfing. Records in 1989 show that the cost of a bed for the night was £5, which was increased to £8 due to rising costs. However, the twenty-first century saw a change in direction because of falling patronage. In 1999, architects were hired to look at the bedrooms, regarding their future use. The result in 2001 was that the bedrooms were converted into eight self-contained apartments, finished to a high degree and fitted with all modern conveniences. Most of these were let to long-term clients via letting agents, while others were retained as short-term lettings to facilitate members.

Associations linked to Garda Club

Over the past four decades the Garda Club on Harrington Street was eminently suitable as a temporary home for many a police organisation or society, prominent on the national or international stage. With ample space to hold meetings or conduct business or to avail of a postal address, sometimes it afforded a means for these organisations to consolidate themselves before moving on to more permanent premises. When it was set up in 1961, the Garda Pensioners Association, now the Garda Síochána Retired Members Association (GSRMA), did not have a permanent office. Initially it located to 43 Dawson Street before moving on to 32 Nassau Street and eventually in 1999 to its current and natural home at 8 Harrington Street. A portrait of Ned Garvey was generously commissioned by the Garda pensioners in the 1970s in recognition of his dedication to meeting their needs. The painting still holds pride of place at Harrington Street.

Many a Garda organisation also used the spacious ballrooms for AGMs and functions over the years, notably Coiste Siamsa. In its calendar of events a particular highlight was the annual Garda Sports Week. The week culminated in a memorable prize-giving night in Harrington Street each year, which saw participants and guests celebrate the joys of victory or the pain of defeat.

Above: Delegates at a Coiste Siamsa AGM in the early 1980s

Harrington Street was also home to St Paul's Benefit Society Ltd from March 1978 until 1980. In tending to the medical needs of serving and retired members of the force and their dependants, St Paul's had a long association with the Passionist Fathers at Mount Argus, chaplains to the force. A letting agreement between St Paul's and the Garda Club in 1978 allowed for three rooms in 8 Harrington Street to be used for office accommodation. In 1980, the society amalgamated with the Garda Síochána Medical Aid Society to become St Paul's Garda Medical Aid Society, looking after the health insurance needs of its members. Subsequently, it moved to Phibsboro Tower. The rooms occupied by St Paul's were then converted into a recreation area, comprising snooker tables, darts, and such like.

The first link between Harrington Street and the Garda Holiday and Travel Club was when Sergeant Fergus B McGuinness, serving in Pearse Street Garda Station, arranged a meeting at the Garda Club on 6 October 1990. A notice had been circulated throughout the force outlining plans to set up a club to provide holidays and travel at home and abroad at attractive prices. The inaugural meeting was a resounding success. A committee was elected and included Fergus McGuinness, Derek Byrne, Patrick Mullin, PJ Riordan and Michael Gibbs as well as Tom Roddy, Frank Mulligan, Patrick Morgan and Jim Hoban. The club officially opened for business on 7 January 1991, operating from an office in Harrington Street during the weekday hours of 10 am to 1 pm. From the outset, the club organised its own long-haul packages, many associated with St Patrick's Day festivities worldwide. Such was its success that in June 1992 the club became a limited company, a fully bonded tour operator and an approved member of the International Air Transport Association (IATA). Nowadays the club operates from the sixth floor of Phibsboro Tower.

Another longstanding association with Harrington Street is the International Police Association (IPA). Formed on 1 January 1950 by Arthur Troop, the IPA is the largest police organisation in the world. Its raison d'être, as envisioned by Troop – a police sergeant from Lincolnshire, England – was to create a channel for friendship and international co-operation among police officers. The turmoil of World War II had been a springboard for Troop to promote friendship above fighting and destruction. In a spirit of plurality, it adopted the Esperanto words *Servo per amikeco* (service through friendship) as its motto. Harrington Street was made available to the Irish section of the IPA as a postal address and a venue for meetings when required. It was thus in one room in Harrington Street that the magazine of the Irish section, *Police Friendship*, was founded and developed. In 1978/9, it ran a memorable national Garda Quiz. Organised by social secretary Fergus McGuinness, the semi-finals and final were held at Harrington Street with generous prizes of Waterford Crystal and cash. Questions were set by RTÉ's Peter Murphy of *Cross Country Quiz* fame, who also was quizmaster on the night. Members of the public were welcome to attend for an entrance fee of 60 pence. In 1980, the hall and restaurant at Harrington Street were put at the IPA's disposal for the seventeenth International Executive Council Meeting. The association nowadays provides a vast range of services for serving and retired members of the force, such as sports events, group travel, social activities and accommodation in IPA houses. The organisation later moved to its permanent address in IPA House in Glasnevin. The deep debt of gratitude to the Garda Club did not go unrecognised. To mark his magnanimity and loyal support, Edmund Garvey is cited as one of the association's benefactors. He was awarded an honorary life membership and was considered a staunch friend of the IPA. In 1997, the association presented the then chairman of the Garda Club, Jim Murphy, with a painting to hang in the foyer at the Westmanstown complex.

Another police organisation that had a small office in Harrington Street for a time was the Fraternal Order of Police (FOP). The largest organisation of policemen in the United States, the Fraternal Order of Police has more than 325,000 members in 2,100 local chapters (lodges). Having some characteristics of a trade union, it represents the interests of policeman and lobbies the US Congress on issues such as improved working conditions and the security of its members. It represents all branches of policing in the US, including harbour police, traffic police and airport police. The FOP was set up in 1915 by two Pittsburgh police officers, Martin Toole and Delbert Nagle, who sought to improve the lot of policemen, in particular the onerous twelve-hour working day all year round with no overtime. Given the traditional links between Irish emigrants and the US police force, it comes as no surprise that an affiliate lodge was also set up in Ireland as indeed it was in Canada and Germany. In 1994, a room in the Garda Club was made available to the FOP for the exclusive use of its members as an office and meeting room. From the office, the FOP ran successful darts tournaments, in some cases grant aided by the Garda Club.

The Garda Club also forged valuable links with many of the county associations based in Dublin. In the days when most Garda recruits came from outside Dublin, these associations were often a lifeline to the home county. Every county in Ireland could claim a Garda son or nephew or neighbour, and so the club was a home from home for the Mayo Association, the Kerry Association, the Offaly Association, the Sligo Association, the Beara Association, to name but a few. Their meetings and fundraisers brought life to the club many a time. One of the best supported and active county associations in the country was then and continues to be the Mayo Association. An added bonus was that Garda Club chairman Jim Murphy was also a former Association chairman and is still an active member to this day.

When pioneering the building of Knock Airport in the early 1980s, Monsignor James Horan, through the Dublin branch of the Mayo Association, held a fundraiser in the Garda Club that was filled to capacity. It is fulfilling to feel that the Garda Club contributed in a small way to that outstanding project, completed in August 1985.

Below: The Garda Male Voice Choir on the steps of the Garda Club with conductor Maureen Reilly for the Garda Jubilee in 1972

On the entertainment front, the Garda Male Voice Choir has been in permanent residence at Harrington Street since 1972. The venue affords ample space for the choir to raise the rafters practising its vast repertoire – ranging from the quiet haunting airs of Thomas Moore to the majestic operatic choruses of Mozart and Wagner and to the traditional songs of people the world over. Its presence was also something of a godsend to the Divisional Committee in the early years of the club. Monday night was habitually one of the choir's practice nights. Once a month this coincided with the Divisional Committee meetings and annually with the club AGM. Whenever a quorum could not be formed on the night, due to the absence or delay of members, some of the choir's finest tenors and baritones were pressed into service so

Garda Male Voice Choir

In 1972, as the fiftieth anniversary of the foundation of An Garda Síochána was approaching, a religious celebration was planned to mark '50 years a growing' from 1922 to 1972. The late Fr Clarence Daly CP of the Passionist Order in Mount Argus was commissioned to organise some singers to perform at the celebration. The late Fr Clarence was chaplain to the Gardaí in the Dublin Metropolitan Area at the time. The big, jolly priest was a regular visitor to the Aliens' Registration Office in Dublin Castle and went there in search of advice.

The late Detective Garda Jack Reilly from County Longford was deployed in that office and Fr Clarence was aware that Jack's wife, Maureen, a schoolteacher in Dublin at the time, was also the musical director of a children's choir. Jack was requested to approach Maureen with a view to her providing the choral music at the forthcoming religious anniversary celebration. Maureen Reilly (neé Dillon), from Kiltimagh in County Mayo, was most accommodating and a meeting was arranged to establish what was required. When Maureen heard the request for the services of her choir, her response was, 'Can the Gardaí not sing themselves?'

From that spark of genius, a fire ignited and the Garda Síochána Male Voice Choir arose from its flames. Jack Reilly went to the Phones Office situated in the small yard at Dublin Castle and had an 'All Stations Bulletin' or 'Route' circulated to all stations, requesting all prospective singers to 'parade their bodies' in Dublin Castle on a specific evening to audition.

Then, one cold winter's evening in February, about a dozen stout-hearted men gathered around a battered old piano in a recreation room at Dublin Castle. A few bars of various hymns and songs were sung and, as the word spread, the numbers increased. A suitable venue for rehearsal had to be found and an approach was made to the Garda Recreation Club in Harrington Street for the use of their facilities. This was granted without question and free of charge. Rehearsals were then arranged for Monday and Wednesday nights. A piano was also provided, until the choir was in a position to provide its own – from fundraising and contributions by its members to a monthly raffle. Soon the ranks of the choir had swollen to about seventy members.

The performance of the Garda Male Voice Choir, conducted by Maureen Reilly, both at Mount Argus and at St Patrick's Cathedral, Dublin, is remembered as the highlight of the anniversary celebrations in 1972 and was regarded by all as a resounding success. During its early days the choir enjoyed the ardent support of the then Garda Commissioner, Edmund P Garvey. The Garda Recreation Club is credited with the provision of the very first set of blazers and slacks worn by the choir in 1980.

There have been numerous memorable events in the annals of the choir. In the autumn of 1972 the choral group reassembled in the Garda Club, after a short summer break, and their first task was to begin rehearsals for a commissioned fifty-minute programme to be broadcast on Telefís Éireann at prime viewing time on Christmas Night. This programme, recorded in Clonliffe College, proved to be a successful venture. On that same Christmas Night, the Garda Male Voice Choir, directed by Maureen Reilly, also sang *Ambrán na bhFiann* at the closing down of the station. This was considered a very prestigious event in those days of monochrome television. A number of appearances followed on *The Late Late Show* with Gay Byrne and the Garda Male Voice Choir was in much demand throughout Ireland.

Another important event was the broadcast of a Mass written specially for the choir by the late Philip Greene. This was transmitted on live television across Europe from Belfield Church in Dublin on 15 August 1975. The event was recorded and released on an LP record entitled *The Man from Galilee* with tenor Frank Patterson as soloist.

The choir has performed far and near: a US tour in 1976 for the American Bicentennial celebrations, singing in Pittsburgh, Boston and Washington; another US tour in 1980 in which the well-known bass baritone, Peter McBrien, accompanied the choir as a soloist as well as the enthralling fifteen-year-old soprano, Catherine Kennedy; and a most enjoyable US and Canada tour in 1997.

A particularly moving experience for the choir was on 11 September 2002, when as guests of the NYPD Choir they performed at a religious service at the edge of Ground Zero in New York to mark the first anniversary of the Twin Towers terrorist attack.

The law of the land, North and South, were in unison on 7 October 1983 when the Garda Choir joined the RUC Choir and Band, in the celebration of the latter's Diamond Jubilee at the Ulster Hall in Belfast. When the Garda Choir took to the stage, the audience rose in a thunderous, standing ovation that continued for over five minutes. In 1990, at the prestigious Royal Albert Hall in London, the Garda Choir blended with a choir of one thousand police voices from all over Britain and Ireland, as a fundraiser for Great Ormond Street Hospital for Children.

The choir has enjoyed success in several competitions and has taken gold three times: in 2003 at the Sligo International Choral Festival, where the performance was humorously described by adjudicators as 'an arresting performance and always on the right beat'; at Enniscorthy, County Wexford; and at the Chester Music Festival.

Tony Ruane, Garda Male Voice Choir

that meetings could proceed. Club business may not have been as melodious as choir practice but it could still offer many a high note and dramatics. Later when the club drew up plans for its proposed golf courses, Garda golfers packed into the AGMs and quorum problems were consigned to the past.

Celebrating the 1972 Jubilee

The year 1972 was a special one for the Garda Club with the celebration of the Garda Síochána Jubilee in mid-June. Earlier that year on 21 February 1972, a reception was held in Harrington Street to recall the historic event fifty years previously when the first members of the Civic Guard were enrolled. The assembled gathering was addressed by Commissioner Michael Wymes who paid tribute to the high standards of self-sacrifice and devotion to duty that the first members of the force had set themselves in 1922, and which was the proud heritage of the Gardaí in 1972.

The Jubilee celebrations also concluded at the Garda Club at the end of Garda Week in June and was recorded in the commemorative brochure, *An Garda Síochána: Golden Jubilee 1922–1972.* It featured an inspiring opening speech by Ned Garvey, then chief superintendent, that likened the spirit of athletic endeavour to religious vows.

We are coming to the end of a week of memories; to this end, too, of a week that will itself be long remembered. The occasion of the Jubilee celebrations of the Garda Síochána has been signalised with every mark of esteem and goodwill from Church and State and the whole community. As we enter the second half century of our service, our hope must be that we will continue, as a Force, to deserve those golden opinions which have, in the last few days, been voiced so generously and enthusiastically.

Now our athletes and sportsmen of yesterday and today have contributed more than their share to this favourable public image of the Force. And that is one good reason why Garda Sports Week must always have a special importance in our calendar. It is, one might say, an annual renewal of vows, when our young and not so young Gardaí, by the hundred, re-dedicate themselves to the splendid spirit of athletic endeavour and emulation, thereby giving the assurance of a future as storied and gloried as the past. Its success, then, is vital, if we are to preserve and transmit our Garda heritage on field and track.

And despite many pressures and many distractions, Garda Week 1972 has been a very successful one indeed. For this, there are many to whom a tribute of thanks is due. The list of those to whom we are indebted is a long one, from the organising committee and sub-committees who set the ball rolling in the first instance, to the staff and volunteer personnel of our Social Club, who have done so much to make this closing night a pleasant one for all. But one thing is certain, that the lion's share of the credit must go to the competitors. Without them, there could be no Garda Sports Week. And this applies to all who competed, whether prize-winners or not. Our gratitude goes in the same measure, to winners and losers: to all we say – Well Done!

Commissioner Wymes then presented the prizes to the winners of the Garda Sports Week, praising the high standard held in the sixteen branches of sport. Garda Michael Gillespie of Mountmellick Garda Station was singled out for special mention, having won the Athlete of the Year award. In conclusion, the Commissioner paid tribute to the Garda sportsmen and women who had added glory and lustre to the name of the Garda Síochána over the previous fifty years.

Sport funds and grants

Funds are inevitably required by all sporting bodies to stay afloat. The granting of funds to different sporting bodies within the force and for various articles relating to sport and relaxation was therefore an integral part of the raison d'être of the Garda Recreation Club. The cultural aspect of sports was not overlooked either. In fact, any activity that would enhance the reputation of the force was generously assisted and encouraged by the club.

President Éamon de Valera inspecting a guard of honour at Mount Argus during the 1972 Garda Jubilee celebrations

The second annual report presented at the AGM in 1963 by the assistant honorary secretary, Tom Ryan, detailed the grants provided for the year 1962/63:

> *The sum of £300 was given to Garda organisations by way of grants. The Garda Scholarship scheme was granted the sum of £100. £25 was given for the promotion of hurling in the Division. £40 to the Soccer Club, £25 to the basketball club, an individual grant of £10 was given to Garda B McKenna, Kilmainham Station, the well-known cyclist, and a similar grant to Garda PJ Kenny, Dublin Castle. The Garda GAA Football Club was given a grant of £25 together with the sum of £44, the proceeds of a dance held for their benefit. Medals costing £32.17 were bought for the following sports: hurling, football, handball, and the A District sports. A grant of £83.17.6 was made to Coiste Siamsa last year to assist in the promotion of Garda athletic activities.*

The following year's balance sheet showed that £235-worth of grants was paid out as well as £105.4.9 for billiards, £106.10.10 for footballs and sports goods, £44.8.9 to the GAA Garda Club (half of which were dance proceeds), £51 7*s* for radio repairs and TV licences, and a loan of £264 was given to the Garda Sub Aqua Club.

Over the years one of the most recurring expenses was for recovering or repair of snooker tables and the purchase of darts boards or radios or TV licences for the stations within the DMA. There were fourteen billiard tables in DMA stations in 1976 and the club took care of their repair and maintenance. At the AGM that year, the honorary secretary Jim Daly exhorted the members to ensure these tables were not damaged as the cost of cloths and cushions was then in the region of £200. Other sundry sport items supplied included footballs, jerseys, tennis balls and rackets, and badminton nets.

Grants were also extended to gym equipment or gym repairs in Divisional stations. For example in February 1976, a grant of £1,000 was given towards the cost of a new gymnasium in Fitzgibbon Street Station and in 1998 to Blanchardstown Station. Because the Garda Recreation Club did not have an inexhaustible supply of funds at its disposal, Garda sporting clubs were restricted to applying for grants every five years. This included substantial loans for new boats to the Garda Angling Club or Garda Sub Aqua Club down through the years.

They say that success breeds success and this was certainly true of the Garda Club. It was always exciting when a sporting club was on a winning streak and grants were forthcoming so as to not to hinder their progress. For example, a grant of £600 was given to the five-man team of the Garda Midlands Tug-of-War Club, which was representing Ireland in the World Games at Santa Clara, California, in 1981. Similarly, a grant of £300 was given to the Garda Soccer Club for their trip to play

Derry at the Brandywell in the FAI Cup qualifier in 1986 or when the Garda GAA football team won the Dublin Intermediate Football Championship in 1986. Funds were also made available to Garda sports clubs for promotional and goodwill tours to help defray costs, such as when the Garda GAA Club went to the USA in 1987.

Sometimes stations were unlucky with their applications, especially if facilities existed elsewhere. A grant towards the purchase of a piano for the Garda Technical Bureau in 1980 was turned down on the grounds that pianos were available at the Garda Club for practice and rehearsal. As Dublin city expanded during the 1980s, the DMA was restructured and new districts such as U and W were created. This meant that the new stations, such as Ronanstown and Santry, needed extra resources allocated to them for sport and relaxation. This was also true when the Q district was created in 1997.

The treasurer's report from 1983 shows that the club paid out £7,064.66 in grants and recreational facilities for the year 1982/3. There were many beneficiaries of the grants system. One, in particular, was the Garda Darts Club. For many years, Garda stations throughout the DMA had and continue to have facilities for darts, thanks mainly to the Garda Club. This allowed gardaí to develop their skills in the sport and progress further. Since the 1980s, darts championships within the DMA were organised by various associations or individuals. However, in 1992, it achieved greater recognition and the sport of darts was encompassed within the DMA Coiste Roinne. In 9 Harrington Street there were now facilities for darts as well as snooker. A games room for members was located behind the office on the ground floor. Later this was converted into a boardroom. Inside it today proudly hangs the portraits of President Éamon de Valera, Commissioner Edmund Garvey, Commissioner Michael Wymes and Fr Clarence Daly CP.

Charities and fundraisers

Given the tradition of charitable giving in the force as a whole, it was inevitable that the Garda Recreation Club would be prevailed upon from time to time. Many and varied were the requests for sponsorship from charities or charitable causes that landed on the honorary secretary's desk. Some of Ireland's oldest and much-loved charities and even fledgling ones benefited from the Garda Club's generosity. The Divisional Committee, on behalf of the club members, always endeavoured to accommodate such requests where possible. If sponsorship was not feasible, the committee would offer the use of the hall for a fundraiser free of charge. Priority was certainly given to fundraisers for members of the force injured or killed in the line of duty.

Many fundraisers were held by the Passionist Fathers of the nearby Mount Argus in Harold's Cross. The order has enjoyed a long association with An Garda Síochána and its antecedents. The link between the order and policemen sprang from the time

Preaching the peace

The Garda Club has a special place in the hearts of my Passionist colleagues at Mount Argus, and particularly in the hearts of men like the late, great Fr Clarence Daly CP, and more recently Fr Dermot Patrick Cleary CP.

Fr Clarence was a most distinguished Garda chaplain, having served in that capacity for a record twenty-six years. Born in Castlerea, County Roscommon in 1928, he was the grandson, son and nephew of constables in the RIC. As a Garda chaplain, his large stature and bluff personality were perfectly suited to the manners of the everyday policeman. The charistmatic Passionist was also deeply committed to the welfare of the rank and file garda and he never forgot a name. In times of turmoil within the force, he often acted as buffer between the man and their officers, which earned him widespread respect and esteem. His death in 1998 was greeted with deep sadness and loss in An Garda Síochána.

Another man who has a great affection for the Garda Club is Fr Ralph Egan CP, former chaplain to the force, now ministering in the new Passionist parish of Huntstown. He, too, has special memories of many a Garda function in 'the Club'.

I have good memories of attending Garda functions in the Garda Club. Fr Clarence – great orator and preacher that he was – was very much in demand by parish priests to conduct parish missions and retreats. That meant he was away a lot from Mount Argus, sometimes every other week, all over the country, preaching missions as only he could preach. Fr Clarence would often ask me to represent him at Garda functions held in the Garda Club, especially during the 1970s.

I can recall making the short journey from Mount Argus, down Harold's Cross Road, turning right as soon as I crossed over Robert Emmet Bridge, and travelling down past Longwood Avenue, and slipping into the Garda Club through the back roads on my Lambretta scooter. No helmet needed.
I was surely mad then!

Fr Joe Kennedy CP, Garda Chaplain, Mount Argus

Left: Fr Joe Kennedy

Above: Fr Clarence Daly

when the Italian founder of the order, St Paul of the Cross, was saved in a snowstorm by a policeman. As a result, by the mid-1700s the order was entrusted with the care of the Italian police by Pope Benedict XIV. The Irish connection stretched back to 1876 when the DMP band gave a recital in the Rotunda Rooms on Sackville Street (now O'Connell Street) to raise money for the roof of the new monastery at Mount Argus. Later in 1893 the Passionists conducted a retreat for members of the Dublin Metropolitan Police, the first of many. The bond was further strengthened in 1896 when the Obsequies Association of the DMP was formed (now the Garda Obsequies Association). It is a harsh reflection of the times that many a policeman could not afford a plot or burial costs. By paying a small sum per year, it gave members the privilege of availing of Requiem Mass and other rites at Mount Argus. As chaplains to the force, the Passionists have led Garda pilgrimages to Lourdes and Rome, conducted funerals in Mount Argus of members who died in the line of duty, and celebrated centenary thanksgiving Masses of the force. The chaplain most associated with the force is Fr Clarence Daly, who from 1957 ministered to the spiritual needs of members for twenty-six years with extraordinary zeal and dedication. Many a memorable fundraising night was held at the Garda Club with the jovial priest in attendance, and he is remembered with much love and affection.

The Garda Club, ever conscious of its role to promote good community relations, also offered a welcoming hand to immigrant communities. The South Circular Road area of Dublin 8 has traditionally been home to many Jewish and Muslim people relocating to Irish shores, especially since the nineteenth century. In 1976, the Dublin Islamic Society, later called the Islamic Foundation of Ireland, purchased No 7 Harrington Street, next door to the Garda Club. The society mainly comprised medical students at the Royal College of Surgeons in Ireland (RCSI), and the premises on Harrington Street became the first mosque in Ireland. Later when the mosque was unable to accommodate large-scale events, such as Eid prayers at the end of Ramadan, the society was given permission to use Garda Club facilities, which continued for two years. This, according to the society, helped to form a splendid relationship between the Muslim community and gardaí. In 1983, the mosque moved to 163 South Circular Road and 7 Harrington Street was sold in 1985.

Governing body

Undoubtedly, the nerve centre of the Garda Club is the governing body. Its duty is to implement club policy, oversee management and deal with any problems that may arise in the day-to-day running of the club. Underlying its actions is an unquenching desire to propel the club forward and uphold its values. According to former assistant secretary Tom Ryan, 'the dynamic necessary for progress was always there; it was a case of onward ever onward, the summit of our endeavours had yet to be reached'. These sentiments are as true today as in the early days of the club. Those with the longest stewardship of the club have also been their most dedicated chairmen. From its inception in 1961, Ned Garvey steered the club for seventeen years, clearing all its debts by 1978 and leaving the club premises in a healthy financial state with lands valued in excess of £1 million. From 1987 until 2001 Jim Murphy boldly pushed through expansion plans at Westmanstown until it was one of the most modern and enviable golf and sports complexes in the country. In the wake of Ned Garvey's resignation from the governing body in 1978, successive chairmen included Denis Devine, Noel McDermott from 1982, Brian Prendergast from 1984, Jim Murphy from 1987, Mick Feehan from 2001 and Dave Dowling from 2008. Each contributed enormously to the development of the club.

Returning to the late 1960s, the club had reached the stage where the running of its affairs became a matter of routine for the committee. Subcommittees had been set up to look after the bingo, dancing and card playing, which all operated as distinct entities under the control of the central committee. Social or house committees were set up later to organise the cabaret and other social functions. Matters mundane and mighty all came under the scrutiny of the Divisional Committee at their monthly meetings. The ongoing upkeep of the premises was a constant concern. At a business level, the committee had to decide what price to set on drink, how to improve attendances at weekly functions, deal with complaints and negotiate insurance premiums, apart from dealing with expansion plans at Stackstown and Westmanstown and their funding. At times it could reach lofty heights when the committee debated the exigencies of providing sandwiches for sale at the cabaret, or crisps and peanuts in the members' bar.

Above left: Committee Room and
Above right: Members' Bar at Harrington Street

Running an entertainment venue was certainly a colossal task. Applications would pile in, ranging from Garda clubs to the general public, for the use of function rooms for fundraisers and meetings. These were always granted at the discretion of the Divisional Committee, though no meetings of a political nature were sanctioned. Given the weight of matters for deliberation, it is little wonder that committee meetings had a habit of stretching late into the evening. On occasion these got out of hand and necessitated various proposals to limit talking time.

The security of the club was uppermost, ensuring that functions and events were well supervised and that patrons behaved in a responsible and fitting manner. Crowd control outside the club became an issue in the early 1980s but, on the whole, relations between the club and the local residents on Harrington Street and adjoining streets were good. In proportion to the volume of patrons that passed through the club doors, the amount of 'aggro' or hassle was minor. The committee regularly appealed to its members to be sensitive to the rights of others, in relation to where they parked their cars, and to keep noise at a minimum in the interest of harmony. From time to time infractions did arise, which the club was at pains to resolve quickly. In fact, any member found guilty of misdemeanour or conduct unfitting a member on or outside the premises was swiftly hauled in front of the committee to give an account of him or herself. Depending on the misdemeanour, mostly of a drunk and disorderly nature, members could find themselves suspended for a week, a month, six months or even a year. A severe misdemeanour could result in membership not being renewed, but, happily, this was a rare occurrence. In February 1988, the Garda

Time, gentlemen, time...

The chairman said that reference had to be made to termination of meetings at 10 pm. It was decided after a short discussion that meetings should not be more than three hours' duration.

Minutes of Divisional Committee meeting, 23 November 1978

Brian Prendergast motioned the times for termination of meetings and as a standing order made the following proposal: 'That meetings end at 10 pm, and that if an important matter is under discussion that a motion to suspend the standing order be moved to extend the time by one half-hour.'

Minutes of Divisional Committee meeting, 16 January 1980

Pat Mullin stated that an effort should be made to start meetings on time. It was decided to make an effort to start on time and meetings to finish at 11 pm, no matter what time they began at.

Minutes of Divisional Committee meeting, 7 June 1981

Club hit the headlines when the notorious Dublin gangland leader Martin Cahill (aka The General) was responsible for a spate of tyre slashing outside the Garda Club and around the city. It was believed to have been in retaliation for increased Garda surveillance of his gang members. Prior to the tyre-slashing incident, the greens in the Garda-owned Stackstown Golf Club had also been vandalised.

Like any committee there were sometimes thorny issues to be tackled. A perennial issue was increasing the subscription base, especially as the club embarked on ambitious expansion plans, purchasing No 8 Harrington Street in 1968 and acquiring land at Stackstown in 1973 and at Westmanstown in 1985. Continual efforts were made to sign up new Garda recruits who were to be assigned to DMA stations. It became a regular practice for officers of the club, such as the assistant honorary secretary and honorary treasurer, to travel to the Garda Training College at Templemore every six months or so to acquaint recruits with the finer points of the Garda Club and the facilities on offer. The grounds for increasing subscription rates were often due to meeting overdraft payments and inflation caused by the expansion programme. One memorable increase in 1989 almost led to a mutiny. Such was the opposition to the proposal to increase the rate from £1 to £2 per week that a extraordinary general meeting was called. Members threatened to cancel their membership en masse if the change was implemented. The upshot was that a compromise was reached and the rate increased to £1.50 per week.

Initially, the Divisional Committee was responsible for hiring staff to run the club and, indeed, in the early days some staff lived on the premises. Nonetheless, over time the club was restructured and refurbished and the accommodation space utilised for other purposes. In the early days many of the members assisted with running various functions, the security of the club and helping out in the bar on a voluntary basis; however, with the burgeoning catering and bar functions more staff were hired. The responsibility for hiring staff then fell to civilian management. Civilian managers could attend to the day-to-day tasks necessary for running the club on a proper commercial basis. In this respect the club has seen a succession of bar managers and catering managers over the years. Miss Ita Bodkin was the first manageress of the Garda Club. Upon her resignation to get married, management

Damage limitation

A request from a woman in Phibsborough for compensation for damage caused to her coat during the cabaret was discussed and it was agreed to pay her £3, this being half of what it cost her to get the coat cleaned.

Minutes of Divisional Committee meeting, 14 December 1977

transferred to Con and Betty Lean, coinciding with the opening of the restaurant. When Mr and Mrs Lean departed in 1979, Miss Catherine Griffin took their place, along with Mrs Helen Corrigan in administration. Upon Miss Griffin leaving in 1982, the new manager became Helen Corrigan. With extensive experience in catering and dealing with committees, Helen was one of the most capable and best-loved managers whose service was marked by great commitment and loyalty. The idea of providing a home from home for the members was certainly recognised by her, working closely with the Divisional Committee and attending their weekly Monday meetings to clarify matters or request changes and so forth. After so many years of loyal service, members were deeply saddened when she retired in March 1998.

It was a proud moment in 1985 when the club celebrated twenty-one years at Harrington Street. The occasion was marked by a Mass and a reception at the club, with many of the founders and members in attendance as well as invited guests. By then the club had 3,600 members, two ballrooms, a restaurant, six bars and various meeting rooms. In its accommodation wing, there were twenty-two bedrooms of various sizes to cater for visiting policemen.

There was and is no resting on laurels for the committee, who have stayed faithful to the rules of the club in maintaining the clubhouse and promoting recreational needs. The work is neverending, however. With the arrival of new technology, such as computerisation, the club had to keep abreast. In 1988, it set up a subcommittee to look into the computerisation of club affairs, both at Harrington Street and Westmanstown. This was effected gradually and full computerisation came in 1999 at a cost of £20,000.

The upgrading and modernisation of Harrington Street has continued, from improving bathroom facilities and bar counters to installing double glazing and new sound and lighting systems. Both the top and bottom halls were extensively renovated in 1986 and in 1994. A new system of heating was installed in 1994,

Trouble in paradise

There followed a major discussion on the proposed increase of £1 [to £2 per week] on the weekly subscription agreed at this year's AGM. Each District Representative expressed the negative vibes they were getting to such an increase and the possible repercussions of membership fall-off if the increase of £1 per week was implemented. The meeting felt after listening to all the contributions that before any further developments take place that a special general meeting be called to get the feelings of the members at large.

Minutes of Divisional Committee meeting, 27 September 1989

Size matters

Mount Argus priest Fr Clarence Daly CP was presented with a cheque [at the twenty-first birthday celebrations of the Garda Club].

'Many's the priest wouldn't get as much at a Station', he told the crowd. 'Wouldn't you know he was a Garda's son by the size of his feet,' remarked a member of the force.

Liam Collins, Ad-lib column, Evening Herald, *1 January 1985*

turning over from oil to gas. Rewiring of the electrical system of the house took place in 1994 as did the refurbishment of the VIP Room. More extensive refurbishment of Harrington Street took place in 1997 and over £250,000 was spent on making it one of the finest police clubs in the world. The building was reopened on September 4th to much fanfare. A reception was held on the day and members and invited guests, including civil servants employed in Garda stations, were greeted at the Garda Club by two doormen in dress suits. The guest of honour at the opening ceremony was the Minister for Justice, Equality and Law Reform, Mr John O'Donoghue TD.

With the provision of extensive function rooms at Westmanstown in the 1990s and changing lifestyles, Harrington Street entered a quieter period. From humble origins, the club certainly became the focal point for Garda social life in Dublin city. All told, the Garda Recreation Club has grown over the past fifty years due to the foresight of the early governing body, who set out on a bold programme of expansion. Today as members and guests stroll along the sycamore-lined Harrington Street and step through the club's canopied doorway, greeted by an oak-panelled interior, they come upon an oasis from the hustle and bustle of the city, an inviting retreat from the cares of the world. But the story of the Garda Club was set to expand even further and reach dizzying heights with the acquisition of land at Stackstown and Westmanstown.

Right: Pictured at the reopening of the refurbished Garda Club in September 1997, *from left,* Dublin City Manager Frank Feely, Marian McGuinness TD, Lord Mayor of Dublin Ben Briscoe and Garda Commissioner Patrick Culligan

16 Evening Herald, Tuesday, Wednesday, January 1, 2, 1985

People. . .News. . .Gossip. . .Pictures. . .the column they always read

Boys on the beat join the millionaire set

ad-lib Liam Collins

YOU SEE them every day — and they're not driving Rolls Royces, they're on their feet.

They are the least assuming and most unusual members of the new "Millionaires Club".

They are the Dublin Metropolitan Garda Recreation Club.

Already the 3,600 members own the Garda Club in Harrington Street — which celebrated its 21st birthday last night — the £1,000 a new member Strokestown Golf Club and they have multi-million pound plans for the future.

The Club is in the throes of completing a deal that will buy them a 50-acre prime site in Lucan.

"We are now talking about millions" says Club chairman Brian Prendergast who is attached to Cabra station. "Thank God I'm out of it" added Edmund Garvey the ex-Garda Commissioner who started it all and says he was "kicked out" by Fianna Fail.

To celebrate their "coming of age" current Commissioner, the cool, clean Larry Wren, came along to Harrington Street's Garda Club, with its six bars and numerous function rooms to join in the celebrations.

There are 52 [illegible] in the Garda [illegible] all over the world [illegible] when they visit Dublin.

Twenty-one years ago a group of Gardai walked into the Georgian house near Kelly's Corner to start it all. Immediately they sent a circular to every Garda station in the country asking members of the force what they did in their "private lives."

Anyone who replied that they were a brickie, spark, plumber, painter or had any building skill was pressed into service and within months the club was open.

Among the original members celebrating the 21st birthday last night were Edmund Garvey, Brian Prendergast, Supt. Tom Ryan, Jim Daly, John O'Gara, Frank Kiernan and Cyril Daly. Dundalk Superintendent Sean O'Mahony from Dundalk couldn't be there and Detective Garda Sean O'Mahony has since died.

Accompanying the Commissioner was genial Assistant Commissioner Eamon Doherty, Charlie Gaffney from the Technical Bureau, and Assistant Commissioner Fleming who is President of the club.

Mount Argus priest Fr. Clarence Daly, C.P. was presented with a cheque. "Mine's the priest wouldn't get as much at a Station" he told the crowd. "Wouldn't you know he was a Garda's son by the size of his feet" remarked a member of the force.

Why did he set it up? "Young members of the force were drinking and going into dirty old pubs" said Garvey. "We thought if they were going to do anything wrong they might as well [illegible]."

★ ★ ★

A PRESS BALL wouldn't be complete without a story — and unfortunately charming Kate O'Toole of the Government Information Service provided it.

During one of the dances she fell and broke her leg.

Big Tom McGurk decided to play doctor until the ambulance arrived.

Otherwise it was an uneventful night with almost 400 people packing the Burlington Hotel.

Dancing out the old year were Brendan Martin, one time RTE Gaelic writer, who left a [illegible] for the [illegible] cigar smoking Alden Doyle of Annabelle's; actress Deirdre Raftery recently returned from an Arts Council visit to London where she studied at LAMDA; Supt. Jim Murphy of Store Street and the lovely person Ann O'Callaghan.

Viewers of RTE's New Year's night extravaganza will be glad to hear that Tadhg de Brun — who was warming up the audience — insulted Maurice Pratt, without knowing that the Quinnsworth voice was in the audience.

Whiskey people Jameson invited the entire top of the National Concert Hall to a free Bowing evening — where black tie had to be worn.

Joining the masses on the bottom tier — where you had to pay for your own drink were Labour Party friends Barry Desmond, Minister for Health and one-time MEP Brendan Halligan, who sat slightly apart in the Choir Seats.

★ ★ ★

"WRAP THAT" said the Gallagher Bros. firm of Killybegs, when they bought a snooker table from Abbey Billiards for one of their clients as a small Christmas gift.

It cost £600 plus VAT — and that [illegible] to wrap it.

The table — transported by road as far as Dublin and by [illegible] trailer to [illegible] £1,600.

When Gallaghers rang to place the order — and then ordered "wrap it" the Abbey Billiards people thought it was a joke. But now they're laughing all the way to the bank.

Just to show how bad things are in the retail trade a Cavan woman who runs a shop in the town ordered a full-sized table for her 15 year old son.

But with the cost of playing snooker running at £3.50 an hour maybe that was just a sound investment. Who knows, could be a Cavan Alex Higgins.

Mother and daughter attending the Press Ball in the Burlington Hotel, Dublin, were: ISABELLA STAINES with MARIA, Windy Arbour, Dublin.

Attending the 21st anniversary celebrations of the Garda Club in Harrington Street last night were (from left: former station sergeant JOHN O'GARA (Kevin Street); former Garda Commissioner and founder of the Garda Club, EDWARD GARVEY; Sgt. BRIAN PRENDERGAST (Cabra), present Chairman, and Garda Commissioner LAURENCE WREN.

Also at the 21st anniversary of the Garda Club in Harrington Street were (from left), members of [illegible]

Above: The *Evening Herald* in 1985 reports on the twenty-first birthday celebrations of the Garda Club with the club now worth over a million pounds

Below: Members celebrate twenty-one years of the Garda Club in 1985

Above: Exterior of Harrington Street, Dublin

Keeping in touch, exchanging stories, building friendships...

My connections with the Garda Recreation Club go back to the very earliest days of my career in An Garda Síochána. From the outset, the Garda Club in Harrington Street provided an important social outlet for An Garda Síochána, especially for young members from the country deployed to the Dublin Metropolitan Area. After my allocation from the Garda Training Centre to Crumlin in September 1967, it was a natural focal point for meetings of all kinds, be they social, sporting or organisational. I have very happy memories of attending dances in Harrington Street, usually on a Saturday night where, in the era of less sophisticated communications systems, members availed of the opportunity to keep in touch, exchange stories and build friendships which lasted throughout their service.

Over the course of the subsequent years I learned and fully appreciated the vision of those who founded the 'Club' and the significant contribution it has made to the social and recreational life of members of An Garda Síochána and their families.

Fachtna Murphy, Former Garda Commissioner

Bringing Golf to the Mountain

Stackstown Golf Club

Chapter

5

No man really dies if he leaves behind something that other men may share.

Chapter 5
Bringing Golf to the Mountain

THE Divisional Committee was not one to let the grass grow under its feet, especially if it involved fine golfing greens. In the early 1970s, with Harrington Street well established as a private members' club and entertainment hotspot, and its finances in rude good health, the committee looked at further expansion. The idea of a golf and sports club located on a dedicated site was foremost in their thoughts. In Ireland, golf had been enjoyed by relatively small groups in exclusive clubs in the first half of the twentieth century but all that began to change in the early 1960s after Irish golfers Christy O'Connor Snr and Harry Bradshaw won the Canada Cup – a forerunner to the World Cup of Golf – in 1958, and when it was staged two years later in Portmarnock, Dublin, in 1960. Golf courses began to spring up all over the country, many designed by the renowned Irish golf architect, Mr Eddie Hackett.

The sport was particularly popular with senior members of An Garda Síochána and having their own golf course was a greatly cherished dream. An added incentive was that many Garda golfers were finding it nigh on impossible to gain admittance to existing golf clubs, many of which were overcrowded. Having their own golf club became a much-discussed topic among committee members and a number of options were examined. In fact, any landbank in the greater Dublin area that went on sale was promptly visited and scrutinised. In his reminiscences, Tom Ryan recalls accompanying Ned Garvey on several visits to land in the vicinity of South County Dublin and being particularly interested in land in the Slade Valley. However, this interest waned during 1973 when another tract of land, located at Ballyboughal, County Dublin, was examined. Committee members, including Ned Garvey, Tom Ryan, Jim Daly and Charlie Gaffney, visited Ballyboughal and walked the land to get a feel for its potential development. After numerous visits to the property and much debate, however, it was decided not to go ahead with this intended purchase. Nonetheless, it was not long before another appealing piece of land came to the attention of the prospective buyers.

This land on high ground at the foothills of the Dublin Mountains, specifically Kilmashogue Mountain, came on the market in early 1975. As customary by now, Ned Garvey, Tom Ryan and other members visited it and from its plentiful gorse ditches surveyed all before them. No doubt the beauty and scale of the land nestled at the foothills of the mountains appealed to Garvey, who quickly made up his mind that it should be purchased. The tract amounted to 112 acres on the side of Kilmashogue Mountain – more hill than mountain – at a distance of some nine miles from the centre of Dublin. It was mostly located in the townland of Stackstown, with a small portion in the townland of Taylor's Grange, in the parishes of Rathfarnham and Whitechurch and in the barony of Rathdown. It was bounded on the east by Kellystown Road, to the north lay St Columba's College, while to the south and west boundaries were formed by woodlands owned by Coillte, the semi-state company responsible for forestry. The vendor was Mr William Taylor, whose family had owned the land in the area for generations. There were breathtaking views of Dublin Bay and city, though the chief beneficiaries of that panorama at the time were the sheep that grazed there.

The fact that the site was on a mountain incline did not appear to matter to the club representatives who entered negotiations for its purchase. When some of the membership inspected the land, they were aghast at the idea of even contemplating the laying of a golf course on such hilly ground. A number of committee meetings followed and a groundswell of opinion emerged against this proposed venture. Needless to say, Ned Garvey was not in the 'O ye of little faith' brigade. The opposition only served to fire his determination further since he had by now made up his mind to close the deal. A good portion of the committee and those close to Garvey knew only too well that he made up his mind quickly and then acted accordingly. Before most of the committee knew what was happening, they were the part owners of a piece of mountainside. The owner Mr Taylor had sold it to Ned Garvey at an agreed price of £68,000. In today's money, this translates to approximately £600 per acre or €900. When fees were included, the total sum amounted to £70,000.

Despite the naysayers, there were plenty who saw the value of having a golf club of their own at Stackstown. These were sufficient in number to allow work to progress on the initial development. With 112 acres, Stackstown had the acreage required to lay a golf course and build ancillary facilities. It was intended to devote 108 acres to the layout of the golf course and the remainder to a sports complex, which would in time include a swimming pool and tennis and squash courts for the use of wives and families of members of the Garda Recreation Club.

Preparing the land

A golf subcommittee was formed in June 1975 to prepare the grounds and to look into the practicalities and legalities of setting up a golf club. These members included Denis Devine, Paddy Harrington, Oliver Nugent, Dan Buggy and Dan Kennedy. The most pressing job was getting the land into shape. Before long, work began on a temporary nine hole course, marking tees and cutting greens, and constructing a hut as a temporary changing facility. The initial course was chiefly laid out by Denis Devine and willing members such as Dan Corcoran, Jim Mahoney and others who volunteered their services.

It is a great mark of the men that they transformed the stony soil into a magnificent golf course. With picks and shovels, they pried rocks from the hillsides, cleared stones, gorse, shrubs and trees, and moved mounds of earth to shape the fairways and greens. It is nearly impossible to understand the scale of the undertaking today. Day after day for months on end, these dedicated men toiled and moiled. In 2005, Paddy Harrington relayed to Dermot Gilleece in the *Sunday Independent* that 'with the indulgence of my superiors, there was hardly a day when myself and about eight or nine colleagues weren't up there moving earth and shaping greens'. It was a true labour of love for Paddy Harrington, who also pressed his five sons into service. The youngest, Padraig, was just at the tender age of four but would later go on to scale the dizzying heights of professional golf. As Padraig himself revealed to Tom Callahan in *Golf Digest* in February 2008: 'One of my earliest memories was at four years of age, helping to level a green with my feet. I was lucky. My four older brothers had to pick up stones.' The assiduous work clearly paid off in more ways than one.

Bridge of dreams

When I first laid eyes on the land at Stackstown in 1975 at the side of Kilmashogue Mountain, there was nothing but rocks, stones and whins all around. One of the first tasks facing us was to clear the land and build a bridge over the Little Dargle river at the Kellystown end to gain access.

It all began when my brother Mike Murphy arrived up in his JCB, having driven it all the way across the city from Clontarf. I stood waiting for him along with Seamus Hoban and Donie O'Riordan, who had all taken annual leave to build the bridge. Mike jumped down from the cab and instructed me to 'Get in there, drive it, just pull this lever and pull that lever, it's easy. Off you go.' I had never driven a JCB in my life before! But off I went.

It took us a couple of days to divert the stream, put in the foundations and form the bridge. The bridge was constructed entirely from concrete and the only steel used was from farm gates found on the land. During the construction we had to endure all sorts of resistance – mostly in the form of laughter from the opposition. 'That won't stay up!' they sniggered, but stay up she did. To our pride, she has withstood all sorts of heavy vehicles over the years and is still there.

We persevered with the hard work for a few days but all of us were delighted with our efforts – not least because of the financial savings. The bridge was constructed for a mere £500; the estimates were £10,000! And nothing could beat the great fun we had building it!

John Murphy, former Honorary Secretary, Garda Recreation Club and first Honorary Treasurer, Stackstown Golf Club

Above: Denis Devine, John Murphy (in JCB), Frank Kiernan and Jim Mahoney, c1975
Below: John Murphy (right) and Donie O'Riordan constructing the bridge, c1975

Memorable photographs of the time record volunteers constructing a bridge over the Little Dargle river to gain access to the golf lands beyond it. This Trojan work, accomplished by John Murphy in a JCB along with Seamas Hoban and Donie O'Riordan, is there for all to see. Behind all the work on the course was the galvanising force of Ned Garvey. The foresight of the club founder is recognised today by former club captain Noel Burke: 'It is remarkable that Edmund Garvey, a non-golfer, could see the potential of this as a site for a golf course, when others saw the project as too daunting. Willing hands set to work and sculptured the lands into an extraordinary golf course, which has been nurtured and refined over the years into a top class facility.'

A tale of two rivers

There are two small rivers running through Stackstown: the Peacock and the Little Dargle. The former enters the course beside the third green and flows through the course through four manmade lakes before entering Kilmashogue Golf Course and thereafter Marley Park. The Peacock was reputed to have cures for foot welts. In order to be cured, people had to walk upstream from Stackstown towards the mountain wearing their boots. Just beyond Stackstown they would get onto the bank and, without removing their shoes, sat there until they were dry and their foot ailments hopefully cured!

The more substantive Little Dargle river is found at the Kellystown end of the course. It initially forms the course boundary on the left of the sixth green, is culverted to go underneath the seventeenth tee box before continuing on through the course, through 'Danesmoate' property and onwards to Marley Park and beyond. One of the first tasks facing the club developers was to bridge this river to gain access to the majority of the golf course lands that lay beyond it. Over the years the Little Dargle has claimed many wayward balls off the seventeenth tee, as the river side of that fairway seems to act like a magnet in claiming errant shots. Many promising cards were ruined at this hole, and many tales of woe about this hole recounted in the clubhouse.

One such tale involved Joe Holden, who could never master this hole and put many balls out of bounds. He resolved that he would get his own back by requesting that when he died his ashes would be spread on the seventeenth green. Thereby, he hoped to achieve in death what he had failed so many times to do in life. Shortly after, he did pass on; his friends received his ashes and stood with the urn in the middle of the green. It was a calm sunny day and Joe was about to get his wish. But when the lid was removed from the urn, a breeze came from nowhere and blew the ashes away over the white stakes. Joe was out of bounds for the last time!

Noel Burke, Honorary Captain, Stackstown Golf Club, 2008/9

Right: Stackstown's first 'clubhouse'

Stackstown Golf Club established

At the AGM of the Garda Club in 1976, the honorary secretary, Jim Daly, reported on the progress thus far:

> *On 18th June 1975 a meeting was held at the club with a view to forming a working committee for the promotion of golf in our lands at Taylor's Grange. Meeting was well attended and a number of similar meetings took place. Work is in progress at the grounds and nine temporary holes are laid out with tees marked and greens cut. A full eighteen hole course will be ready within a relatively short time. It is planned to open the course on Easter Sunday, 18th April 1976.*
>
> *On 10th March 1976 the golf members held their first AGM in the Garda Club. Officers and committee members were elected. Rules prepared by Mr Vincent Landy SC on behalf of the parent club were placed before this meeting and adopted. The rules provide that no member shall be eligible for election as an ordinary member of the Golf Club unless he is also a member of the parent club. It is proposed that the lands be leased on a yearly lease to the new club.*
>
> *Owing to the enormous cost of developing these lands and construction of clubhouse the parent club will be committed to giving financial assistance to the golfers or some years to come. I have no doubt that it will eventually be one of the finest golf clubs in Europe. All members should give it their support and they should feel proud that we are the only police force in the world to have its own golf course. I think it is only right to place on record our thanks to our chairman Commissioner Garvey for his courage and foresight in making all this possible.*

At the AGM, the members elected Ned Garvey as the first club president, Denis Devine its first captain and Paddy Harrington its first greens officer. Thus, Stackstown Golf Club officially came into existence in 1976. It drew up its club

Below: Early golf course plan for Stackstown

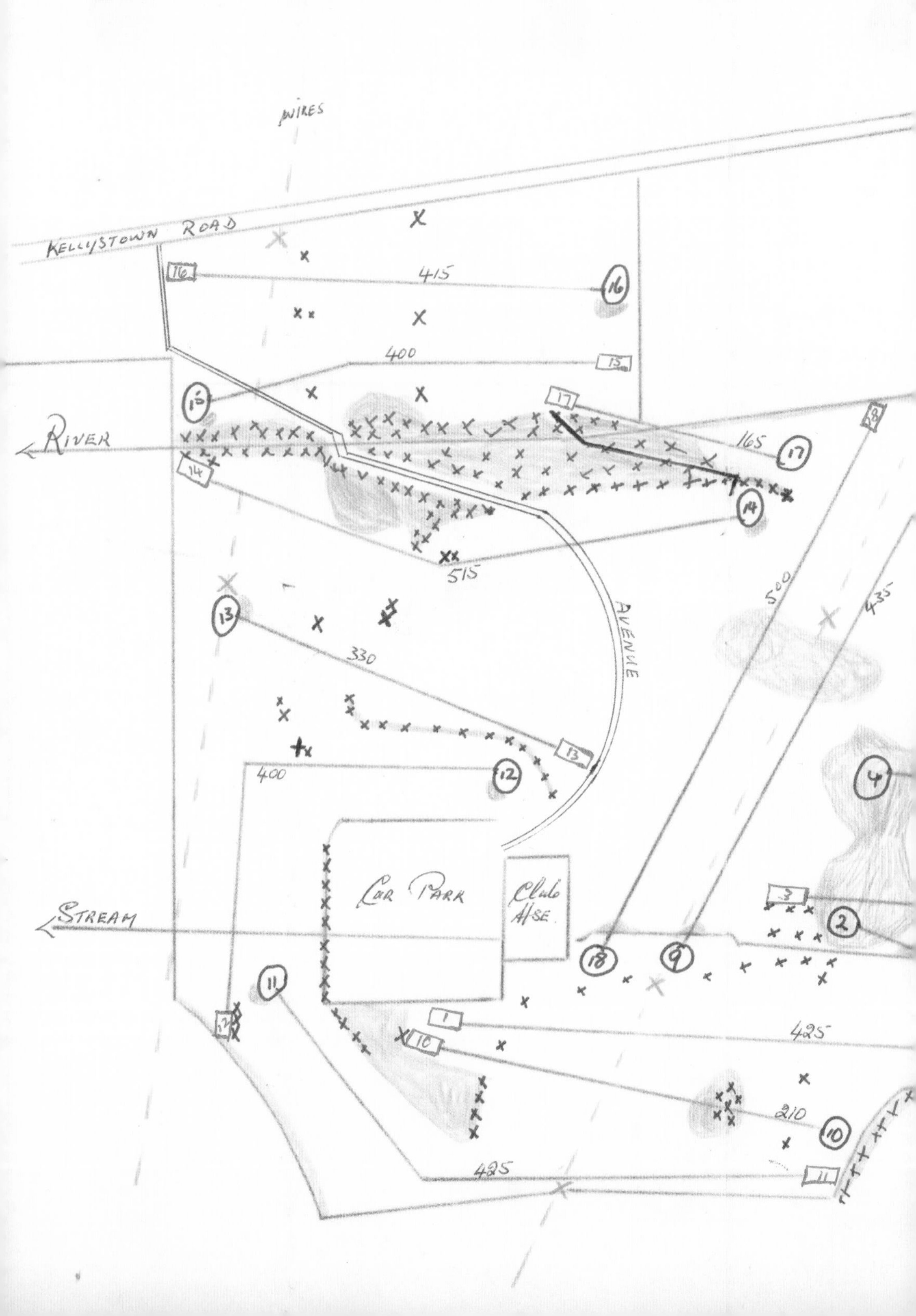

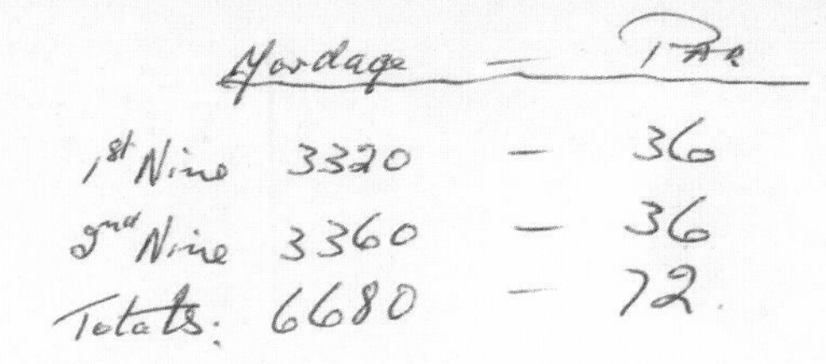

Yardage	Par
1st Nine 3320	36
2nd Nine 3360	36
Totals: 6680	72.

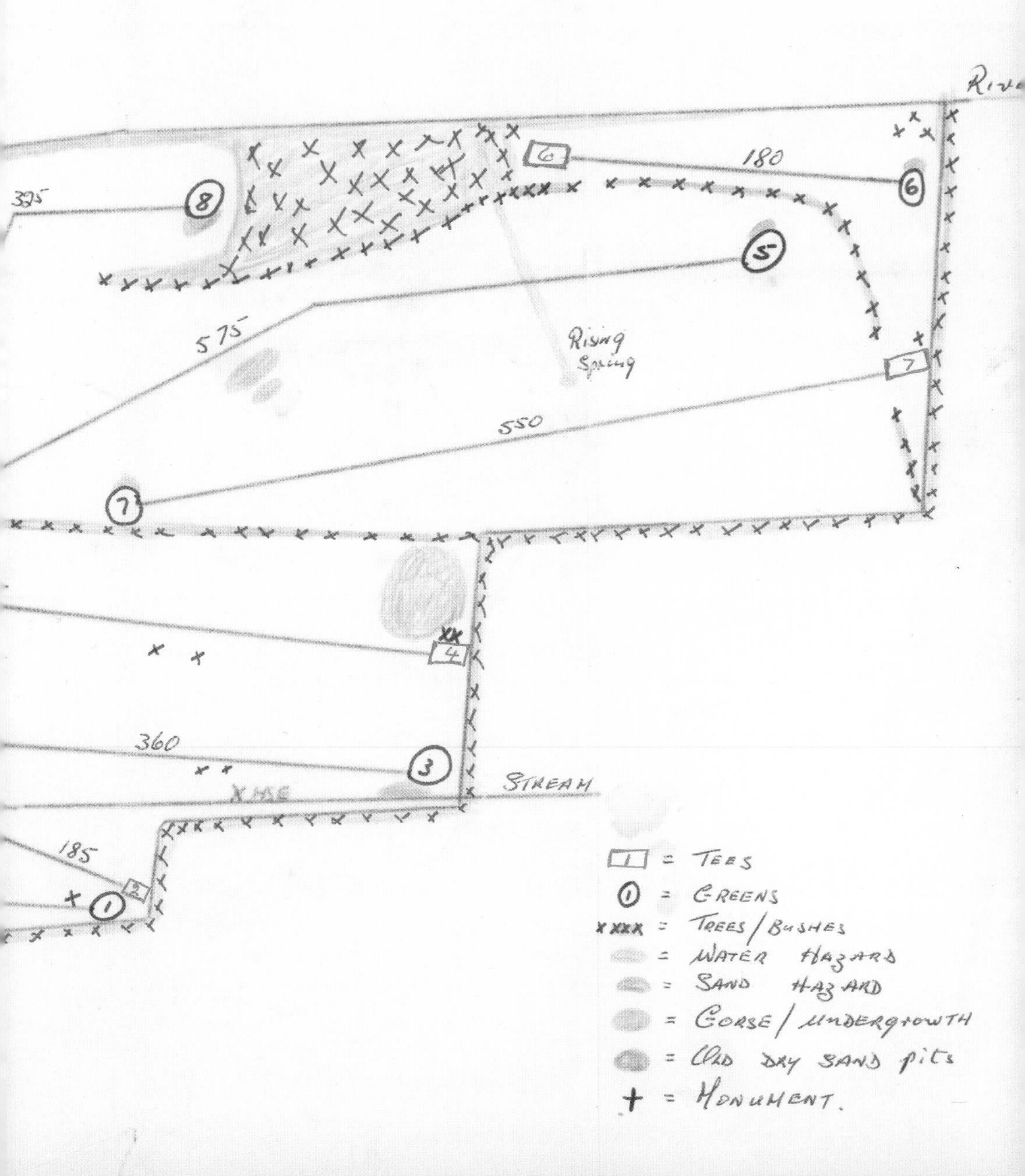

rules, which were all subsequently adopted, and the club was affiliated to the Golf Union of Ireland in 1976. The members took to the greens with great gusto and by 1977 had entered teams for the Metropolitan Trophy, the Barton Cup, the Junior Cup and the Pierce Purcell Shield. At first the facilities at Stackstown were to be available only to members and their families on payment of a separate membership fee. Preference was given to paid-up members of the Garda Recreation Club. Later in 1977, however, the membership was extended to non-Garda members, as only 250 Garda members had signed up. It was agreed to accept 100 civilian members initially but this number grew over time. The year 1978 saw the formation of the ladies' section, headed by its first captain, Rita Quinn.

Living legacy

There is an abiding photograph of Edmund Garvey complete with hat and coat holding a golf club ready, as on a tee box, posed to strike an imaginary ball. In the background lies the virgin unkempt land; it is perhaps the first photograph of Stackstown in its then raw state. When I see that photograph of Edmund Garvey again, I think of his vision and all the work that went into the initial effort to develop Stackstown into a golf course worthy of his dream. There is a plaque with an inscription at a monument at Snowy Mountain Park in Australia commemorating the giant hydroelectric scheme there. The citation could have been written about our founder: 'No man really dies if he leaves behind something that other men may share. If aught he does shall benefit mankind some part of him shall live forever there.'

Noel Burke, Honorary Captain, Stackstown Golf Club, 2009

Eighteen-hole golf course

Work continued on creating the permanent eighteen-hole course, which was designed by Eddie Hackett and completed in 1979. Hackett's trademark style was evident everywhere. Always sensitive to the natural terrain, the layout had the look and feel of something that nature intended. The course was long from the back tees, with plainly visible landing areas, large greens and impressive elevated tees. Mature woodland bordered every hole and helped to shield golfers on wild windy days. The meandering mountain streams – Peacock and Little Dargle – were harnessed to add to the golfing challenge. Set against woodland, it became a par-72 course, consisting of four par 5, ten par 4 and four par 3 holes. Additional adjoining lands were purchased over the years to add length and challenge to the course, now measuring 6,500 yards. In addition, the course has been modified to make it less hilly, and while it still presents a challenge to test the skills of golfers, it is also more pleasurable. In particular, two

Above: **Ned Garvey feigning to tee off in 1976**
Below: **Denis Devine teeing off in 1976**

Above: Paddy Harrington preparing to tee off in 1976

more holes were added in 1999, specifically the fifteenth and sixteenth holes, to make it the twenty-hole parkland it is today. The sixteenth was the most difficult hole on the course with few birdies ever recorded there. The added bonus of the proximity to mountains and woodland was that wild deer and pheasant frequently appeared on the course, much to the delight of golfers – admittedly not when taking a shot. It comes as no surprise that a stag and three trees became part of the club emblem.

The greens were a source of immense pride to the honorary greens officer, Paddy Harrington. They were built to 'a revolutionary new concept', he declared in the 1983 *Stackstown Golf Club Commemorative Book*. The combination of materials used was stone, gravel, pebble, white lime-free sand, peat moss and a sprinkling of soil, which was to serve the club well over the years. The transformation had been truly miraculous, as Harrington revealed in 1983.

> *Members now see an 18 hole golf course, well manicured and maintained, giving no indication of what the basic raw material was like. Step back to 1976: then it was simply 100 acres of Dublin mountain. Look at the hill on the left of Kellystown Road or the land on the left of the 11th fairway, that is exactly what our course was like before work began. In addition, a massive gravel pit extended from the present pits, at the first bridge on the road, right across the 14th, 18th and 19th fairways into the areas of the present 2nd and 4th greens. It is probably no exaggeration to say that a million tons of rock were removed and buried in those pits.*

Some idea of the size of the project can be gained from the mass of rocks on the left of the 12th fairway. They were left over after the same amount of rock had been used to build up the fairway itself and the left side of the 12th green. Almost all the fourteen fairways were built by bulldozing the land and then topsoiling and seeding it. In fact, if you think there are hills in Stackstown now, you should have seen the hills that were removed. One cannot finish without giving special mention to the 6th and 17th holes. Where you now see golf holes, in 1976 there was just space or a river valley into which thousands of tons of rock, subsoil, etc. was poured, creating golf holes where no land existed.

Seeking autonomy

As time moved on, the golf club sought more autonomy to run its affairs. For a number of years the amount of rent to be paid to the Garda Recreation Club was disputed. In 1978, Ned Garvey had received legal advice that the club should rent out the land at Stackstown to the golf club for £7,000 each year and when the clubhouse was built this should rise to £25,000. Clearly, many members felt the golf club should have a greater say in these matters. Hence in June 1979, the Divisional Committee decided to grant Stackstown Golf Club a lengthy lease, subject to the approval of the members, and once the trustees and solicitors of both clubs had prepared the finer details. At a special general meeting on 10 March 1980 under the chairmanship of Denis Devine, the members debated the long lease motion. Like all matters relating to Garda Recreation Club business, the decision was not unanimous. Many members favoured retaining the lands in Garda Club possession as an asset for further development. There was also the fear expressed by some that civilians would eventually take over the club.

When the motion was put to the members, an overwhelming majority voted in favour of entering into a leasing arrangement with the golf club. The lease allowed Stackstown to operate independently and raise its own loans and generally finance day-to-day operations. When the lands were leased, one triangular field at the entrance to Stackstown along Kellystown Road was retained by the Garda Recreation Club. It was envisaged then that this section would be developed as a sports centre with tennis courts and possibly a swimming pool. In the event, this did not happen as this facility was later developed in Westmanstown by the Garda Recreation Club. This four and a half acres is now called 'the Harrington Field'. It was left fallow for many years with little usage, although sods from the land were used to augment the golf course in 1986.

Garda Recreation Club

Telephone 753764

8-9-10 HARRINGTON STREET,
DUBLIN 8.

29th. April, 1983.

Mr. P. Shovlin,
Secretary,
Stackstown Golf Club.

Dear Paddy,

I am writing to you on behalf of the Officers and Committee of the Garda Recreation Club, 8,9,10 Harrington Street.

Please let me known the position in relation to members of Harrington Street, who go to Stackstown Golf Club for the purpose of playing Golf, what is the position in relation to Green Fees ? What is the position in relation to members of Harrington Street, entering Stackstown for the purpose of using Bar facilities ?

I would appreciate an early reply.

Yours sincerely,

HON. SECRETARY.

Above and right: **Correspondence between the Garda Recreation Club regarding the status of its members at the golf club**

STACKSTOWN GOLF CLUB

Kellystown Road, Rathfarnham Dublin 16. Phone :942338

Your Ref: Our Ref: Date 14th. May. 1983.

The Hon. Secretary,
Garda Recreation Club,
8/9/10 Harrington Street,
Dublin 8.

Dear John,

Thank you for your letter of 24th. April, 1983. The matters raised therein were placed before a full Committee meeting, who, after discussion, instructed me to reply as hereunder :-

1. Members of your Club are entitled to play golf at Stackstown Golf Club on payment of half normal green fees i.e.

   Monday to Friday = £2.50.

   Weekends & Bank Holidays = £3. 00.

   This also entitles them to the use of the Bar and Dining Room facilities.

2. No one is entitled, by law, to enter and use bar facilities at Stackstown Golf Club except those listed hereunder :-

   a) All members of the Club.
   b) Green Fee paying persons.
   c) Pavilion members.
   d) Guests of Club members.
   e) Members of Golfing Societies booked into the Club.

I trust that the foregoing is satisfactory to your Officer and Committe. May I take this opportunity to advise you that no previous letters relating to this matter were received by me.

Yours Sincerely,

Patrick J. Shovlin

Patrick J. Shovlin.
Hon. Secretary.

Constructing the clubhouse

One of most important aspects of having the lease was that it paved the way for the golf club to fund and build its own clubhouse. To this end, the Divisional Committee passed a resolution in 1 April 1981 granting the golf club permission to erect a clubhouse, which Garda Club members could have access to at suitable times. James O'Toole of Lynch O'Toole Walsh Architects, a keen golfer himself, was commissioned to design the building and during the summer of 1983 the construction of an impressive three-storey clubhouse was completed. It had a comprehensive range of facilities and could boast the finest views of Dublin city and bay from its front windows. The golfers were glad to swap the temporary hut hitherto squeezed into for this magnificent new clubhouse. The social outlet of the club was not neglected either. The clubhouse could offer members the ultimate in modern facilities such as a members' bar and lounge, restaurant, ballroom, functions area and bar, snooker and pool rooms, men's and ladies' locker rooms, sauna, penthouse, and pro shop as well as a car park. As the facilities improved, the Garvey vision realised its full potential.

The clubhouse was formally opened on 10 September 1983 by the then Taoiseach Dr Garret FitzGerald TD. Praising the voluntary work of the gardaí, he noted that over one million hours of hard work had gone into the golf club. Renowned more for his intellect than sporting prowess, the Taoiseach revealed: 'I am not adept at any sport but the one sport I would like to have been good at is golf.' He was attended at the ribbon-cutting ceremony by club president Mr Oliver Nugent and club captain Mr Aiden Browne, and unveiled a plaque to mark the occasion. Commissioner Eamonn Doherty and Mr Michael Fitzpatrick, president of the Golfing Union of Ireland, were also in attendance. The clubhouse was conjointly blessed by Fr Sean Carey PP Ballinteer and Rev Kenneth Todd. It was a unique and proud day for Garda members, as Stackstown was now the only golf course in the world developed by a police force.

To mark the occasion, a game of golf was played by two professionals. These were Ireland's Christy O'Connor Snr and Australia's Peter Thomson, five-times

Ball in play

'That the trustees of the Dublin Metropolitan Garda Recreation Club, Harrington Street, be directed to grant leases to the Trustees of Stackstown Golf Club to enable them to build their own Clubhouse, and to have autonomy over that area and portion of the lands which is under golf at Stackstown and Taylor's Grange, Rathfarnham.'

Resolution passed at special general meeting of Dublin Metropolitan Garda Recreation Club on 10 March 1980

Above: **Members' bar at Stackstown**
Below: **Aiden Browne enjoying a game of snooker at Stackstown clubhouse in 1976**

Clubhouse and golf course at Stackstown

Above: Foyer of Stackstown clubhouse

winner of the British Open. Thomson, though retired from tournament golf, was still in the top ten on the American Seniors Tours. Despite Thomson entertaining the 700-strong crowd, the canny O'Connor emerged the winner with some marvellous shots. This encounter between two greats of the game was a fitting prelude for what was to come. It was clear that the two golfers had enjoyed the challenge, with the victorious O'Connor revealing the secret of the new course, as reported by Paddy Harrington in the *Stackstown Golf Club Commemorative Book.*

> *Thomson afterwards described the course as awkward and qualified this by saying awkward in terms of difficulty. He was highly complimentary on its condition for such a young course. O'Connor disagreed that the course was awkward or terribly difficult. He stressed that taking the correct line off the tee at most of the holes was the secret for setting up relatively easy shots. He was also complimentary on the excellent condition of such a young course.*

By 1983, the club was fully subscribed with a total membership of 958. Ordinary membership was confined to gardaí and totalled 380, non-Garda or seven-day membership was 270, lady associates numbered 141, juveniles 120, pavilion members 40, five-day members were five and there were two country members. The golf club was now in a position to act as hosts to other clubs on its Open Days when the clubhouse was officially open. The total development cost of the golf club was in the region of £1.01 million, with the clubhouse costing £280,000. The greater part of that expenditure was met by fundraising, sponsorship, patrons' contributions and a bank loan for £175,000. A number of fundraising activities, such as discos, were often held in Harrington Street and were well patronised. The Garda Club sponsored one day in the Stackstown Open Week in September 1983 to the tune of £1,000 as part of the official opening. This was a tradition that continued in subsequent Open Weeks.

Golfing success

The growing popularity of golf among the force led to the formation of a Garda Recreation Club Golfing Society in March 1986. The Divisional Committee granted £330 for getting the society off the ground and established. It meant that an Inter-District Golf competition could be held annually in Stackstown and receive sponsorship from the Garda Club. In 1992, the Garda Recreation Club gave Stackstown a small piece of its adjoining land at no cost so the club could fence off their entrance from Kellystown Road.

The Stackstown course went on to produce the great professional Padraig Harrington. With great dedication and resilience, Padraig honed his golfing skills from a very young age on the hills and dales of Kilmashogue Mountain. It was a day of tremendous pride and joy for his family and club when he turned professional in 1995, just after winning the Walker Cup with the Great Britain & Ireland team. As he bogeyed and birdied, little did he think that he would become British Open champion in 2007 and 2008 and US PGA champion in 2008. By his own admission, the course that he cut his teeth on was 'a very tricky, winding golf course'. Nonetheless, it stood him in good stead for all the challenging courses that lay ahead.

Aside from Padraig Harrington, the club has enjoyed considerable success at provincial and national level and got off to a good start in 1978 by winning the inaugural Jimmy Bruen Shield. In this amateur competition, clubs are represented by five pairs playing foursomes, with a combined handicap of 23 – the individual minimum handicap of 6 and with a maximum handicap of 17. The winning 1978 team comprised John Nealon, Dermot McCormack, Jim Kavanagh, Pat Waters, Aiden Browne, John McLoughney, Tom O'Connor, Patsy O'Connor, Tom O'Donoghue, Martin Hynes, and team manager Dan Buggy. Despite their great efforts, the club was beaten in the All-Ireland semi-final in 1980 but won the competition again in 1982.

Other notable successes for the club include winning the All-Ireland Irish Junior Cup in 1996, the JB Carr Diamond Trophy in 1996, the Barton Cup in 1998 and the Metropolitan Cup in 1992 and 1999. Further honours arrived in 2002, with winning the Bloom Cup, and in 2003 winning the Leinster Final of the Barton Shield, with a team comprising Michael and John McDermott, Mark Campbell and Liam Ryan. Great celebrations ensued in 2005 when the club won the Tenth All-Ireland JB Carr

Above: **A youthful Padraig Harrington with his mother Breda Harrington and Captain Paddy Shovlin (centre)**

Below: **Padraig Harrington billboard gracing the entrance to Stackstown Golf Club**

Stackstown Golf Clu
Proud of our 3 times Major Champion
Padraig Harrington

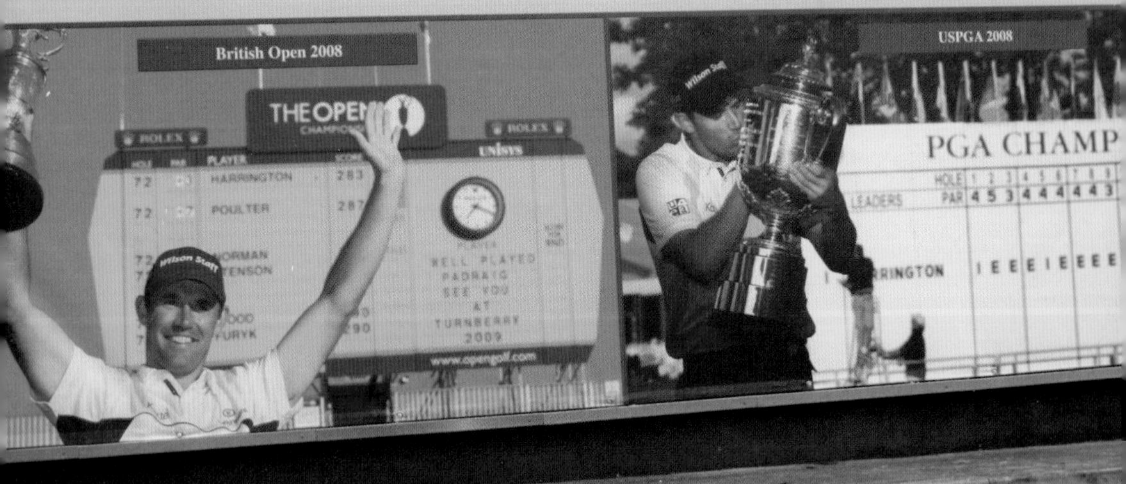

Diamond Trophy, featuring Pat Malone, Tony O'Mahoney, John Kavanagh, Sean O'Dwyer, Tom O'Donoghue, John Mahony, Pat McNiallais, Patsy O'Connor, Frank Kavanagh and Tom Kiely.

Acclaim has also been heaped on the club through the efforts of individual golfers such as Tom O'Donohue, Mark Campbell and Michael McDermott, who have won major honours. Tom O'Donohue was Leinster Senior Champion in 1990, 1991 and 1992. In 1993, he was runner-up in the Leinster Senior Championship and in 1994 was also runner-up in the Irish Seniors Amateur Open Championship. Mark Campbell has the distinction of being the youngest player ever to win the Irish Shell South of Ireland Amateur Open Championship in 1999. He went on to win the East of Ireland in 2004 and has played in the 101st All-Indian Amateur Championship and Nations Cup match in 2002 and in the Mexican Amateur Stroke Play Championship in 2002. For his part, Michael McDermott won the West of Ireland Championships in 2001 and has represented Ireland in numerous amateur events such as the Lytham Trophy and the European Team Championship in 2001.

As for ladies golf, Lady Captain Mary Randles and her captain's prize winner Sinéad Kearney were placed third in the regional qualifiers of the Volkswagen-Irish Independent Lady Captain's Classic in 2001. The ladies also won the Mark Bloom Cup in 2002 and the girls won the Leinster Smurfit Junior Girls in 1995. Lorna Browne in particular has brought much distinction to ladies golf at Stackstown. In 1991 and 1992 she was a member of the Leinster Girls team and in 1992 represented Ireland in the Irish Girls team. In 1993, she was also a member of the Leinster Girls and Irish Junior team and in 1995 represented her country on the Irish Student International team.

Stackstown Golf Club continues in its ever-upwards spirit, constantly developing the course. Thus, in 2006, Padraig Harrington officially opened the redevelopment of six greens and tee boxes. In 2009, plans got underway to open a new 'Harrington Room' at the club in honour of the three-time major champion Padraig Harrington. The room, opened in March 2011, features items from Harrington's career to date, a gallery and a library housing memorabilia donated by Padraig and the Harrington family.

In the space of thirty years the club has come a very long way. Today it is a top class golf course that presents its own unique challenges to both novice and experienced golfers alike. One thing for sure is that a premium is placed on the accuracy of the tee. To that end, guidance and practice facilities are at hand in the practice range, putting green, chipping green and, not least, the resident PGA professional, Michael Kavanagh. The success of Padraig Harrington, in particular, has catapulted Stackstown to national prominence and now visitors from near and far can strike a ball and wish for glory on the greens, too. It is truly testament to the vision and drive of Ned Garvey.

Five years a-growing

The ladies' section of Stackstown Golf Club has been going strong since its inception in April 1978. A group of eleven ladies, mostly wives of members, with very little knowledge of golf with the exception of Rita Quinn but perhaps with the motto 'If you can't beat them join them', came together at a meeting in the Garda Club on Harrington Street. There, with the help of two male members, Paddy Harrington and Dan Buggy, the Lady Associates of Stackstown Golf Club was born. Rita Quinn took the helm as Lady Captain, an office she held for the first two years of our existence. With Rita's knowledge of golf, complete dedication and selflessness, she eventually got us round to some kind of standard; sometimes the going was rough, counting of shots became a major task and such aids as counters used by ladies for their knitting, etc. were suggested – pocket calculators were not so readily available then.

The fun we had in the little cabin afterwards made up for it all. Rita's hard work paid off and we are now able to take our place with the best, some of our ladies playing off handicaps as low as 16 and one of our junior members off single figures. Anne Marron took over from Rita and again with the same dedication to the office of Lady Captain, and I think ladies and men alike will always remember Anne's night held under the stars in Stackstown on 21 June 1980.

Brideen Buggy followed on after Anne and I think Brideen's highlight will always be when she led her gallant band of the fifth Autumn team to the finals in Killiney where we were beaten on points only. Ursula Forristal succeeded Brideen and had the privilege of being the first Lady Captain in our new clubhouse, even if it was not quite finished.

Our successes to date are modest but we are coming on and in future years will be a force to be reckoned with. Our greatest achievement so far was last September [1982] when Pat Hynes and Yvonne McQuillan (mother and daughter) brought home the Golden Rose from Killarney as winners of the Lancôme Final and went on to represent Ireland in Paris. Last year also two of our ladies, Kathleen Kelly and Rita Quinn, got to the final of the *Daily Mail* competition – no mean feat. We are glad to report this year we have two representatives going to Killarney again, Sadie Garvey and Ita O'Brien, and we wish them both every success in September.

Teresa Mahoney, former Lady Captain, Stackstown Golf Club, 1983

Officers of Stackstown Golf Club

Year	Presidents	Captains
2011	Tommy O'Rourke	Richie Ryan
2010	Larry O'Connor	Felix McKenna
2009	William Herlihy	Noel Burke
2008	Eddie Ryan	Gerry Carter
2007	Tom Daly	Tom Collins
2006	Michael Fitzpatrick	Philip Bond
2005	Willie Hogan	Tony O'Loughlin
2004	Gerry Blake	Larry O'Connor
2003	James Maguire	Gerry Mullins
2002	Patrick King	Michael Flynn
2001	Tom O'Connor	Willie Hogan
2000	Terry McMahon	Larry McCormack
1999	Mick Walsh	Joe Sullivan
1998	Tom Culligan	Ken Duncan
1997	Sean Flanagan	Tom O'Connor
1996	Martin Hynes	Michael Greville
1995	Brian Kelly	Noel McDermott
1994	Patrick A Power	Tom Culligan
1993	Michael Feerick	Sean Flanagan
1992	Pat Millea	Martin Hynes
1991	Jim O'Malley	Paddy Power
1990	Dan McCallion	Michael Feerick
1989	Edmund Garvey	Pat Millea
1988	Edmund Garvey	Pat Shovlin
1987	Jim Marron	Dan McCallion
1986	Aiden Browne	Dermot McCormack
1985	Patsy O'Connor	Oliver Nugent
1984	William Kelly	John Naughton
1983	Oliver Nugent	Aiden Browne
1982	Jim Mahoney	Jim McGuane
1981	Dan Corcoran	Patsy O'Connor
1980	Dan Buggy	Jim Mahoney
1979	Denis Devine	Dan Buggy
1978	Paddy Harrington	Denis Devine
1977	Edmund Garvey	Paddy Harrington
1976	Edmund Garvey	Denis Devine

Year	Lady Presidents
2011	Joan O'Brien
2010	Pat Doherty
2009	Valerie Hobson
2008	Nancy Aherne
2007	Helen Collins
2006	Marie Lavelle
2005	Breda Harrington
2004	Sheila Byrne
2003	Doreen Naughton
2002	Mai Branagan

Left: First ladies committee of Stackstown Golf Club in October 1978.

Back row (left to right): Brid Walsh, Mai Branagan, Anna Marron, Kathleen Kelly, Imelda Kenny and Brideen Buggy.
Front row (left to right): Teresa Mahoney, Joanne Farrell, Rita Quinn (lady captain), Maureen O'Carroll and Ursula Forristal

Year	Lady Captains
2011	Minda Walsh
2010	Catherine O'Donovan
2009	Mary McDonnell
2008	Muriel O'Shea
2007	Betty Smith
2006	Mary McGettrick-Lovegrove
2005	Mary O'Flynn
2004	Anna Deignan
2003	Kay Deegan
2002	Anne McQuaid
2001	Mary Randles
2000	Margaret Ryan
1999	Helen Flood
1998	Claire O'Carroll
1997	Ann Kavanangh
1996	Eveleen McMahon
1995	Ita O'Brien
1994	Nuala Lucas
1993	Barbara Duncan
1992	Eileen Hearne
1991	Mary Sheahan
1990	Ann Hoban
1989	Ronnie Clarke
1988	Eileen Sullivan
1987	Anne Hennessey
1986	Maura Gorby
1985	Kathleen Kelly
1984	Maureen O'Carroll
1983	Teresa Mahoney
1982	Ursula Forristal
1981	Brideen Buggy
1980	Ann Marron
1979	Rita Quinn
1978	Rita Quinn

Dwellings and denizens of Stackstown

The land at Stackstown and other lands in the area had previously belonged to the Taylor family for generations. The Coillte lands, which form a necklace bordering the course to the south and west and stretching from the sixth to the tenth greens, replaced an oak forest that also extended to some of the lands of Stackstown. The oak forest was cut down during World War I to make pit props for coalmines in Wales. This was at a time when Britain's more mature hardwoods were being harvested to make ships to assist in the war effort. The area was later acquired by the then Department of Lands for the princely sum of £6 per Irish acre. Locals were employed to dig drains in a herringbone fashion and were paid one and a half pennies per perch (five and a half yards). Later when the trees were harvested, local women were employed to take the bark off the trees, earning six shillings per week. The forewoman for her efforts got an extra shilling. Today the area has been replanted with softwood trees by Coillte.

On the higher grounds around Stackstown there were many quarries and several sandpits in the golf course itself. One very large sandpit was located on what is now the fifteenth green and sixteenth tee box and fairway. The sandpit was extensive and very deep where it was extensively worked over the years. Given that the quarries and sandpits gave considerable employment locally, it is not surprising there were several dwellings dotted all around the present golf course. Only one such house remains intact, however: the cottage alongside what is now the third fairway.

By far the most interesting and colourful resident was 'the Hermit of Kilmashogue'. In the early part of the twentieth century, he lived at the top of the sandpit in a wooden house with slits for windows. Of Scottish origin and well educated, his name was Parker. Essentially a hermit, he lived alone and few people were admitted to the house. When he did speak to callers, it was through the window slits. In 1920, the house was destroyed by locals as Parker was suspected of being an informer. He was blamed, wrongly perhaps, of betraying Sean Doyle who was shot by the Black and Tans near Parker's house on 19 September 1920. Doyle was a nineteen-year-old Volunteer with the 4th Battalion Engineers of the IRA. From his home in Inchicore, he had travelled out that morning to join about forty others on manoeuvres in the area and they were surprised by the Black and Tans. They called on Doyle to halt but he refused and was shot and fatally wounded. Afterwards, they took his body away in a wheelbarrow down Sutton's Lane, now Kellystown Road. Hastily thrown on the barrow, his head was hanging forward and rubbing off the wheel. Local women at great risk to themselves blocked the lane and refused to allow the body through until it was rearranged in a more dignified manner.

After they shot Sean Doyle, the soldiers took Parker away from his nearby residence. Locals saw this as a cover-up for Parker's involvement in his death. Parker was held for two weeks and when he returned to Stackstown, his house was gone. The locals had dug underneath it from the sandpit causing it to cascade down to the bottom of the pit. Thereafter, the homeless hermit took to the roads and for the most part slept rough within a large oat sack that he would get into and pull up over his head. He occasionally lodged with 'The Hake' Farrells in Ticknock. (They were so called because they sold fish during Lent.) Today an inscribed monument stands near where Doyle was shot on the left of the fifteenth fairway and is a protected structure under the National Monuments Act. The actual point where he was shot was about 25 yards on the fairway side of the monument. The Doyle monument, the hermit's house, and the sixteenth tee box – built on the site of the sandpit – are all in close proximity to each other.

The site of the sixteenth tee box was built up by transporting thousands of tons of rubble from the original Hill 16 in Croke Park when it was being redeveloped. Hill 16 itself had been formed from rubble from Sackville Street (now O'Connell Street) after the 1916 Rising.

When the golf course lands were purchased, the cottage on the right of the third fairway was occupied by a Miss Hannon, who later moved to Rathfarnham. The roof and windows of the cottage have been repaired and the cottage has been largely preserved in its original state. It has a unique setting, sitting high on the course, its whitewashed walls making it stand out against the greenery of the Coillte forest to the rear. There was a path from the house to Courtney's house, which is now surrounded by the forest and still occupied by the same family. Over the years the cottage was rented to different tenants. Brothers George and Charlie Gilmore lived there for a long time; George was a dock policeman, while Charlie was interned during the Troubles. Peader or Peter Dixon and his wife Mairéad and family resided there in the 1930s. The Dixons started a garden to the front of the house and part of a privet hedge forming one boundary of the garden can still be seen there today.

The cottage was also home to Mick and Sal Saunders. Their children Pat and Michael were born in the cottage in the late 1930s. They also had a sister

Ann who entered a convent in Wales and died in recent years. Mike Saunders later got a position as caretaker of Dublin Castle. The job came with a house within the castle, beside what is now the Garda National Drugs Unit. Pat and Michael have happy memories of growing up there. They knew many gardaí that worked in the various units and both learned to drive cars and motorcycles, driving Garda vehicles within the confines of the castle. The brothers knew Edmund Garvey well and when he discovered their connection to Stackstown, he offered them membership!

They returned for the first time to Stackstown in March 2009 in the company of Ita and Pat Deacy, pavilion members in Stackstown. Another link in the chain is that Ita is their aunt. They visited the cottage and recalled many tales of their youth and their neighbours in Stackstown at the time. All these families, except the Courtneys, have long since left.

Noel Burke, former Honorary Captain, Stackstown Golf Club, 2009

Above: The picturesque cottage along the third fairway

Left: Pat and Michael Saunders pay a trip to the cottage with Ita and Pat Deacy in 2008

Man of Vision

Edmund Garvey and the Garda Club

Chapter

6

Mr Garvey's physical energy was matched by a similar mental energy and without his drive and determination to get things done it is doubtful if the Garda Club project would have ever got off the ground.

Chapter 6
Man of Vision

ONE name will be forever synonymous with the Garda Club. Edmund Garvey – Eddie to his family and friends or Ned to the media and public, though few in person called him such. The club's existence today is largely owed to his singular vision, courage, drive, energy, organising flair and business acumen. In his seventeen-year stewardship of the club, the hand of Ned Garvey was evident at every turn. Today, older members and staff look back fondly on extraordinary times with an extraordinary person at the helm. Some claim him to be a genius in policing and operational matters. Others remember a true gentleman, who, despite his tough and blunt exterior, was a great humanitarian. Most agree that he displayed fierce loyalty to the force and to his friends. There can be no doubt, however, that he was immensely proud of the Garda Club, what it represented, what it achieved, and its vast potential waiting to be tapped by successive chairmen and committees.

Truly 'something else'

Ned Garvey's link with the Garda Club is well known and documented. Over the years, I have heard many people talk about his sense of vision, about his ability to see the big picture, about his initiative and fearless courage in getting the Garda Recreation and Social Club off the ground. Ned, God rest him, would be the first man, however, to acknowledge the immense contribution made by a relatively small number of his Garda colleagues to the growth and development of the Garda Club and how it was to give birth to the magnificent complex that is Stackstown Golf Club in the Dublin mountains and the amazing facility that is Westmanstown Sports, Conference and Leisure Centre in the Clonsilla area of West Dublin.

I have heard nothing but admiration and praise from visiting police forces to our shores when they see the social and sporting facilities that are now part and parcel of the everyday life of our gardaí, serving and retired. I used the phrase 'fearless courage and initiative' in reference to Ned Garvey. You could say the same about Tom Ryan and Jim Daly. Cliché it might be, but they truly were 'something else'!

Fr Joe Kennedy CP, Garda Chaplain, Mount Argus

His advice to the organising committee of Stackstown Golf Club in 1975, to 'think big but spend wisely', captures his pragmatic idealism.

His career in An Garda Síochána was equally successful. He rose to its highest office – Garda Commissioner – during one of the most turbulent periods of the modern Irish state. The 1970s brought unparalleled violent crime in the shape of armed robberies, kidnappings and assassinations, principally at the hands of the Irish Republican Army (IRA). It presented great challenges to Commissioner Garvey and his force to ensure the security of the nation was not undermined. But what should have been a distinguished career was marred by a single event in 1978. He was summarily dismissed from office on 19 January 1978 by the Lynch Government that had swept to power some months before. No explanation was given other than a loss of confidence in him by the Government. Speculation abounded as to the cause; a mixture of personality and politics, some said. Either way, it was to cast a long shadow over his outstanding career and involvement with the Garda Club. Aside from bringing a premature end to an otherwise unblemished career, his dismissal from office set in train a period of intense disharmony within the Garda Club and a rift that would not be healed until December 1983.

Distinguished career

Edmund Patrick Garvey was born in Bradford, Yorkshire, on 1 February 1915 and not Ballinlough, County Roscommon, contrary to popular belief. His parents had previously lived in America before moving to Yorkshire, but finally returned when he was a baby to their native Ballinlough, where the Garvey family had a grocery business. Times were decidedly tough, money scarce, and the small community not immune to the struggle for Ireland's freedom. Ned Garvey once recalled to Henry Kelly in *The Irish Times* of 13 September 1975 how the Black and Tans had twice raided the family shop when he was a boy and had taken his father out to be shot on both occasions but had relented at the last minute. They had once nearly burned the whole village, forcing the villagers to sleep in open fields. Garvey's formal education ended at sixteen whereupon he took up a variety of jobs – helping out in the family shop and delivering newspapers. A lifelong interest in motorcars led him to work as a mechanic and driver with 'a few cars on the road' before joining Taca Síochána in 1939 at the age of twenty-four. Taca was a Garda auxiliary group recruited at the start of 'the Emergency' to assist the force in wartime. It was later disbanded and its members subsumed into An Garda Síochána.

Dublin was where Ned Garvey would spend most of his career, based first in College Street (present day Pearse Street) Station. In 1944, he joined the Central Detective Unit (CDU) and was placed on housebreaking detail for Dublin South. In the CDU, he earned a reputation in the investigation of serious crime and rose swiftly through the ranks. Beneath the diligence and industry that characterised his

Above: Taca reunion in Harrington Street on 5 June 1976, showing Edmund Garvey *(front row, fourth right)* beside Garda chaplain Fr Clarence Daly

work was also the ambition to succeed. Promoted to detective sergeant in 1953, four years later he became detective inspector with responsibility for larcenies in the DMA. In 1961, he was appointed superintendent and transferred to Kevin Street. His extraordinary talent as an organiser and administrator marked him out for a special task. He became the first housing officer appointed by the force and served in that capacity from 1961 to 1965. With his strong humanitarian streak, he was committed and energetic in promoting the welfare of guards and ensuring that standards of accommodation were raised, always with the maxim: 'Only the best is good enough for the guards.' During this time, 500 houses were constructed for members of the force. This period coincided with his setting up the Garda Club along with a small committee, and the purchase of the premises on Harrington Street.

As chief superintendent in charge of the Longford/Westmeath Division, he moved to Mullingar in 1968. But by 1972 he was back in the DMA North after the divisions were reorganised. One of his personal highlights that year was helping to organise the Golden Jubilee celebrations of the force, with great success. The Garda Club on Harrington Street became a focal point for the launch and finale of the celebrations, much to Garvey's gratification. The following year in January 1973, Desmond O'Malley TD, the Fianna Fáil Minister for Justice, appointed him Assistant Commissioner and in 1974 he was put in charge of the anti-subversive unit, C3, following a dramatic helicopter escape of prisoners from Mountjoy Prison. Within a short space of time, he succeeded Patrick Malone to become the force's tenth commissioner, when the National Coalition of 1973–77 was in power. The strength of the force was then 8,500 men. His time as commissioner, from September 1975 to January 1978, was during the height of paramilitary activity in the State. In an interview with Jim Farrelly in the *Sunday Independent* of 16 March 1984, Garvey revealed that he believed he got the top job because the IRA were 'rampant' around the country at the time and he had a 'reputation for leading my men against the IRA'. In fact, the security of the State became his top priority while in office.

As a detective, much of his career was spent in plain clothes, working assiduously and earning great distinction in the process. By his own admission, he found detective work rewarding and satisfying and had developed a 'near-photographic memory' after twenty years in the job. He was involved in many important investigations, even at commissioner level. One in particular gripped the nation in 1975. Dutch industrialist Tiede Herrema was sensationally kidnapped at Monaleen, County Limerick on 3 October 1975 by paramilitaries and held captive in Monasterevin during a seventeen-day armed siege at a house. Garvey's successful closure of the case brought a surprise royal honour some weeks later: he was decorated as Commander of the Order of Orange-Nassau by the Dutch ambassador, Mr Felix van Raalte, on behalf of Queen Juliana of the Netherlands. On the same occasion, the Minister for Justice, Mr Patrick Cooney TD, received the Grand Cross of the

Crime detection and common sense

Some of Mr Garvey's feats while he was a detective are still recalled. At Dublin Castle on one occasion glancing through the English *Police Gazette*, he noticed that a man (a native of County Donegal) was wanted by the Glasgow police in connection with a number of robberies with violence. He mentioned to his subordinates that a number of similar robberies had occurred a few days before in Counties Donegal and Monaghan. Deducing that the wanted man had arrived in Dublin for a spree, he sent out a team of detectives who discovered that the wanted man had been staying at a Talbot Street hotel but had checked out that morning.

Continuing their enquiries they went to car hire firms and struck oil at one in Westland Row. The wanted man had hired a car and was due back that evening. When he returned detectives, dressed as petrol attendants in white coats, grabbed him. On the back seat of the car was a suitcase containing thousands of pounds which he had stolen.

'Crime detection is a matter of common sense,' Mr Garvey remarked afterwards.

Evening Herald, *21 January 1978*

Order of Orange-Nassau. A cheque for £5,000 for the Garda Benevolent Fund was subsequently presented to Garvey in January 1976 by the Dutch ambassador in recognition of the part played by gardaí in the favourable outcome of the siege.

In January 1978, Ned Garvey was summoned to the Department of Justice to be informed by the then Minister for Justice Gerry Collins that the Government wished to have his resignation within two hours. Failing that, he would be removed from office. No explanation was offered. He was informed that he had lost the confidence of the Government but would still be entitled to a full pension and gratuity rights, an indication that his removal from office was not based on misconduct.

Ned Garvey's dismissal has to be read in light of the times and his personality. His term of office was characterised by a tough approach to crime and to establishing greater levels of discipline within the force. Years of demoralisation among rank and file gardaí he sought to change and likewise a certain inertia at Garda Headquarters. His hands-on approach ensured he was familiar with the workings of every Garda station in the country, which he visited during his term of office and met personnel in every division. The visits afforded him an opportunity to change the prevailing culture in many divisions. However, the personal tours were much resented by the Garda Representative Body, especially his urge for gardaí to hand out more summonses – going from an average of forty to two hundred per man per year. For his efforts, Garvey did not always enjoy the full support of the force, with accusations of operating a blunt and an insensitive transfer policy and harsh discipline. The transfer policy was particularly resented in the Donegal division. It made headlines when one member, Garda Kevin Towey from Buncrana, was sacked from the force in dramatic fashion because he failed to comply with a transfer order.

With his reputation as a man who wanted action and results, Garvey repeatedly clashed with two of the four Garda representative bodies, specifically those that represented the more junior ranks. These bodies had numerous differences of opinion on various matters prior to his dismissal – including issues affecting Garda welfare, morale and public attitudes towards the force – that were often hampered by his tough approach to discipline. Nonetheless, he had survived their no-confidence motion in him in 1976. However, it could be said that they failed to acknowledge his more humanitarian side, which sought to care for all members of the force. When news of his dismissal reached the representative bodies, they gave limited support. While recognising his many achievements, they claimed that he did not always steer the Garda Síochána in the right direction. On the Government's side, there were accusations of fingerprint irregularities in the Garda Technical Bureau and Garda brutality – the existence of a 'heavy gang' – during the interrogation of criminals. Garvey clashed with Gerry Collins over a proposed inquiry into the matter and also a promotions deadlock. According to Conor Brady, writing in *The Irish Times* on 21 January 1978, Garvey was 'subjected to pressure quite unlike anything his

Above: Presentation to Ned Garvey *(right)* in the 1970s accompanied by Jim and Mary Daly
Below: (left to right) Jack Reilly, Bridget Garvey, Ned Garvey, Maureen O'Reilly and Fr Clarence Daly at the Garda Club in the 1970s

Intensity of idealism

As the song says 'memories are made of this', and I often think that history itself is in a sense memory formulated in different ways. The instant case (memoir) may be described as an attempt to recall the progress of a project in positive terms; a project distinguished by the intensity of its idealism. Mr Garvey realised this; and showed that realisation in his capacity for work which was enormous. His physical energy was matched by a similar mental energy and without his drive and determination to get things done it is doubtful if the Garda Club project would have ever got off the ground.

Tom Ryan, 'Personal Reminiscences', c1997

predecessors had experienced from their political masters. He was sent in by the Coalition Government because he was, as Patrick Cooney put it, a "tough cop" '. But the downfall of the tough cop was that he was equally uncompromising with his political masters and intent on remaining independent as a professional policeman. His job, as he saw it, was to get results.

For a man who gave such distinguished service to the force, Garvey's dismissal came as something of a shock to the nation. Though he may have had an inkling that all was not well, since relations between him and the Department of Justice had been strained for some time, the swiftness of his dismissal was indeed surprising. When news of it reached the media, he told them: 'The honour and the honour of my family are at stake. I have done nothing to deserve this.' There was no honourable option open to him but to fight his removal from office through the courts. The outcome of his High Court action, after being represented by Mr RJ O'Hanlon SC and junior counsel Mr Peter Sutherland, saw his dismissal declared null and void in 1978. On appeal, the decision was confirmed by the Supreme Court in 1979 and he was awarded £1,704 for wrongful dismissal plus costs. The Government was also forced to pay him a further £11,309, making legal history in the process. A measure of the esteem in which colleagues held Garvey was a 'fighting fund' of £5,000 that was collected from about 1,200 supporters to meet his legal costs. In the event, the money was not required and subsequently returned to the donors.

Earned his keep

After joining the Garda Mr Garvey's first station was Pearse Street and he later took up plain clothes duties. He enjoyed this work and was to comment: 'I think I had a good record on crime work. I don't know that anybody could say I didn't earn my keep at it, anyway.'

Obituary, Garda Review, *December 1989*

Personality and politics

Much has been said of the toughness of Ned Garvey, whether displayed in office or in pushing through Garda Club policy and objectives. For many, Ned Garvey the man was summed up succinctly in an *Evening Herald* headline on 20 January 1978: 'Chief who was feared but admired.' While there was much to fear, given he did not suffer fools gladly, had no time for slackers and was brusque and economical with words, there was also plenty to admire. As a person of high integrity and with an acute sense of right and wrong, he displayed a humanitarianism that stretched far and wide. Coming from the west of Ireland, he had witnessed grinding poverty, emigration and the harsh conditions of the early decades of the twentieth century, which had left its mark. His compassion for people was not solely reserved for members of the force but for the community at large. Much of it was born out of a deep-seated religious faith, espousing Christian values. He was kind-hearted, liked young people, took an interest in their welfare, and was immensely proud of the force. In fact, he considered it his extended family. Similarly, he had a great regard for the 'man on the beat' and in avuncular tones called young guards 'the lads'.

Like Jim 'Lugs' Branigan, who equally shared a tough reputation, Garvey often attempted to rehabilitate criminals on release from prison and find them suitable employment. This altruistic spirit also had resonances in a Garda figure from another era, namely Commissioner Eoin O'Duffy. Alarmed at the rate of tuberculosis in the force in 1928, O'Duffy held a meeting with the representative body, which in turn led to the Garda Medical Aid Society being founded. Both men also had an innate talent for organisation, with boundless energy and imagination, and were men of decisive and effective action, strict disciplinarians, idealists and committed Christians. O'Duffy often stated that 'the Gardaí were not merely men carrying out an ordinary job but policemen doing a Christian duty'. It is ironic that both men were dismissed from office – O'Duffy in 1933 – and indeed on the same legal basis. Section 6(2) of the Police Forces Amalgamation Act, 1925, which stipulated that the Commissioner 'may at any time be removed by the Executive Council', was used by the Government in defence of its action in 1978.

Physically, Ned Garvey was a commanding figure: tall, broad and heavy-set. He had few personal vices, neither drank nor smoke and indeed was a lifelong pioneer. In June 1944, he had married Bridget (Breta) Kenny, a native of Louisburgh, County Mayo, and they had seven children: Eamonn, Regina, Eva, Ann, Mary, Christopher (Chris) and Deirdre. His extraordinary work and Garda Club commitments left little time for family life but trips to All-Ireland finals were certainly a treat for his children. If Ned Garvey did have hobbies, you could say it was for 'doing things' – setting up clubs and organising events, and keeping things going with his phenomenal energy. It was remarkable for a man who did not play sports at all that he provided for those that did, and went on to become the first chairman of the Garda Sea Angling Club, founded in 1965, as well as the first president of Stackstown Golf Club.

Boxing clever

Jim Branigan also had a great regard for Ned Garvey, former Commissioner. 'He was a hard-working yet friendly man. His promotion all along was due to his hard work and it was one of the most popular promotions ever in the force.' He is a lifelong friend of Mr Garvey.

Bernard Neary, Lugs: The Life and Times of Jim Branigan, *1985*

Many have argued that Ned Garvey was removed from office for political reasons. Yet those who knew him closely would say he was the most apolitical of people. His refusal to play ball with his political masters, regardless of political party, signalled his end. Garvey was his own man, uncompromising, and guided by his own inner lights of duty, right and justice.

At his eventual retirement function on 30 May 1980 at the Burlington Hotel, Assistant Commissioner Daniel Devitt paid tribute to the career of his close friend and railed against the forces that had brought him low, as recounted by Gregory Allen in *The Garda Síochána: Policing Independent Ireland 1922–1982:*

> *A prophet, it is said, is not accepted in his own country. Jealousy of his ability, his uprightness and his integrity made lesser men come to the conclusion that he should be removed from office. His ability in all aspects of policing, administrative and operational, was in my view approaching closely to genius. And, as the great Dublin writer Jonathan Swift once said: 'When a genius comes on the scene, all the dunces conspire against him.'*

Certainly, the genius had something Messianic in his disposition. The *Evening Herald* on 20 January 1981 described him as 'an austere disciplinarian who drove himself with an almost puritanical zeal'. Yet the austere disciplinarian is likened by those that remember him best to that of an old schoolmaster who always had the best interests of the pupils at heart. This puritanical zeal was certainly in evidence when trying to set up the Garda Club on Harrington Street. To this end, Garvey often adopted an aggressive stance to get things done, which naturally did not always sit well with some of his fellow club officers and members. Former chairman Brian Prendergast believes this combative stance originated in Garvey's early dealings with the Board of Works as housing officer in the 1960s. The welfare of Garda members was not always a priority for the Board of Works as it was for Ned Garvey. Despite his high-handed nature, he nonetheless had many redeeming features. Prendergast recalls, for example, that if someone could prove there was a better way of doing something, Ned Garvey would stop acting 'the Inspector' and become more consultative. Indeed when he would arrive to see what work had been done, he was often congratulatory and thankful.

Above: Ned Garvey expressing his gratitude to the Garda Pensioners' Association for the portrait presented to him in 1980

Garvey's purchase of land at Stackstown, situated at the foothills of the Dublin Mountains, also gave rise to innumerable rows among committee members because of its perceived unsuitability as a golf course and playing fields. Yet he persevered. Later attempts by Stackstown Golf Club to acquire greater autonomy were not always supported by Garvey and meetings could be fraught at times.

Action of Divisional Committee

The question of Ned Garvey and the chairmanship of the Garda Club was to become as controversial as his dismissal from office. Perhaps it was the growing antipathy to Garvey from some quarters for his inflexibility about certain Garda Club decisions that precipitated the crisis in the club. Or perhaps it was the genuine view held by some members that Garvey should no longer hold the post of chairman given his dismissal from office.

The governing body in retrospect allowed for no period of careful reflection on the impact of Garvey's dismissal from office. Within four days of the announcement, a special Divisional Committee meeting was convened on 23 January 1978 to discuss the commissioner's removal from office. It was attended by Seán O'Mahoney, Harry Thynne, J Collins, Hugh McNulty, Charlie Gaffney, John F Sexton, Dan Hanrahan, John Murphy, John Irving, Tony O'Grady, Brian Prendergast, Ollie Nugent, John O'Gara, Paddy Harrington, Denis Devine and Mick Coyne. At the meeting, certain members expressed the view that Garvey could no longer hold the position of chairman of the Garda Club. That said, the committee clearly agonised over what it should do and members were divided on the issue. There was total sympathy that his dismissal was a great injustice; nonetheless, his position was regarded as untenable. This was based on the fact that he had been sacked from office, and so was no longer a serving member of An Garda Síochána, was neither a retired nor honorary member and thus by the rules of the club did not qualify for membership and by extension hold the position of chairman. No regard was given to the fact that Garvey had initiated proceedings to take the matter before the High Court for judicial determination.

During the debate, due recognition was given to Ned Garvey for establishing the Garda Recreation Club and steering it to what it had become, as well as purchasing the land at Stackstown for a golf club, which was on its way to becoming one of the best in the country. It was felt by some committee members that his removal would create a great void that could not readily be filled. One committee member declared the Garda Club could not carry on without him. Finally, the meeting proceeded to elect a new chairman and John Irving was unanimously elected. Committee member Denis Devine proposed that Garvey be made an honorary member of the club, which was agreed by all. In light of the fact that Garvey still had unfinished business with the club, the new chairman was asked to approach him with a view to employing him to finish the work he had started, offering him a contract and negotiating a salary.

When news of this development was communicated to Garvey, he took great offence and decided to fight back. In hindsight, it would appear the governing body had acted with indecent haste and ran the risk of prejudicing Garvey's court case. Nonetheless, some saw it as a timely opportunity to wrest power from what was perceived as an all-controlling chairman.

Events took a dramatic turn at the Divisional Committee meeting on 12 April 1978 when Garvey turned up to chair it. Before it commenced, John Irving said he wished to make a statement. He stated that the committee might have presumed too much in thinking that the previous chairman was no longer available for the position. More importantly, he added that the committee was not in a position to prejudice the matter at that stage and in order not to lay the committee open to a charge of contempt of court and not to prejudice any court proceedings, he would be vacating

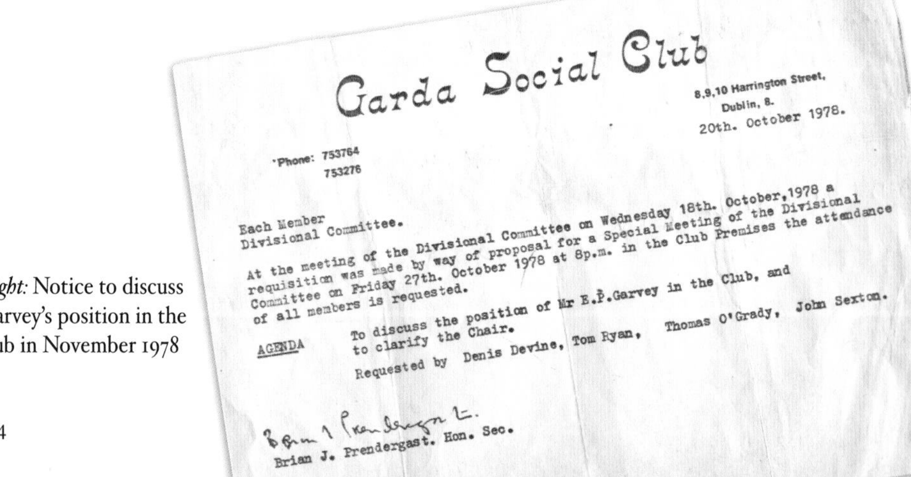

Garda Social Club

8,9,10 Harrington Street,
Dublin, 8.
20th. October 1978.

'Phone: 753764
753276

Each Member
Divisional Committee.

At the meeting of the Divisional Committee on Wednesday 18th. October,1978 a requisition was made by way of proposal for a Special Meeting of the Divisional Committee on Friday 27th. October 1978 at 8p.m. in the Club Premises the attendance of all members is requested.

AGENDA To discuss the position of Mr E.P.Garvey in the Club, and to clarify the Chair.

Requested by Denis Devine, Tom Ryan, Thomas O'Grady, John Sexton.

Brian J. Prendergast.

Brian J. Prendergast. Hon. Sec.

Right: Notice to discuss Garvey's position in the club in November 1978

GARDA CLUB DROPS GARVEY

SACKED Garda Commissioner Edmund Garvey, who is expecting to hear the result of his High Court action against the Government next week, has been removed from his position as chairman of the Garda Social Club.

The decision to stand him down from the post at the Harrington Street Club was taken last night by the Divisional Committee of the club's governing body.

There was almost a full attendance of Committee members at the meeting, and the removal decision was passed by more than a two-thirds majority.

When told of the decision today, a surprised Mr. Garvey said: "This is the first I have heard of it. I didn't even know the meeting was taking place. Anyway, I have more important things on my mind at present."

But a member of the Committee, who was present at last night's meeting, said: "Mr. Garvey knew the meeting was taking place and he knew what was being discussed but he didn't turn up."

A motion passed at last night's meeting means, in effect, that the committee did not recognise Mr. Garvey was entitled to be in the chair since he was sacked by the Government last January.

Mr. Garvey, in fact, resigned as club chairman at that time but several weeks later the man who replaced him, Detective Inspector John Irving, stepped down to let Mr. Garvey resume as chairman.

This move upset a number of club members and resulted in a rift within the club, which ended with club secretary, Det. Inspector John Murphy, and assistant secretary, Charlie Gaffney of the Technical Bureau, both resigning.

A new secretary was appointed and Mr. Garvey assumed control of the affairs of the club, which is open to the 2,000 serving members of the force in the Metropolitan area generally.

The membership will have the chance to elect a completely new committee when the annual meeting takes place on Monday week, November 6.

One committee member said to-day: "We felt Mr. Garvey should not be in the chair for that meeting. It is now up to the members to elect whoever they wish."

MR. GARVEY

Above: Evening Press **news story on Saturday, 28 October 1978**

the chair. As there was no dissenter to Garvey's nomination to the chair, he duly took the chair and the meeting commenced.

While members did agree to Garvey's reinstatement, there was certainly still some hostility towards him. There were suggestions at the meeting of a 'clique' in existence that was and had been involved in running club affairs. Nonetheless, Garvey addressed the meeting and explained the importance he attached to being club chairman. Having regard to his forthcoming court case, he had adopted his stance on the advice of his legal advisers. He also referred to his part in the foundation of the club and deplored attempts to force him to relinquish his association with the organisation.

The hostility resulted in the honorary secretary and honorary treasurer resigning from the committee. Some of these members felt that their loyalty to Garvey had been unquestioned hitherto but that their position and views had been misconstrued by other members, who had effectively poisoned Garvey's ear against them. As the months progressed, the antagonism grew, culminating in some members at a Divisional Committee meeting on 10 May 1978 expressing the view that Garvey was making a mistake by being chairman. As ever, Ned Garvey stressed the importance of the matter to his court case, pointing out that his case was due for hearing in July 1978 and that he intended leaving the club at that point. In the event, it would be October that year before the High Court would give its judgment. The minutes of the Divisional Committee on 18 October 1978 noted that the issue was raised again regarding the question of Garvey's position and the need for clarification.

Events came to a head on 27 October 1978 at a special meeting of the Divisional Committee, at which Garvey was not present. The annual general meeting was coming up and certain members did not want Garvey to chair the meeting. A proposal was put to the meeting that the committee did not recognise Garvey as chairman of the club at that time, nor since his removal from office as commissioner on 19 January 1978. Despite warnings from some members about the legal implications of this proposal, given there was a *de jure* commissioner and a *de facto* commissioner (Mr Garvey and Mr McLoughlin, respectively), the proposal went to a vote. It was by no means unanimous: eleven voted for, four against, with one abstention. Ned Garvey for the first time since founding the club in 1961 would not chair an AGM. The next day, 28 October, the news quickly made its way onto the front page of the *Evening Herald* in a sensational heading: 'GARDA CLUB DROPS GARVEY.' It went on to report the events of the previous nine months and the rift that had developed within the club.

When the day of the AGM arrived on 6 November 1978, amid much advance publicity, it drew large crowds with 423 members in attendance. Liam Ryan of the *Irish Independent* reported that one hundred retired members of the force turned up unexpectedly just to vote for Mr Garvey. Never one to shirk his responsibilities, Garvey was present. His name was put forward to chair the meeting as were the names of three others, but despite getting 166 votes it was Denis Devine who was

Bottom letter: **Garvey resigns as a club trustee in November 1978**
Top letter: **The Garda Club acknowledges Garvey's resignation**

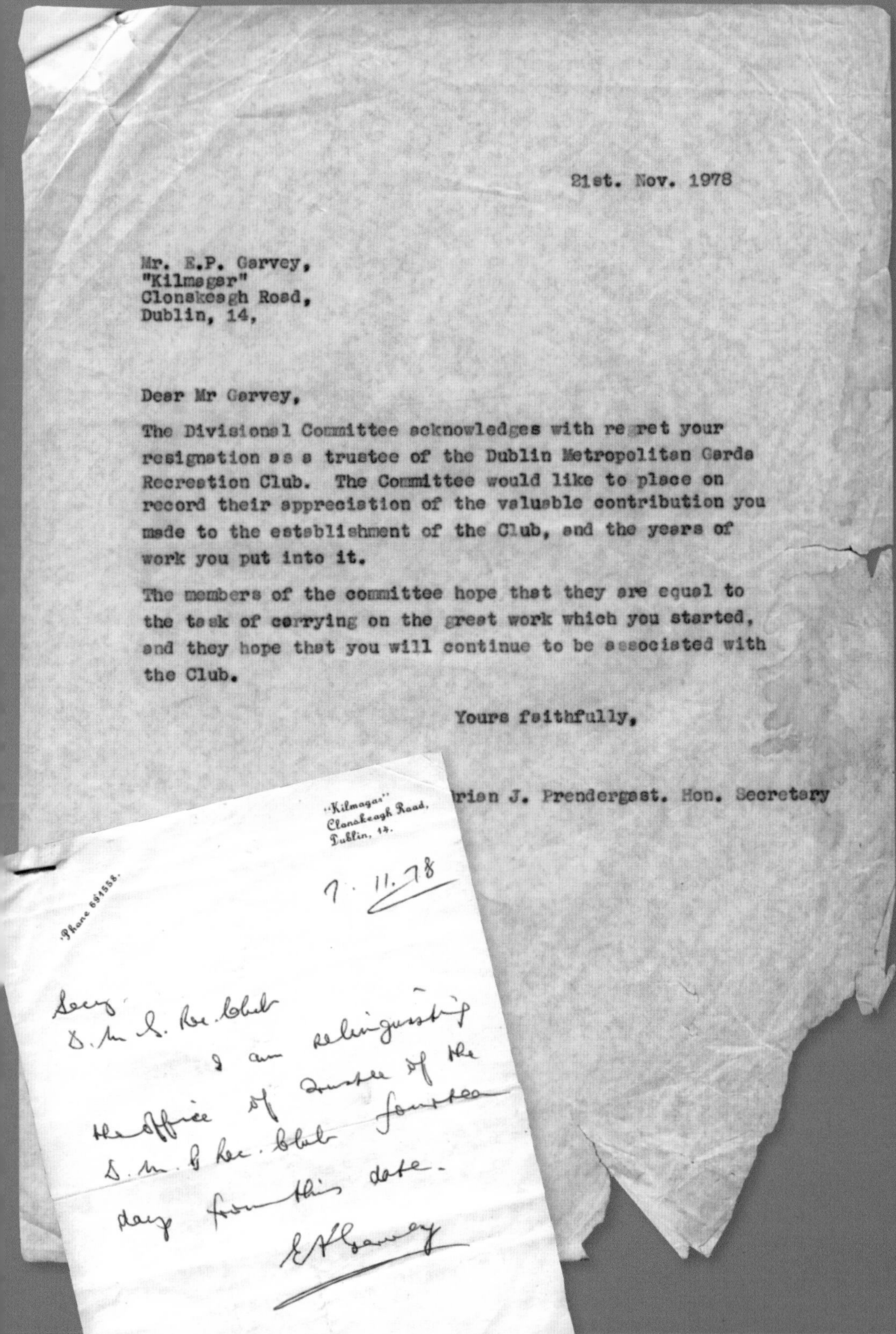

21st. Nov. 1978

Mr. E.P. Garvey,
"Kilmagar"
Clonskeagh Road,
Dublin, 14,

Dear Mr Garvey,

The Divisional Committee acknowledges with regret your resignation as a trustee of the Dublin Metropolitan Garda Recreation Club. The Committee would like to place on record their appreciation of the valuable contribution you made to the establishment of the Club, and the years of work you put into it.

The members of the committee hope that they are equal to the task of carrying on the great work which you started, and they hope that you will continue to be associated with the Club.

Yours faithfully,

[B]rian J. Prendergast. Hon. Secretary

"Kilmagar"
Clonskeagh Road,
Dublin, 14.

Phone 694558.

7. 11. 78

Secy.
D.M.G. Rec. Club
I am relinquishing the office of trustee of the D.M.G. Rec. Club fourteen days from this date.

E.P. Garvey

elected chairman on 216 votes. Garvey's defeat was further compounded later: when it came to elect a chairman for the Garda Club, his name was not proposed. In the event, Devine was again elected chairman. The rest of the club officers were duly elected and the committee members ratified. One of the first actions of the new chairman was to adjourn the meeting for six months so that new club rules could be drawn up, in particular to stipulate that honorary members would not have voting rights. (In later years, voting rights of honorary members were reinstated.) In fact, the AGM did not take place until 3 March 1980 because of the legal difficulties that arose. The AGM of 6 November 1978 was a watershed moment for the Garda Club. At one level, it was a sweeping out of the old and in with the new. It led to the subsequent resignation of the club trustees: Edmund Garvey, Tom Ryan and John O'Gara, who were now no longer members of the governing body.

The much-heralded Garvey legal case, when it had finally begun on October 10th, had drawn a good deal of media attention down at the law courts. The issue of whether the Government had the right to dismiss the commissioner was never in question but that of being denied natural justice and constitutional justice was. It was a major issue and the courts found accordingly. Mr Justice Herbert McWilliam in the High Court found that Garvey should have been given prior notice and a reason for his dismissal as well as an opportunity to make representations on his behalf and had thus been denied natural justice. The result of the High Court action saw his dismissal declared null and void. On appeal, the decision was upheld in the Supreme Court on 9 March 1979 by a 4–1 majority. After his case had gone back and forth from the High Court and Supreme Court over two years, he was finally awarded £1,704 for wrongful dismissal, plus costs. The Government was also forced to pay him a further £11,309. Having been vindicated, Mr Garvey was officially reinstated as commissioner. Needless to say, this did not happen in practice but spawned another legal limbo. It necessitated the passing of the Garda Síochána Act 1979 to retrospectively validate the actions of Mr Garvey's successor, Patrick McLaughlin, as commissioner. Garvey's 'retirement' or 'resignation' was accepted as being from 14 May 1979 and McLaughlin was formally reappointed as commissioner from the following day, namely 15 May.

All the months of legal wrangling did little to clarify Garvey's position in the Garda Club. However, the High Court ruling vindicating Garvey gave the governing body confidence to decide a certain course of action. At a meeting on 23 November 1978, a committee was set up to look at new club rules and a proposal that Garvey again be made an honorary member within the rules was carried.

The matter could have rested there but alas did not. The fallout from the Garvey affair had witnessed the resignation of many a club officer and committee member who had poured blood, sweat and tears into the club from its inception. However, another issue arose that was to deepen the rancour further.

Longwood House affair

As annual general meetings go, the one held on 26 May 1980 is unlikely to be forgotten in Garda Club annals. It set off a protracted legal battle that fortunately, despite the bitterness it engendered, was amicably settled in the end. On the day, club chairman Denis Devine informed the assembled members that he was obliged to tell them, on the advice of the club solicitor, that certain matters had come to his notice since becoming chairman in 1978. In particular, he mentioned that a house at 46 Longwood Avenue, off South Circular Road – bought to temporarily house the sitting tenants at 8 Harrington Street in 1968 – did not appear on the balance sheet as an asset, that it had been subsequently sold and that the proceeds appeared nowhere. Furthermore, the previous auditor had been unable to supply certain documents to facilitate a proper audit and there were incomplete records. The club solicitor, fearful that a fraud had been committed, was of the opinion that an investigation should be carried out. At the AGM, several members stated that they had been on the committee when the house was purchased and sold and were satisfied that all was in order. In the event, it was decided to take no further action. However, a month later, the Garda Representative Association demanded an investigation into the affairs of the Garda Recreation Club since its inception.

Given that Ned Garvey, Tom Ryan and Jim Daly had been trustees of the property at Longwood Avenue, it was only a matter of time before these allegations reached their ears. When they did, Garvey took umbrage at the mere suggestion that all was not above board. His honour and integrity had been called into question for a second time and he would defend it again at all costs. At a special Divisional Committee meeting on 12 February 1981, a letter from Mr Garvey's solicitor was read out. It concerned 'slanderous remarks' made by the chairman about the previous trustees of the club, in particular, regarding a house at Longwood Avenue. On reading the letter and on the advice of the club solicitor, the committee decided that the matter should be defended and the chairman indemnified. The club chairman claimed that his words had been misrepresented and that he had not called Mr Garvey and the other trustees dishonest, nor that anything sinister had taken place during their trusteeship.

In recompense, Ned Garvey and the other trustees wanted a published apology and the payment of damages for the humiliation and injury caused to their good names. In the event of not receiving one, they were prepared to take further legal action. In the early days, attempts, such as they were, to resolve the matter amicably proved unsuccessful. A full civil action followed. By 2 October 1981, the chairman Denis Devine had been served with a summons from the High Court by the three previous trustees for damages for slander and the cost of proceedings. For the next year or so the case wound its way slowly through the court, and was proving to be a long arduous process. By November 1982, Denis Devine had resigned as chairman of the club following his retirement from An Garda Síochána and Noel McDermott had been elected to the chair. The following January saw Jim Murphy elected vice chairman.

Above: **Fr Clarence Daly, Commissioner Laurence Wren, Ned Garvey and Assistant Commissioner John Fleming at the Garvey presentation in December 1983**
Below: **Assistant Commissioner John Fleming making a presentation to Ned Garvey in December 1983**

Presentation to E. P. GARVEY, Founder Chairman of Dublin Metropolitan Garda Recreation Club

The Committee of the above Club cordially invite

____

to be present at the Garda Club, Harrington Street
on Sunday, 4th. December, 1983 at 8 p.m.
on the occasion of a Presentation
to honour the Founding Member.

Dress informal —— Buffet Meal
R.S.V.P. before 1st. December, 1983

Above: **An invitation to Mr Ned Garvey's presentation 1983**

In their new roles, both Noel McDermott and Jim Murphy were keen to get the 'pending litigation', as the matter had been dubbed, resolved once and for all. Several months later in July 1983, the opportunity to adopt a more conciliatory approach presented itself. The idea of making a presentation to former officers of the club, including Garvey, was discussed by the Divisional Committee at their monthly meeting. A presentation for Garvey got the backing of several members and at subsequent meetings gathered momentum. One member was keen to express the view that but for the former chairman's leadership, there would be no club. As a result, a subcommittee was formed on 30 August 1983 to arrange the presentation, which included Sean O'Mahoney, Jim Murphy, Con McCarthy, Ned Grace, William Dwyer and Mick Leenane. These members were fully aware that much groundwork had to be covered and some decisions faced up to before Garvey would consent to the presentation.

Over the next few months, the subcommittee set to work. At first, Jim Murphy broached the subject of the presentation with Garvey and reported that his initial response had been quite good. A second meeting between them led to the former chairman, Mr Garvey, agreeing to meet members of the subcommittee. Much thought was given to the presentation itself and the particulars, such as type of function, the date, invitees, and choice of gift. December 4th was decided as a suitable date.

Clearly, the subcommittee, chiefly Ned Grace, Jim Murphy and William Dwyer, had made excellent progress. Jim Murphy at a Divisional Committee meeting on 10 October 1983 spoke of how Garvey had told them of his pleasure at the gesture of the club. Indeed, he had referred to the current members of the committee in a most complimentary way. He was agreeable to the presentation in the Garda Club on December 4th and to the nature of the invitees, for example, members who had worked in the club and former members of the committee. On the presentation itself, when asked what he would like, the members reported that Garvey would be visiting the USA on December 10th, six days after the presentation, and would welcome the gift of plane tickets for himself and his wife. As a more lasting tribute, he wished to have something for his home, namely armchairs, to complement a portrait of himself previously presented by the Garda Síochána Retired Members Association.

Meanwhile, the pending litigation was making its own progress. The day in court was finally set for 24/25 November 1983. The Garda Club solicitor, on the advice of two counsels, felt the case could be successfully defended on the grounds of technical privilege. At a committee meeting on November 8th the advancing court date weighed heavily on the minds of the members. Just how close the day of reckoning had become was pressed home when the club solicitor served summonses on a number of committee members present at the meeting. The reality of adverse publicity for the club no doubt also concentrated the minds of members on halting the proceedings if at all possible. Jim Murphy offered the view that Ned Garvey was open to negotiation on the matter and the case could be settled. After much discussion, assistant secretary Cyril Doyle and Sean O'Mahoney were nominated to meet Garvey and explore the entire situation. Pending the outcome, arrangements for the presentation could go ahead.

A meeting of the Divisional Committee just three days before the court date heard that Cyril Doyle and Sean O'Mahoney had duly met with Garvey on Thursday, 17 November and later in the office of William Fry, solicitors for the former trustees, with Tom Ryan also in attendance. The club solicitor Mr Veale was present to try to work out an agreement. After discussion, the situation was that the former trustees sought £7,000 in damages, plus costs. After consideration of this position, another meeting was held on 21 November. The final word was damages of £5,000, plus costs. The matter of a public vindication was also sought by the trustees and agreement reached that an apology would be published, most likely at the next AGM.

When club chairman Noel McDermott asked how Garvey had felt, Sean O'Mahoney replied that Garvey was very hurt and that his family had suffered greatly. Clearly, the committee was disappointed that money was required in damages and that the litigation could have been settled when costs were low. By the conclusion of the meeting, the committee had voted not to accept the settlement proposal and to carry the costs of both plaintiff and defendant, plus £5,000 in damages. At this point, the plans for the presentation function were put in serious jeopardy. During the final two days before the case went before the High Court, frantic efforts were made to resolve the matter in a last-ditch attempt. A hastily convened meeting on 23 November 1983 was to bear fruit, however. Jim Murphy, keen for the club to make peace with Garvey, stated that he had heard from Garvey that the presentation was most important to him. He had already invited the Commissioner, who had accepted as had many others. Also, if damages had been paid, it was his intention to hand them back on the night of the presentation. He had no difficulty with the apology but felt that the matter should be decided once and for all.

The committee was still in two minds: the chairman had it on good advice from a senior counsel that the case could still be successfully defended; Jim Murphy argued that a conciliatory gesture was needed. The single-most important fact was that Ned Garvey wanted to stay out of court and wanted the presentation to go ahead. It was clear that the presentation would represent the culmination and recognition of his life's work with the Garda Club, an achievement that meant more to him than anything else. Obviously, the committee wanted the presentation to go ahead as well. It finally came down to a vote. Proposed by Jim Murphy and seconded by William Dwyer, the members voted that the Garda Club pay the costs of the plaintiff to a maximum of £8,000, on settlement of the litigation on the clear understanding that the damages would be paid. Fifteen voted for the motion and four against. The motion was carried, though it would eventually cost the club £15,000 in legal fees. The greatest irony of all was that club records eventually surfaced showing, as had been believed by the majority of the membership, that there had been no impropriety in the purchase and resale of the Longwood Avenue house. On the locating of those records, Garvey felt that he had been resoundingly vindicated and was happy the resultant explanations answered the case satisfactorily.

Oil painting of Ned Garvey by George Colley RHA, commissioned by the Garda Pensioners' Association in 198[illegible]

An IPA friendship

On the day of final reckoning when the 'good book' is opened, it is certain that the late Commissioner Mr EP Garvey will be listed therein, and the record will show many, many credits.

Obituary, Police Friendship: The Journal of the International Police Association Irish Section, *Vol. 3, No. 1, 1990*

Honouring his achievements

The presentation function on 4 December 1983 at the Garda Club was a resounding success and brought great pleasure to Ned Garvey and his family. For him, it was a salve on the wounds of bitterness and betrayal and an opportunity to finally set aside all the aggravation. With it came a sense of vindication, relief and an acknowledgement that his toil of many years had not been in vain. With the passage of time, many members expressed regret for the way events had unfolded in the Garda Club, feeling that a great wrong had been inflicted on their esteemed founder. Like the Government, they too had denied him natural justice.

The presentation was not to close the chapter on Ned Garvey's association with the club, however. Now that bygones were bygones, he could quietly and confidently savour the club and all its successes. He became a regular visitor to Harrington Street in the remaining years of his life, bumping into old colleagues and friends, lunching with manageress Helen Corrigan, and catching up on all the news and plans for the future. The onset of Parkinson's disease did little to curtail his visits to a place he called a home from home, 'the Club'. His health deteriorated, however, and following a brain infarction he died in St Michael's Hospital, Dún Laoghaire, on 29 November 1989 at the age of seventy-four. His passing was marked by the Divisional Committee a week later at its monthly meeting. Club chairman Jim Murphy proposed a vote of sympathy for the founding member of the Garda Recreation Club. It was seconded by Oliver Nugent and passed unanimously. One minute's silence was then observed in honour of the founding chairman.

The final act in the drama of Ned Garvey was played out six months later at the AGM on 29 May 1990. The meeting approved a motion proposed by Oliver Nugent and seconded by John O'Malley to delete Rule 3b and substitute it with a new rule that 'retired members of An Garda Síochána who were ordinary members of the club at the time of retirement shall become honorary members and shall have full voting rights'. It was a final effort to right the wrong that had been done. For all his faults, history will be kinder to Ned Garvey in light of his marvellous legacy.

A Golden Era: Westmanstown

Chapter

7

Many hours of hard work, planning and even haggling had to be gone through.

Chapter 7
A Golden Era: Westmanstown

THE limited sporting success by the three Garda football clubs, namely GAA, rugby and soccer, became a focus of concern in the Garda Recreation Club during the 1980s. The paucity of silverware belied the large numbers of athletic young men, and indeed women, passing through the force at the time. The main reason identified for this lack of success was a shortage of facilities, as none of the clubs owned or controlled their own pitches. The period also coincided with a growing Garda Club membership, with Harrington Street busier than ever, hosting many a social function. Indeed, the patronage of the members assured constant activity on the premises: the field sports brought their competitive teams and followers back to celebrate or drown their sorrows. Furthermore, All-Irelands, rugby weekends and visiting police soccer teams from other countries added to the excitement of the already established calendar of social events at Harrington Street.

The needs grew greater and many sporting groups within the force and under the umbrella of the Coiste Siamsa began to seek facilities required for field, tennis, bowls, swimming, golf and other pursuits. Though the lands at Stackstown in 1975 were initially purchased with a view to catering for field sports, this in practice did not materialise, partly because the location and terrain were not suitable. The question of golf was also thrown into the mix. Interest in the sport had been growing apace with the advent of Stackstown Golf Club and its popular appeal.

The idea of an all-encompassing sports facility never once disappeared off the agenda of the Harrington Street committee. In the early 1980s, the then committee and its sucessors had been keen to embark on a venture that would fulfil the true meaning of the Garda Recreation Club. Moves to find land to facilitate the sporting groups gathered momentum and a subcommittee had been set up to look into acquiring land. In the meantime, a drive was made to encourage new membership among the gardaí. Members on the northside of Dublin, in particular, felt neglected with the arrival of the new golf club in Stackstown and having to trek so far south of the city. As a result, getting land on the northside became a priority. After Stackstown was completed, various plots of land for sale were inspected on the northside of Dublin in the early 1980s. These included land at Santry, Shangan Hill, Castleknock, Ballymun, Willsbrook, Westfield in Lucan, and Ballyboughal, but as it turned out neither land nor terms were suitable in most cases. The most serious contender was a parcel of land close to Dublin Airport. Despite initial inspections and price enquiries, progress stalled until Brian Prendergast became chairman in 1984. A subsequent survey, however, found this land at Cloghran unsuitable for Garda Club purposes. Under Brian's stewardship, the land subcommittee was reconstituted in February 1984 to include Jim Murphy, Noel McDermott, John O'Malley, Cyril Doyle, Michael Barrins and George Trenier. With renewed vigour, the subcommittee set to work.

First purchase of land at Westmanstown

In 1984, land became available at Westmanstown in West Dublin and serendipity must surely have played a hand in its discovery. Two Garda GAA Club members, PJ Gallagher and George Heneghan, when travelling along the back road between Lucan and Clonsilla one day, saw a for sale notice on the property. It was prime pasture land situated less than a mile north of Lucan, opposite the walls of Luttrellstown Estate and adjoining the railway line and the Royal Canal. Excited at the prospect, they quickly brought it to the attention of their GAA chairman Jim Murphy, who also happened to be vice chairman of the Garda Club at the time. As the land looked promising, the committee was keen to expedite matters and numerous inspections by the land subcommittee soon followed.

With road frontage of approximately 1,520 ft, the 48.2 acres were deemed an ideal site to fulfil the aims of the Garda Recreation Club to provide outdoor recreation facilities for its members. Needless to say, many naysayers on the committee objected to the proposed purchase. Strong concerns were expressed by some committee members about the potential for this piece of land to become flooded during rainy weather. These concerns were eventually put aside in the belief that good drainage could remedy any existing flooding problems. As it was proposed to distribute sections of the land to the various football clubs – GAA, rugby and soccer – the respective clubs also inspected the land and found it to be suitable.

At a meeting of the Divisional Committee on 24 October 1984, proposed by Eddie Boland and seconded by Mick Leenane, the executive was instructed to negotiate a price with a view to purchase. The owner of the land was Mr John J Smyth of Barrettstown House in Newbridge, County Kildare. A price of £240,000 was negotiated for the 48.2 acres that had road frontage. Shortly afterwards at a meeting of 21 November 1984, it was decided unanimously to make the purchase. It came as a great relief to the Garda GAA, soccer and rugby clubs who could now settle down to developing their games in a place of their own and no longer have to depend on shared, rented accommodation in various parts of the city.

The leftover land was earmarked for pitch and putt. This was to accommodate the less serious golfer, seeing that the facility at Stackstown Golf Club could cater for the golf enthusiasts. However, demand dictated that it be changed to a nine hole golf course should more land became available. Indeed, as it transpired, such was the demand for golf among the members that on 26 March 1986 the Garda Recreation Club Golfing Society was formed.

Westmanstown motion passed
The following proposal was put to the meeting:

'The meeting is asked to authorise the purchase of a parcel of land at Westmanstown, County Dublin, to be developed for sporting and recreation purposes of An Garda Síochána and their families.'

Proposed by Eddie Boland, seconded by Michael Linnane. Carried unanimously.

Minutes of Divisional Committee meeting, 24 October 1984

By April 1985, the sale had gone through and by February 1986 design maps had been drawn up by the architects and engineers to show the designated pitch areas. Planning permission was lodged with Dublin County Council in April 1986 (later to become Fingal County Council in 1993). The advice and expertise of local councillor Ned Ryan, one-time chairman of Dublin County Council, regarding planning matters was of considerable help to the committee as was that of local politician, Mr Brian Lenihan Snr TD. Outline planning permission was granted in May 1986, and meetings held with the city manager to acquaint him with the club's ambitions for development proved beneficial. So much so that by July of that year it had progressed to the stage of getting full planning permission.

Leasing land to Garda football clubs

In keeping with the democratic structure of the Garda Recreation Club, an AGM on 28 May 1986 ratified the decision to sell portions of the land to the GAA, rugby and soccer clubs. Not surprisingly, some disputes arose over the land selected for the pitches, when models prepared by the architects and engineers were viewed. By June 1987, however, the final plans had been drawn up for the agreed selling of the parcels of land, which met with widespread approval. It was agreed with the three clubs that they would each buy their pitches by way of a long lease agreement at approximately £5,000 per acre. The Garda Recreation Club would cover all the legal costs involved. The money raised from the leasing would also help the Garda Recreation Club to pay some of the costs of developing the land. The monies paid by the individual clubs were: £46,250 by the GAA Club for 9.25 acres; £29,500 by the Rugby Club for 5.9 acres; and £15,000 by the Soccer Club for 3.49 acres. The monies released from this venture not only helped to defray the development costs but also assured the independence of the three clubs concerned. Further development of the pitches was completed by the respective clubs, such as the planting of trees around the perimeter.

In 1988, contracts of sale were duly drawn up between the Garda Club and the GAA, rugby and soccer clubs, respectively. One important detail in the allocation was that the final location of the pitches was such that the remainder of the land was not landlocked in the event of further adjoining plots becoming available in the future. This in fact did come to pass, whereby the Soccer Club had to relocate their pitch and take down dugouts and railings in March 1991. However, the Garda Club agreed to compensate the club by £2,000. Another condition of sale was in the event that a football club ceased activity and wished to resell the land, it would have to be resold to the Garda Recreation Club. A change to Garda Club rules in the 1980s had extended the power of the club trustees to lease any property for and on behalf of the club. The three football clubs took possession and completed some major improvements to their newly acquired sites.

Acquiring more land

The purchase of 48.2 acres at Westmanstown was just the beginning. Though it was enough to accommodate the needs of the football clubs, it was not adequate to fulfil the entire ambitions of the committee. While the land was being cleared and prepared for the playing pitches and a pitch and putt course initially, the question of acquiring more land to enhance the development was never sidelined. The 48.2 acres would be just the first of four parcels of land purchased at Westmanstown.

Moves to purchase more adjacent land were set in train in 1987. Negotiations began with Mr Gerard Flynn, owner of 30.5 acres that bordered the Royal Canal and the Western Railway line to the west and Westmanstown Road to the south, and also stretching along the Westmanstown River. One impediment was that Mr Flynn had taken up residence in New York so transatlantic negotiations proved long and drawn out. However, an opportunity to expedite the matter soon presented itself. It was certainly a case of being in the right place at the right time or as Mahatma Gandhi said, ‘providence has its appointed hour for everything’. In October 1988 when on a goodwill tour to America, chairman Jim Murphy got the opportunity to visit Mr Flynn and to persuade him to sell his holding to the Garda Club for £100,650. On returning to Ireland, negotiations continued until shortly after Christmas 1988, when Bosco Muldoon remembers travelling with Jim Murphy, John O’Malley, Ollie Nugent, Cyril Doyle and Christy McCarthy to a pub in Newcastle to seal the deal with Mr Flynn. Legalities were subsequently concluded in 1989. This now paved the way for developing a nine hole golf course.

While negotiations were ongoing regarding the Flynn land, it had come to the attention of the committee in early 1988 that the previous owner of Westmanstown, John Smyth, was considering selling 7.4 acres adjoining Garda Club land. This was a barley field located near the corner of Woodwall Road and Westmanstown Road. The winds of fortune were certainly prevailing for the Garda Club and the sale was completed in June 1988 at a cost of £43,000.

Now that the momentum had fully gathered, a discussion took place in January 1989 to purchase approximately 43 adjoining acres at Westmanstown again from Gerard Flynn for £276,250. The deal progressed smoothly and the land was purchased in May 1989. This afforded the extension of the golf course to eighteen holes and some pockets of land to facilitate tennis and bowls. In Westmanstown, the entire tract of land solely bounded by rail and road encompassed 148 acres. However, attempts to secure the remaining land and further consolidate the Garda Club holdings has proved unsuccessful to date.

Nonetheless, taking every opportunity to increase the value of the Garda Club's holdings was a cornerstone of the committee. The prospect of buying one of the two-storey cottages at the entrance to Westmanstown complex became possible in early 1994 with an asking price of £59,000. In the inimitable fashion of the committee, matters were expedited in record time and in June 1994 the house, known as Nead an Dreoilín, became Garda Club property. Many years later, in 2011, the adjoining cottage was purchased.

History of Westmanstown and the kestrel

Following the arrival of the Normans in Ireland in 1169, Henry II gave a vast tract of land to one of his retainers, Hugh de Lacy. This land stretched from Dublin to the Shannon. De Lacy in turn granted the lands of Castleknock (Cnucha) and the surrounding district by charter to his liegeman, Hugh Tyrrel. His grant of land included what is now the Phoenix Park, in addition to Clonsilla and Mulhuddart. Tyrrel began fortification of Cnucha in 1173.

In 1299, an inquisition into the estate of Hugh Tyrrel, the fifth baron who had died, shows that his estate at Castleknock was something in the region of 7,000 acres. Before the end of the thirteenth century various families had settled in the district and their names are well known in the place names of the surrounding areas: Abbot, Blanchard, Keppock, Luttrell, Pilate (Pellet), Deuswell (Diswell). The Luttrells were a Norman family who first came to Ireland in 1204. At that time Geoffrey Luttrell was granted the castle and manor of Luttrellstown by King John in reward for faithful service.

Richard Tyrrel, the sixth baron of Castleknock, took over in 1299. His period of control was full of incident, including his involvement in a State trial.

It appears that a falcon, a bird of prey, owned by the Chief Justice in Ireland, escaped and flew to Castleknock. Richard kept the bird, although he knew whose it was and that a reward was offered for its recovery. He eventually escaped conviction by handing back the bird. It is believed that Robert Tyrrel, eighth and last baron of Castleknock, and his wife and son and heir all died in the plague of 1370. With the demise of the Tyrrel line the estate was divided.

In former years the area was noted for its wildlife. Scald Wood, the great wood of Blanchardstown, was a favourite place for the hunting of wolves. In 1652, the wolves had become so numerous that the government of the day ordered a public hunt of these animals at Castleknock. The assembled inhabitants of the barony were ordered to join to destroy 'the wolves lying in the wood of the ward'.

In earlier times the Phoenix Park formed part of the lands of the Earl of Stafford. One of the pastimes in vogue was the flying of hawks after blackbirds, which attracted as many as two hundred spectators to the park. The name Westmanstown is first mentioned in records in 1821. It is believed to be a corruption of the name Waspayle, a Norman family who are recorded in the area in the sixteenth century.

The kestrel (*Falco tinnunculus*) is a member of the falcon family and is our commonest bird of prey; it is readily identifiable when hovering as though suspended from an invisible line. The male is beautifully marked with a blue-grey head and tail, the latter with a black and white tip, and red-brown upper parts, spotted with black. Many will be familiar with the sight of a kestrel quartering the area of the new golf course in Westmanstown.

Michael B Carroll, Technical Bureau, 1988

Right: Michael Carroll

Golfers Peter Synnott and Jim Muldoon lend a hand clearing the golf lands

Golf steward Gerry Creagh outside the very first clubhouse – a portacabin!

Teamwork – planting trees on the golf course in November 1990

Team leader – Gerry Byrne, first greenkeeper, leading his team planting trees in 1990

Eddie Hackett, renowned Irish golf architect

Right: An aerial view of the purchased land at Westmanstown before development began

Preparing the land

Returning to 1985, the scale of the task to transform the prime agricultural land into playing pitches and a golf course, not to mention building a clubhouse and later a sports and leisure centre, was colossal. It was all a far cry from the old iron gate that wobbled between wooden posts holding the gate upright with pieces of rusty, barbed wire, as recalled by Bosco Muldoon when he first stepped foot on the land. The entire project was managed from the Garda Club in Harrington Street with all the expenditure for the development also coming from Harrington Street. This included the golf course designer, water and sewage disposal, portacabins for dressing rooms, both mens and ladies, an office canteen, shower and toilet facilities, a tractor and a machinery shed.

Before a tree could be planted or a trench dug, the land had to be cleared. Hedges and ditches had to be cut and cleared and large stones removed from the soil. Playing fields had to be laid out, a golf course designed and pegged, land drained, trees planted, an access road built, water piped, electricity supplied and sewerage disposal organised. The task was truly enormous and it was a question of all hands to the wheel. But true to form, the spirit of generosity among club members so evident from the early days surfaced once more. To name but a few, Mick Dunne and George Trenier – a devoted member of the Garda Rugby Club – and golf enthusiasts Jim Tymond and Bosco Muldoon put in Trojan work clearing the land, getting the ground ready and preparing for the installation of the various services.

These were times of great camaraderie and fun, with one highlight of the early years being the first barbeque held on the premises. Bosco Muldoon recalls that 'the finest of steaks were served and our tables and seats consisted of bales of straw and hay. Refreshments were served by Paddy O'Reilly from the nearby Roselawn Inn

Of stones and white coats

Stone picking was very hard on the back and it reminded me of footing turf on the bog. After about two hours you'd have enough of it. One day I decided to bring my two sons, Brian and Connor, who were about twelve and thirteen years old at that time, as I thought they'd be nearer the ground and great at stone picking. I promised them an ice cream when we finished, but after about half an hour they were already looking for their ice cream!

By now we had picked a few heaps of stones and George Trenier came along on the tractor. The young lads wanted a lift and as we travelled back towards the clubhouse, Brian said to me: 'Dad, look, there's a doctor picking stones.' When George and myself looked, we saw a man wearing a long white coat picking stones. George quickly turned to me and said: 'Come on, you know it's time to get out of here when you see the fellows with white coats coming!'

We had a good laugh, even though the young fellows did not know what we were laughing at. The fellow with the white coat turned out to be Jim Tymond, who worked in the Technical Bureau at that time where they wore white coats.

Bosco Muldoon

and staff and people still to this day talk about that night.'

As chairman, Brian Prendergast oversaw the early purchase of the lands but retired from the club at a meeting of the committee on 28 January 1987, after many years of loyal work and service. In addition to taking part in the acquisition of the land at Westmanstown, he was also a well-known member of the Garda Angling Club, working tirelessly for the establishment and success of that club, too. Though there were three chairman spanning the interval between Ned Garvey and Jim Murphy – Denis Devine, Noel McDermott and Brian Prendergast, who admirably furthered the aims of the club – the tenure of Jim Murphy is perhaps the one most linked to the realisation of the Westmanstown project. He was elected to the chair on 28 January 1987, along with Bosco Muldoon as vice chairman. Jim's tenure as chairman came at a remarkable period in the history of the Garda Recreation Club. Many have said that his drive and determination to bring projects to successful completion matched that of the founder Edmund Garvey.

Once the playing fields were ready, the soccer and rugby clubs installed themselves relatively quickly. Having a home of their own spurred them on to establish themselves in serious competition. The idea of a pitch and putt course was a totally new project and was entertained until the acquisition of extra land. With the extra land, it was decided to extend it to a nine hole golf course and later again, upon purchasing more land, to an eighteen hole course. To oversee the development of the course, a golf subcommittee was set up comprising Cyril Doyle, Majella Ryan, Bosco Muldoon, Jim Murphy, Jim Tymond and Oliver Nugent. In time they would become known as the 'founding fathers' of Westmanstown Golf Club. One of the first tasks facing the subcommittee was to appoint a golf architect to design the nine hole course. The renowned golf architect Mr Eddie Hackett, who had designed the golf course at Stackstown, was the inevitable choice. As it turned out, Westmanstown Golf Club has the distinction of being the last golf course that Eddie would design in the Dublin area. The sprightly seventy-three-year-old met the subcommittee in December 1987 to view the golf lands for the first time. With an area of 47.3 acres, Eddie found that the land had many attractive features for a golf course. Before long he was shaping the varying flat and gently undulating pasture land; the sections were divided by bushes, trees, a stream at the northern end of the course and a river at the southern end, which he used to good effect. The layout, he believed, when completed would offer the golfer testing and interesting holes and the variety of shots demanded in a satisfying round of golf.

The land, despite its good grass cover, was waterlogged by surface water to varying extents and had been badly poached by cattle hooves. Surveys by turfgrass and drainage experts, however, showed that the situation was not as bad as had been previously thought. That said, they did advise on necessary drainage measures as the course was likely to become soft in wet weather. To remedy the problem, the topsoil at the site of the greens was removed for building mounds, and drains were cut into the subsoil and covered with gravel and a topsoil of sandy soil and moss peat.

By March 1988 clearing of the major drains was completed and in the following month Eddie pegged the lands, giving an outline for the proposed golf course, now encompassing the extra 7.5 acres that the club was in the process of buying. Sportsturf Specialists Limited carried out the golf course construction. They installed an irrigation system of sprinklers to keep the soil in good condition and constructed access bridges to span streams at all the holes, except the third and sixth. An equipment building was also constructed. Drainage was a constant concern in the early years, to which Westmanstown's greenkeeper Gerry Byrne attests:

> *Tom Sloyan, being a man of the land, advised and guided us all at the club in most matters, but it was drainage he excelled in most. Indeed I had many discussions with Tom Sloyan and Bosco Muldoon on drainage principles in Ireland. The golf course was built on heavy clay and was waterlogged and unplayable for many winter months in its early days. We cleaned all ditches to assist water flow and Tom directed the primary drainage routes to get the course at least playable for the winter months. Additional drainage works improved the land further in subsequent years. This effort was led by Michael McFeely and has resulted in a very dry course today.*

A programme of tree planting was also instituted to enhance the quality of the golf and general ambience of the course. The Herculean efforts came to fruition when the temporary golf course was opened in October 1988 by club president Jim Murphy, with Cyril Doyle, now captain of the newly formed Westmanstown Golf Club, teeing off for the first time. Work commenced in October 1989 and continued throughout 1990 to construct a second set of nine holes, now that the extra land had been acquired. This was undertaken by Leisure Design and Construction Limited in conjunction with Eddie Hackett. Some of the existing nine holes were also redesignated. Liaising with Eddie Hackett had many high points, as Bosco Muldoon remembers:

Eddie Hackett was one of nature's gentlemen. At this stage of his career he was very frail. I remember once while we were working through the mud near the pump house his foot got stuck in the mud and came out of his Wellington boot, leaving the boot stuck in the mud. He was flailing on one foot when I grabbed him and pulled the boot out of the mud. I lifted him back to his car where we had a good laugh about the incident. He thanked me so much and every time we met afterwards he would still thank me.

Against the odds

Nature was not kind to me at Westmanstown, but it will be a most enjoyable course to play on in a few years' time. I am greatly impressed with the enthusiasm out there and you are very lucky to have such an amicable and hard-working greens officer in Gerry Byrne.

Eddie Hackett, Westmanstown Golf Club newsletter, 1990

One extraordinary initiative in the story of the golf course is the involvement of FÁS, the national training and employment authority. It was clear that as the project grew and if work was to progress at a faster pace, it would need many more willing hands and a more formal staffing arrangement. John Gannon was employed and a relationship was forged with the local FÁS co-ordinator Charlie O'Connor in 1988. Jim Tymond, on behalf of the golf committee, applied to FÁS based at Finglas and through the help and direction of Charlie O'Connor got a team of young men to work on the grounds. However, more importantly, they designed a tailor-made greenkeeping course that began in April 1989 and lasted twelve months, the first of its kind in Ireland. Greenkeeper Gerry Byrne recalls the heyday of the project: 'Every thirty-two weeks a new batch of about fifteen trainees would arrive with no training and I would be charged with putting them through the basics of golf course maintenance works. The golf course could not, however, have been maintained to the standard we set without the hard work of so many of these FÁS trainees.' Many supportive members of the training initiative included Bosco Muldoon, Peter Hughes, Tom Sloyan, Jim Muldoon, Dick McDonnell, John Brennan, Dan McInerney and John Kelly. Their contribution and support was much appreciated by FÁS, as indeed was the tremendous support and encouragement of chairman Jim Murphy and Helen Corrigan, who dealt with all records and financial accounts in a very thorough and professional manner.

Many activities, such as preparing the land and building the roadway, happened concurrently. As the playing fields became ready for use and later the temporary golf course, the need for dressing rooms arose. Portacabins were bought, renovated, decorated and furnished in a suitable manner for offices and dressing rooms. They served the purpose very adequately in the short term until the clubhouse was completed in 1992. The question of a water supply was also speedily addressed. By September 1988, a well had been sunk for a separate water supply and a pump installed as well as a pump house constructed.

Keeping the playing fields and greens in pristine condition meant that cutting grass was a regular feature of volunteer work, especially in the Irish climate. Grass cutting at Westmanstown was overseen by George Trenier, who over time gained a certain expertise in the matter. In light of the expense of cutting grass on a hiring basis, the committee decided in 1987 to invest in some much-needed machinery for the first time. In March 1988, a tractor and link box were purchased as were a gang mower and rotary motor for the sum of £4,300. Purchasing the tractor proved to be an adventure in itself, as recounted by Bosco Muldoon:

> *My first mission with John O'Malley as treasurer was a trip to the Cavan/ Monaghan border, home of the late George Trenier. Our mission was to buy a tractor at 'the right price'. Our chairman Jim Murphy told us, before we left, to bargain for the tractor. 'Murph', as we called him, was an expert at bartering and bargaining and over the years had saved the club quite a lot of money with that particular trait. I think he must have acquired this trait from the time he was travelling around the boreens of Mayo in the early 1960s in the then called 'travelling shop'. He expected us to be the same, but as the saying goes, 'You either have it or you don't'.*
>
> *After being fed and watered at George's home, we travelled a few miles on a very narrow road before we came to our destination. To this day I do not know which side of the Border it was on, but we not only bought the tractor but also got a trailer, a loader and a rotary machine!*

Thereafter, George Trenier was to be seen in his spare time driving around on the tractor with great enthusiasm setting out hedges, clearing spaces and keeping an eagle eye on the place. In fact, the tractor became a prized treasure of George's and he took exception to any inappropriate usage, according to Bosco Muldoon: 'George Trenier looked after this machinery as if it were his own. Later, there were a few dust-ups when other enthusiastic members would take out the tractor and mower but would try and cut stones. George finally decided on four designated drivers and everything went smoothly after that.'

At first the tractor was parked in the side entrance of George Strong's house, located beside the twelfth hole, but once the machinery shed was erected in 1990 it had a more permanent home. The shed was constructed at a cost of £26,000 and its erection was not without incident. So much so it went down in Garda Club annals, according to Bosco Muldoon.

The building of the machinery shed was undertaken by Mick Dunne, another committee member. His first day on site with his pals from Kildare caused havoc as they cut the ESB wires, sending fireworks high into the sky. It also left a lot of the neighbours without tea or dinner that evening. The shed was finally built and was used for my own captain's drive-in in 1990. Paddy O'Reilly from the Roselawn Inn supplied the temporary bar facilities and the new concrete floor got a good christening that night; Willie McGee supplied the music and Brian O'Donnell, aka Joe Dolan, and his wife Marie were heard to good effect into the early hours of the next morning.

The provision of an access road into Westmanstown was also a key project. In 1988, when the land was being prepared, a temporary roadway was constructed with the aid of volunteers such as George Trenier, Mick Dunne, Bosco Muldoon and others. By early 1989 meetings took place between the Garda Club and Danny Carr of Cement Roadstone regarding a price for a permanent roadway and car park at Westmanstown to accommodate 200 cars. Negotiations continued with Danny and the contract was awarded to Roadstone in October 1992 for a price of £84,000. The construction was completed in 1992 in time for the opening of the clubhouse.

Money matters

I was fully aware that we were working on a tight budget and spending money was always like spending your own, so respect for the project was always first on everybody's mind. Indeed Jim Murphy lamented many years later that the Fridays I went into Helen in Harrington Street to pick up my wages, the fear was that Thursday's takings in the bar might not cover the wage. Which answers the reason why there was so many pound notes in my bulging envelope!

Gerry Byrne, first greenkeeper, Westmanstown Golf Club

A first of its kind: FÁS greenkeeping course at Westmanstown

In March 1988, I received a phone call from the Fingerprint Section in Garda Headquarters in the Phoenix Park. My first reaction was what kind of trouble was I in now! What a relief when the voice at the other end of the phone was that of Jim Tymond enquiring could FÁS run a greenkeeping course at the new Garda sports ground at Westmanstown.

I am not sure why Jim would have phoned me and FÁS in relation to this request, but perhaps he had heard about a LINC (locally integrated nationally co-ordinated) training programme carried out in the greater Navan area in 1984. This was during a period of high unemployment and the aim of LINC was to identify growth areas and provide appropriate training to satisfy the needs of these areas. Westmanstown Sports Centre was certainly one of these growth areas, with plans for the provision of modern sporting and leisure facilities.

Jim and I agreed to meet onsite and take it from there. Once at Westmanstown, both of us put on the wellies and like two farmers proceeded to walk a portion of the area, with Jim pointing out the proposed layout of the golf course. After this initial survey, Jim again asked the big question, would FÁS be willing to set up a greenkeeping course at Westmanstown? I told him I would fully support his request if he could provide a technical person who could impart the skills and knowledge of greenkeeping to the FÁS students taking part in the training course. Jim explained that the golfing committee was in the process of recruiting a golf course superintendent capable of doing so. On the basis of this commitment, I agreed to set up the course as soon as possible.

The first course commenced in April 1989 with eight students supervised by the new golf course superintendent, Gerry Byrne, and overseen by the first golf committee, comprising Jim Tymond, Majella Ryan and Cyril Doyle. Cyril and the committee also agreed to employ half of the students who successfully completed the course. I am glad to say that the committee honoured their commitment. The duration of each course was twelve months, long enough to ensure that the students had sufficient time to cover all aspects of greenkeeping during the different seasons. Stephen Kelly from Dunboyne – one of the students on the first course and subsequently employed by Westmanstown Golf Club – is now over twenty years at Westmanstown and is a senior member of the current course superintendent Michael Feeley's team. In October 1992, Michael replaced Gerry Byrne and continued to maintain and develop the course until it finished in 1999.

In addition to the technical skills learned on the golf course, the students had to attend a horticultural college to acquire the theory aspects of greenkeeping. As we had difficulty initially securing this training in the Botanic Gardens in Dublin, we sourced another provider abroad. Elmwood

College in Cupar, Scotland, was very supportive and glad to accept our students. Aside from not being able to access the educational modules of this course at the Botanic Gardens, it was actually cheaper to travel to Elmwood College. The partnership approach to the funding of the educational modules was as follows: Westmanstown Golf Club would finance the travel and accommodation costs, while FÁS would finance course fees, course materials and examination costs. In relation to this venture, I would like to sincerely acknowledge the tremendous support and co-operation given by Peter Synnott, the administration and finance person at that time. As a result of this educational input and the practice modules on the golf course given by Gerry Byrne, the course went from strength to strength.

Soon other golf courses in the greater Dublin area heard about the valuable training taking place at Westmanstown and asked could similar training courses be put in place elsewhere. Thus, the following golf courses were approved for training: Corrstown Golf Club, Castle Golf Club, Luttrellstown Golf Club, Swords Golf Club, Lucan Golf Club and Hollystown Golf Club. However, as there was only a maximum of three or four students on each of these golf courses, they were coded to Westmanstown Golf Club as it was the FÁS-approved training centre for greenkeeping. One of these students at Corrstown Golf Club, Robert Kane, came first in Europe on two occasions while studying at Elmwood College and also represented the college in an international competition, receiving a distinction award. Certainly, this achievement highlighted the quality of the training that was taking place at Westmanstown Golf Club.

A major contribution to this quality training was the greenkeeping course syllabus designed by my colleagues George Keeley and Gerry Byrne, which was also accepted by City & Guilds for their Amenity Horticulture Certificate, with the FÁS students majoring in greenkeeping. In time, many of our students secured employment in other golf clubs and some became head greenkeepers. Just a sample includes Gerry Byrne at the K Club, Joe Kinnear at Hermitage Golf Club, John Smith at Headford Golf Club and Mark Murphy at Tullamore Golf Club.

The greenkeeping course at Westmanstown contributed to the development of the golf course but it also gave – during my time in charge – an opportunity to about eighty young people to train, receive a qualification and procure employment in a discipline in which they really wanted to work, and in an era of few job opportunities. For this, FÁS are truly thankful to Westmanstown Golf Club.

Charles O'Connor, FÁS

Right: **Dublin Bus newsletter, November 1992, showing Dr John Lynch, CEO of Dublin Bus, presenting the Love Cup to Captain Jim Murphy**

LOVE CUP FOR WESTMANSTOWN

Dublin Bus presented a trophy to the Garda Golf Club at Westmanstown for competition amongst the members.

The trophy, a Love Cup, in Irish known as a Meadar, was - according to the Assay Office hallmark imprinted on it - made in Dublin in 1900 of sterling silver by a silversmith named Edmond Johnson. It was supplied by the M.M.I. Group of Bluebell, Dublin who had bought it at an auction of old Irish silver.

It is interesting to note that the M.M.I. Group supplies the United Nations with the medals which they award to service people worldwide who serve on U.N. peacekeeping missions. The medal is the same in all cases but the ribbon colour varies depending on the country in which the peacekeeping is performed. The M.M.I. Group won the U.N. contract against stiff international competition.

Below: **Greenkeeper Gerry Byrne**

Greenkeeper extraordinaire

My association with Westmanstown Golf Club started in the late summer of 1988. In many ways, I did not deserve to even get an interview with the club, as I was only third assistant under my father Jim Byrne, who was the long-serving course manager at the Hermitage Golf Club at the time. A call came through to my father from the Botanic Gardens in Dublin informing him of a new nine hole golf course being developed in Clonsilla and that they were looking for a young energetic lad to take on the greenkeeper position. I had finished my greenkeeper educational training at the Botanic Gardens with the second assistant at the time, and was keen to take the position.

I duly applied and was given an interview in the office of Det Supt John Murphy and Det Insp Jim Murphy in Harcourt Street, Dublin. I genuinely felt on arriving at the interview that I was going to be arrested for the way I looked with my long hair and beard! But I was greeted with a smile and made to feel very welcome. Thankfully, the interview went very well and both men took a chance on me and gave me the start I needed to continue my career path.

My level of expectation when I first arrived at Westmanstown on that September day in 1988 took a sudden dip as I drove up a potholed road leading to a 40-foot container that was split in two. One half was used for golf course equipment and the other was a temporary clubhouse that housed a solitary pay phone that would become my lifeline to the outside world for the next two years. On inspection of the course, I saw that the greens were recently built on a wet site and no matter how much I looked I could only find eight holes! For two days, I was under the impression I would have to break the bad news to Jim Murphy that there was a grave mistake in the design until the Tuesday evening I saw a combine harvester arriving onto the adjacent land. To my surprise, it proceeded down by the first hole and on towards a field close to the road and began harvesting wheat only to reveal a green surrounded by the crop at the end of the field. I subsequently figured out that this was the seventh hole, thereby completing the loop and making the total of nine.

Planting trees, many of which are still there today, were from the sweat, tears and laughter of volunteers such as Peter Synnott, Peter Hughes, Dick McDonald, Majella Ryan, George Trenier, Ned Ryan, Jim Tymond, Jim Muldoon, Bosco Muldoon, Ollie Nugent, Ciaran Walsh and the first captain Cyril Doyle. Visits were made to local tree nurseries, purchases made and a Saturday picked for planting. The meeting time was set for 9.30 am and the day would not end until every tree was planted. The banter amongst all the men became legendary and, despite the hard work, the sense of achievement at the end of the day will never be forgotten.

Each spinney on the course has a story to tell, none more so than the large poplars separating the tenth and eleventh holes. These were about to be cut down by a local nursery as they were gone out of control. We made a nominal offer on these and organised transport to the club. Replanting and keeping them alive was always going to be the problem, however. I will never forget digging the holes with all the available volunteers under Ned Ryan's advice and planting the trees, which in hindsight were way too deep to survive. Nonetheless, it kept the trees staple and slowly but surely they all survived and still play an important part in the holes today.

The true personal joy of the development was when I got the opportunity to work with one of the great golf course designers Ireland ever produced, the late Mr Eddie Hackett. Long before the modern greats of Palmer and Nicklaus, a true Irish gentleman was creating masterpieces around the country. Westmanstown can be proud that its name will be forever linked with a legend of golf course architecture.

Modern golf course construction methods were not available or used on the construction of the front nine holes, and putting quality issues soon became apparent in the summer of 1989. The seeded grass quickly died away leaving the indigenous annual meadow grass to take over. The challenge was to keep sustainable surfaces for as long as possible on the seeded greens and encourage the native grasses into the greens as soon as possible. Thankfully, we were successful at this transition over shorter periods of time than expected. As the front nine were growing in, a temporary course was established to facilitate play for new members. These temporary greens became a true focus and their conditioning turned out to be excellent and came in for great praise.

The year 1990 saw the construction of the second nine holes and even at this time modern construction methods were still not perfected in Ireland. We thought we had it right as we went for a soil mix that came out of glasshouses in Malahide, and an excellent silica mix. Problems arose as we ran late into the autumn of 1990, however, because the contractors took the decision to take delivery of all the materials for the project and store them on the proposed green sites to be left until the following season to finish the job off. The winter of 1990 experienced many storms and high winds. In early spring 1991, it was clearly seen that all the sand had blown away! Eddie Hackett had to use his charm once more to convince the contractors to replace the expensive sand to complete the project. Problems arose again, when in the mixing of the sand and soil, the soil, being very wet over the wet winter, mixed in clumps, which before seeding needed to be removed by a team of ten men with potato forks. This was a procedure never seen before in modern day construction.

However, it proved successful as the greens finally grew in with few further problems.

Despite all the teething problems, the new nine and revised eighteen hole route was greeted with high praise and everybody agreed that Eddie Hackett had done a wonderful job with such a limited site and budget.

Working out of the 40-foot dock container continued until the new maintenance facility was built in the winter of 1989/1990. This was truly given the official opening when it was used for the captain's drive-in in 1990. A music band was brought in and a buffet served and the day went on into the late evening. Although the captain's prize nights were hosted at Harrington Street – Cyril Doyle's being most memorable – the true spirit of Westmanstown had arrived that day with many new friendships forged and the club finally found a home.

In 1992, I left Westmanstown for Luttrellstown before finally moving on to the K Club as golf course superintendent in 1996. I can honestly say I could not have been part of the team at the K Club and deliver such major tour events like the Ryder Cup without the experience I gained at Westmanstown. It is with deep pride that I look back on my involvement in Westmanstown and the many great volunteers and members who are still my friends today.

Gerry Byrne, Greenkeeper

Above: Signing the dotted line – Jim Murphy *(seated left)* with building contractor Martin McLoughlin *(seated right)* signing the contract for Westmanstown Sports Centre, surrounded by committee members in 1991

Above: **Construction of the sports complex begins.** *Centre:* **The committee studies the construction plans.** *Bottom left:* **Presentation to Sister Patricia and staff of St Joseph's Hospital, Clonsilla by vice chairman Bosco Muldoon flanked by Jim Murphy and Joe Fallon on right and Dick McDonnell on left.** *Bottom centre:* **Cllr Ned Ryan.** *Bottom right:* **Colm Mohan of Pontederia Limited.**

Story of the sewerage

One of the most challenging and time-consuming problems by far in the development of Westmanstown was the sewerage system. Yet like many of the best ideas, the resolution of the problem was simple and ingenious. Ensconced in prime agricultural land, Westmanstown had one distinct disadvantage – it was remote from any public sewer. Following a meeting with Dublin County Council in late 1988, the club had no alternative but to construct its own septic tank at Westmanstown. The facility, as outlined in the original design plans, was going to be extremely expensive and would involve huge maintenance costs for the future. An added hurdle was that on the design plans, the would-be treatment plant was sited in an area of the playing fields on what was now the 'rugby land'. This would have to be dug up to provide the percolation area. Needless to say, the rugby club was not happy with the proposal.

A chance encounter, however, sometime in 1989 between Bosco Muldoon and his friend Herbie Hughes, from the Dublin County Council Water Department at Ballycoolin, prompted some lateral thinking. After recounting the woes of the sewage disposal system at Westmanstown, Bosco was informed by Herbie that St Joseph's Hospital in Clonsilla had a private sewer connection straight down to Lucan. Needing no encouragement, chairman Jim Murphy, along with Bosco and Cllr Ned Ryan, who was on the hospital board, met with St Joseph's – run by the Daughters of Charity – to discuss their system. Clearly the matter must have been to the liking of the board of management, as it was agreed that the club would endeavour to find an alternative system at no cost to the hospital. If this was successful, the club could then avail of the hospital system exclusively.

A subcommittee was set up consisting of Jim Murphy, Bosco Muldoon and John Murphy for the club and Cllr Ned Ryan for the hospital board of management. Shay Fenton of Fenton-Simons Planning and Development Consultants was commissioned to investigate the matter. Before long he was able to confirm that the existing foul sewer from St Joseph's Hospital discharged to the public sewer on the Lower Lucan Road at the Strawberry Beds via a private drain from the pumping station located in the hospital grounds. It emerged that it was possible to divert the hospital's flow to an existing public sewer known as the Mulhuddart/Clonsilla foul sewer and, secondly, to connect Westmanstown to the would-be redundant private sewer. It was certainly a question of fortune favouring the brave, as the solution met with the approval of the hospital board. Furthermore, all planning and legal costs would be borne by the Garda Recreation Club.

In the event, the project would involve considerable construction and the co-operation of various interested parties. Permission to gain access to lands on the part of the Garda Club was no straightforward matter and took months of negotiations. The first section of sewer entailed clearing a site on the hospital grounds and laying the sewer, whereby the club had to obtain wayleave from the hospital. The second section involved laying the sewer across a public road, Clonsilla Road, and the Royal Canal, and necessitated licences and agreements from Dublin County Council as well as a wayleave from St Joseph's Hospital. In the case of the third section, being within lands owned by Meadowgrove Construction Ltd, it was necessary to obtain the wayleave to enter and construct the sewer. As regards obtaining wayleaves for the fourth section, nearest to the Mulhuddart/Clonsilla foul sewer, it was also on land to which both Meadow Grove Construction and Pontederia Limited had rights.

The legalities of granting wayleaves for the Garda Club to access lands were handled by the club solicitor Mr Maurice Veale. This was a long and complicated process, especially for the fourth section. However, the management team of Cllr Jim Fahey and Colm Mohan in Pontederia was most helpful and co-operative. Eventually, on 15 October 1991, Dublin County Council granted planning permission with one of the conditions being that their Drainage Design Maintenance Department would supervise the project. Subsequently, Clonmel Enterprises Ltd were hired to construct the new sewer, over 310 metres in length, to serve St Joseph's Hospital at a cost of approximately £58,000.

The sewage line for the hospital was completed and performed to their satisfaction by April 1992. The Garda Recreation Club was then free to use the redundant drain downstream of the Royal Canal crossing. The sewer connection on the grounds of Westmanstown to the existing private sewer on Woodwall Road was designed by the club's architect, Mr Anthony O'Neill. An application for planning permission was made on 15 October 1991, after notice appeared in the *Irish Press* of 3 October 1991. Planning permission was granted on 13 December 1991 on several conditions, one of which was that no work would commence until such time as the private sewer was no longer required by St Joseph's Hospital. As St Joseph's was demolishing its pump house, it was intended to sever the sewer at Woodwall Road, to the north of Westmanstown, and build a new hatch box so that the sewer could drain effectively to Tinker's Hill near the Lower Lucan Road. There was great urgency to this application as the clubhouse was due for completion in late 1992.

The work was completed in time much to the relief and satisfaction of the chairman and subcommittee. Their joy was shared by the board of management of St Joseph's Hospital, particularly by Sister Patricia. Their appreciation of the Garda Recreation Club for relieving them of what had been a high-maintenance sewerage system was evident. Now that a goodwill relationship had been forged, Bosco Muldoon and his golf colleagues thereafter presented funds on a regular basis to the hospital, a practice continued on by Dick McDonnell of the golf club.

In the annals of Westmanstown, the story of the sewerage has earned a prominent place. It was a bold initiative where the entire costs of solving the problem were carried by the club. Despite the initial outlay, huge savings were made for generations to come. It was this foresight that propelled Jim Murphy and the subcommittee forward, giving much time and energy to push the project to completion.

Building the clubhouse

In the early years, the idea of the clubhouse was to cater for all the Garda sporting clubs under one roof. It was also envisaged that it would provide social and indoor sporting facilities for the growing membership. In this respect, the clubhouse would be the jewel in the crown of Westmanstown. Before the advent of the Sports and Leisure Centre in 2003, the clubhouse was referred to as Westmanstown Golf and Sports Centre. Like many a project in the Garda Club, its passage was often stormy and not without incident. In the late 1980s the committee was not as one regarding the clubhouse, and a number of committe members voted against it on the grounds of cost. However, when put to the membership at a subsequent well-attended extraordinary general meeting, the motion to build was carried with only a half-dozen objections. At the AGM in 1990 the Garda Recreation Club was also given a mandate to start building a sports complex at Westmanstown.

Work commenced on the building in March 1991 and was completed in July 1992. The large ultramodern two-storey building was designed by Anthony O'Neill and Associates and constructed by PJ McLoughlin and Son. At first the architects had to trim back the design of the building so that it was affordable to the club, at a cost of £2.6 million. It comprised a suite of dressing rooms for each of the football clubs, in addition to changing and locker rooms for the male and female members of Westmanstown Golf Club. Bar, restaurant and function rooms were drawn up and a unique feature of the building was the elegant glass roof at the façade.

In a reflection of the good management and dedication of those involved, the project was delivered on time and within budget. The first section to be completed was the bar, restaurant and function room, as well as the changing rooms for the football clubs. Later the golf changing area, two committee rooms, games rooms and fitness rooms were finalised. Mr Noel Brennan, a member of the Garda Club, was appointed as a full-time manager and a temporary catering contractor was initially hired. This franchise basis was later taken up successfully by Robert O'Boyle. To enhance the excellent gym facilities even more, members could avail of the coaching skills of Brendan Burke of CDU, which was generously sponsored by St Raphael's Credit Union.

The sizeable clubhouse was finished to a high standard and eventually cost in the region of £3.25 million. The sum was raised by a term bank loan, which was to be repaid over twenty-five years at a monthly repayment of £30,000. This meant pooling the resources of both clubs: Harrington Street and Westmanstown.

The first function to be held in the clubhouse was the Westmanstown Golf Captain's Drive-In on 25 April 1992, which was a resounding success. The official opening took place some months later on 1 December 1992 with a special luncheon. On the day, chairman Jim Murphy welcomed over 250 assembled guests, including

Above: Westmanstown clubhouse completed in 1992

Above: A view of the clubhouse in 1992

Above: Enjoying the official opening of the clubhouse in 1992 were *(left to right)* Jim Tymond, Paddy O' Reilly, J Brennan and Cllr Ned Ryan

Above: **Lady golfers accompanied by committee member Tom Rock at the official opening of the clubhouse in 1992**

Deputy Commissioner PJ Moran officiates at the opening of the clubhouse in 1992

Honorary Secretary Christy McCarthy at the official opening of the clubhouse

Chairman Jim Murphy delivers a speech at the opening of the clubhouse

Above: **Pictured at the opening of the clubhouse in 1992 were *(from left)* Brian Prendergast, Tom Ryan, Michael Murphy, Bill Clooney and Paddy Prendergast**

Dickie bows de rigueur

Following a discussion on the new Garda Club ties the meeting decided, following a proposal by PJ Browne, seconded by Jim Tymond, to give a tie to all the bar staff and each committee member, but it was agreed by the meeting following a proposal by John O'Malley that notwithstanding the bar personnel getting ties that the regulatory mode of dress while working would still be the dickie bow.

Minutes of Divisional Committee meeting, 22 May 1991

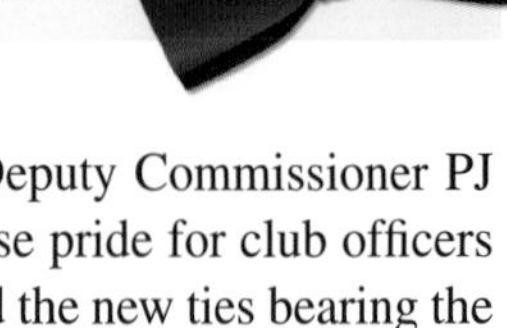

the then Minister for Justice Mr Pádraig Flynn TD and Deputy Commissioner PJ Moran. It was an occasion of unparalleled joy and immense pride for club officers and committee members, resplendent in blazers, slacks and the new ties bearing the club insignia. Jim Murphy began his speech by noting the special importance of the year 1992. It was the seventieth anniversary of the founding of An Garda Síochána and thus was a fitting way to mark a significant milestone in Irish policing history.

An important feature of the sports club was the social membership. The response of the local community was extraordinary and a gym subcommittee was therefore established to draw up rules to accept as many social members as possible. An indication of the success of the sports club was that by 1995 membership stood at 3,668. When various Garda clubs were accommodated in Westmanstown, the position of their honorary members was also clarified in order to regularise their status within the club. The rules stipulated that honorary members had to pay for social membership in order to gain entry to any of the clubs attached to Westmanstown.

The luxurious bar and lounge were popular with members and provided an ideal atmosphere to relax after a round of golf or gym session. The function rooms, capable of catering for all sizes of groups, could be relied upon for various social events from weddings to christening parties to retirements. Cabaret nights, a perennial favourite from Harrington Street days, proved popular in Westmanstown too when they began in October 1993. Over the years Joe Dolan and Björn Again were just two of the acts that were guaranteed crowd-pullers. In the mid-1990s functions at the clubhouse took off in earnest and trading figures were very healthy. Certainly, by 1997 this necessitated the expansion of the catering capacity, with a kitchen extension costing £60,000. A carvery was subsequently purchased in 1999, costing £6,000. The club bar was well established and trading satisfactorily and it too was refurbished in 1998 for £55,229.

Bold and ambitious projects are not without setbacks, however. One occurred in 1994 in relation to the glass roof, which had started to leak in the clubhouse. The architect and building contractor were promptly called to investigate and remedy the situation. Nonetheless, neither accepted responsibility for the flaw. A court case ensued between the club and the architect and builder, which was eventually settled out of court a decade later in the club's favour. The original design of the roof was reworked and a new entrance, bar and office were subsequently constructed.

In time the sports centre firmly established Westmanstown at the heart of the local community. By 1994, with the eighteen hole golf club, GAA, rugby and soccer clubs, as well as tennis and bowling clubs, the centre had 5,000 members. The club could boast a high percentage of non-Garda members too. Membership was open to individuals, corporate clients and families in the surrounding areas of Blanchardstown, Castleknock, Clonsilla, Lucan and Leixlip. This did much to promote good public relations and community spirit. It was also an added advantage when the bus committee, under the chairmanship of Fachtna Murphy, was in negotiation with Dublin Bus to set up a bus service to Westmanstown. The day finally dawned and on 3 February 2000, the 239 bus pulled up alongside the gates of Westmanstown. The 239 had begun its existence as a local-link route around Blanchardstown and Clonsilla in the winter of 1996. With the newly opened Blanchardstown Shopping Centre serving as a hub, it was extended south of the River Liffey in 2000 into Lucan and the Liffey Valley Shopping Centre, serving the back roads of Lucan and Clonsilla. Now Westmanstown was another link in the community chain.

When Jim Murphy's tenure as chairman came to an end in October 2001 on his retirement from the force, he handed over the reins to Michael Feehan, who carried on the grand traditions set by his predecessors. Jim did not sever his connection entirely, however, and took up the post of general manager of Westmanstown until the sports and leisure centre was completed. There was still much work to be done, in particular persuading Bord Gáis to bring a gas connection from Lucan to the new centre. During the 2000s the clubhouse was also upgraded to provide first-class conference and banqueting facilities. In keeping with the parkland theme of Westmanstown, the rooms were bestowed with apt names: Acorn, Cedar, Chestnut, Beech, Willow, Sycamore and Mulberry. The advent of conference facilities also brought a change of name for the premises and thus it became Westmanstown Sports and Conference Centre. It was officially reopened by the then Taoiseach Bertie Ahern on 22 November 2004.

Club rules

In May 1989 a subcommittee had been set up to formulate rules and obtain legal advice regarding the setting up and registering of the Westmanstown Sports Complex, comprising Christy McCarthy and Oliver Nugent. This culminated in the legal drafting of the rules regarding the complex in February 1990. In particular, the rules specified the name of the club, that is, the Dublin Metropolitan Garda Sports Club, and that it would be financed from the resources of the parent club, the Dublin Metropolitan Garda Recreation Club. On foot of legal advice, it was necessary to form a separate club for Westmanstown in order to hold a proprietary licence. By March 1992, the club was registered to sell intoxicating liquor on its premises.

The rules outlined who would be eligible for membership, such as: (a) ordinary members and honorary members of the parent club; (b) all members of Garda sports clubs who pursued their activities on lands at Westmanstown; and (c) any person the committee decided to admit to membership. A change to Rule 5 in 1991, after receiving the support of the members, specified that for any borrowing of monies for the financing of the complex at Westmanstown, the parent club would not be used as collateral and neither would the golfers be levied for monies, in the case of Westmanstown Golf Club. In terms of honorary members of Westmanstown Sports Club, the issue arose in 1995 of whether they were entitled to vote if not paying membership fees. A further rule change was effected in 2000 that allowed for patrons to be appointed by the club, numbering no more than three, and who could be re-elected annually.

Master of wit and law: Christy McCarthy

The position of honorary secretary in any organisation is an onerous one, and this was never more true than when the Garda Club came to establish Westmanstown.

In May 1991, Christy McCarthy took over the position of secretary from Cyril Doyle. Straight away Christy brought to the position his own unique style. Having served on the committee as a representative for the K District, he was all too familiar with what was expected of a committee member, regardless of position. He never missed a meeting and unfailingly kept up-to-date with correspondence and any appointments made on his behalf by the administration of Harrington Street.

Christy was and is an expert on the licensing laws of the land and could always be relied upon to keep everyone abreast of all that had to be complied with in this area. When the important business of licensing Westmanstown occurred, he was of immeasurable help. Without his expertise and direction at the time, it would have been far more difficult for the committee to expedite matters.

Christy is a wit, a man of few words. Those words can make you smile, or think, or both. Furthermore, he can be relied upon to command attention as a witty speaker both *as Béarla agus as Gaeilge*, when the occasion demands. The Garda Club has had a great secretary, a firm friend and a good member in Christy McCarthy, and members were truly sorry to see him retire from the position.

Helen Corrigan

Modus operandi: subcommittee

The essence of leadership is the achievement of goals through others. As chairman, Jim Murphy delegated significant tasks and provided opportunities for initiative, problem solving and decision making among all who served with him in the development of Westmanstown. Side by side, committee members co-created a vision that served to rally and energise the group as a whole. Each individual committee member became a potential leader and manager and indeed today the ship is steered by members who sharpened their business acumen as the Westmanstown complex emerged due to their efforts. From 1987 onwards, especially in 1993, subcommittees were the only way to manage the ever-increasing workload arising from the amount of projects in hand.

Over the following years, subcommittees of various hues were set up and reconstituted as committee members retired, resigned or transferred to other districts and divisions, or else subcommittees disbanded on completion of projects. The importance of keeping the business of Harrington Street afloat and not neglected in the face of the challenge posed by the massive development of Westmanstown was a continuing concern. The club membership had grown and if Harrington Street was not as busy as it used to be, it was still a constant reminder of where the Garda Club had all began.

Though there were many members who contributed enormously to the task of bringing the Westmanstown complex to fruition, a core group of Jim Murphy, Christy McCarthy, Derek Byrne, Bosco Muldoon and George Trenier, in addition to the district representatives, was particularly instrumental. Some of the main subcommittees established were:

Land: Subcommittee included officers of the club in 1987 and Christy McCarthy, Dick Kinsella and M Dunne. Later in March 1988, John Murphy and Majella Ryan joined the committee.

Garda Club, Harrington Street: To administer the draw and circulate results. Subcommittee included Michael Corcoran and John Leahy.

Westmanstown Development Draw: To administer, promote and circulate results. Original subcommittee members included Derek Byrne (treasurer), Dominic Power, Bernie McCarthy and Jim Murphy. This was further strengthened in 1993/4 to include Bosco Muldoon (chairman), Conor McGuinness (secretary), John Murphy, Frank Furlong, Martin Kenny, Dick McDonnell, Geraldine Walsh, Pascal Diskin and Peter Kelly.

Templemore/Harcourt Square Membership: To recruit members from the Garda College, Templemore, and later included the Dublin Metropolitan Region headquarters at Harcourt Square. Subcommittee included John Leahy and PJ Gallagher, initially, and later Dave Dowling, Michael Feehan and Tom Rock.

Westmanstown Tennis Club: To deal with fees, subscriptions and membership. Subcommittee included Jim Murphy, C McCarthy, E McDonnell, R Ryan, G O'Gara, E Grace, M Doyle and J Shannon.

Westmanstown Bowling Club: Subcommittee included Dominic Power and Paschal Diskin.

House Committee Westmanstown: To deal with the ESB and generator. Subcommittee included Eamon O'Reilly, George Trenier, Christy McCarthy, John Leahy and Peter Kelly (chairman).

Harrington Street Entertainment/Promotions: To compile a written programme and deal with bar music and bar inspection and social membership.

Business at Harrington Street: To improve the business at Harrington Street and increase social membership and use of facilities. Subcommittee included Pat McInerney, Ned Grace, Peter Murray and Eamonn McDonnell. Later included Séan Murphy, Noel Brennan, Bernie McCarthy and Tim Meehan.

Fundraising for Harrington Street: Subcommittee included Derek Byrne, Christy McCarthy, Bosco Muldoon, John Leahy and Helen Corrigan.

House Committee Harrington Street: To deal with catering, prices and sanitation in the Garda Club. Subcommittee included Alan Bailey, Eamon O'Reilly, Pat McInernery (chairman) and Trevor Shaw.

Golf Classic: Subcommittee included Jim Murphy, Eamonn McDonnell, Walter O'Connell, Derek Byrne and Eugene Looney.

Bus Service for Westmanstown: To liaise with Dublin Bus to establish a bus service to Westmanstown. Subcommittee included Fachtna Murphy, Paschal Diskin, Ned Grace, Tom Carroll, Tony Sourke, Grainne Doyle and Martin Kenny.

Cabaret and Dinner: To develop the entertainment aspect of Westmanstown. Subcommittee included Christy McCarthy, Noel Brennan, Jim Murphy and Bosco Muldoon.

Membership Committee Harrington Street: Subcommittee included PJ Gallagher, J Duggan, PJ Ruddy, N Vizzard, M Dunne and E Boland.

Membership of A to K Districts: Subcommittee included Walter O'Connell (chairman), Noel Brennan, Aubrey Steadman and Matt Murphy.

Membership of L to W Districts & CDU & Depot: Subcommittee included Kieron Corcoran, Michael Feehan (chairman), Dan Hayes, Donal Watters, Trevor Shaw, Dominic Power and Michael O'Connor.

Membership of Golf Clubs: To liaise with Garda District golfing societies. Subcommittee included Bosco Muldoon and Fergus Healy.

Computerisation: To arrange the computerisation of Harrington Street and later Westmanstown. Subcommittee included Dick Walsh, Mick Corcoran and Eddie Boland.

Westmanstown Gymnasium: To look into hours and supervision in the gym. Subcommittee included Derek Byrne, Dominic Power and Richard Ryan.

Westmanstown Facilities: To oversee the use of facilities by members and monitor same. Subcommittee included Tom Rock and Noel Vizzard.

Funding the Westmanstown project

Organising the funding for the various stages of the development of Westmanstown was a gargantuan task that became ever more complex as the project evolved. Jim Murphy and his committee, particularly the club officers, oversaw it all with Jim ensuring that every penny was well spent. Many avenues of funding were explored to help defray the development costs, ranging from bank loans and Credit Union loans to members' subscriptions and draws to sponsorship and a National Lottery grant.

A unanimous decision to grant permission to the committee to borrow the necessary monies was taken at a Divisional Committee meeting held on 23 March 1988, proposed by Mick Dunne and seconded by Ray McEneaney. Subsequently, Jim Murphy and the executive went to the bank to put forward their request for funds. They must certainly have sold the idea because they got their first loan promptly from AIB. This, along with a contribution from the Golf Club of £53,155, helped to pay for the initial development of the land.

Various fundraising initiatives for the Westmanstown complex got underway in Harrington Street. Since the 1980s, monies from ongoing club monthly membership draws went towards clearing the development debt. By September 1985, the prize fund was increased to £2,000 per month. In January 1987, there was a proposal that 50 pence of members' subscriptions be diverted to a separate Westmanstown Development Account. This was to start when the land was completely paid for. In March 1987, a subcommittee was set up to look at monthly draws as a fundraising initiative. The draw was reconstituted in early 1990 and represented prizes totalling £9,000 annually: £3,500 for the Christmas draw with £500 for each of the other months. However, the yield from the draws was small as the level of subscribers was

Above: At the launch of the members' draw *(left to right)* Conor McGuinness, John Leahy, Declan Foley and Bosco Muldoon

Above: Plans for the new sports complex are unveiled at Westmanstown in 1994 with sponsor Ford Ireland. Pictured *(from left)* Eugene Crowley, Brian Lehane (Ford Ireland), Eddie Murphy (Ford Ireland), Eddie Nolan (Ford Ireland), and Garda Commissioner Eamonn Doherty

Above: Chairman and managing director of Ford Ireland, Eddie Nolan hands over a car for the development draw

Above: Ford Ireland presents another car for the members' draw. Pictured *(left to right)* Bosco Muldoon, Christy McCarthy, Jim Murphy, Eddie Nolan (Ford Ireland), Noel Vizzard, Tony Hickey and Declan Foley (Ford Ireland)

too low, especially as regards the membership of the clubs based at the centre and with regard to some sections of weekly subscribers.

Despite various fundraising subcommittees having been set up over the years to explore the feasibility and viability of some form of continuous fundraising project, new thinking and ideas were sorely needed. Into the picture in 1993 came Conor McGuinness, a member of Westmanstown Golf Club with considerable business acumen. He was at the forefront of a focused campaign to enlist members from the existing club members and introduce sponsorship. Thus the development draw committee was reconstituted in 1993/4 and included Conor McGuinness, J Mahon, Michael Kelly, Jim Murphy, Bosco Muldoon, Michael Dunne, Patsy O'Leary, John Leahy, George Kyne, PJ Gallagher, John Downey, Gus Keating, Richard Ryan, John Murphy, Willie Magee and Martin Kenny. One immediate action was to announce a super monthly members' non-stop development draw in March 1993, which was part of the social entertainment programme at Westmanstown. The draw featured a number of attractive prizes every month such as sun holidays, TVs and videos. The draw was open to the social membership with tickets costing £25 per year. But the really ambitious fundraising drive undertaken by the commitee consisted of a draw for a car. With tickets costing £100 annually, the draw was open to anyone who cared to buy a ticket, and sterling work was done by the committee to encourage members to sign up. One year's free pavilion membership of Westmanstown Sports Centre was even offered as an inducement. A prominent feature of the relaunched development draw was that a main sponsor was identified: from 1994 until 1998, Henry Ford & Son Ltd became the main sponsor. Through the efforts of chairman and managing director Edwin Nolan, Eddie Murphy and Declan Foley and all their colleagues at Ford Ireland, they contributed enormously to the success of the Sports and Leisure Centre.

In the first year of the sponsorship, from January to June 1994, the Ford Escort 4-door 1.4i LX Saloon was on display outside the clubhouse as an enticement to members. On 1 June 1994 the draw took place, coinciding with a media launch of the development programme by Minister for Justice Mrs Máire Geoghegan-Quinn TD and Garda Commissioner Patrick Culligan. In a further boost, Fords committed themselves to the club for five years.

The excellent work of the committee certainly paid off. By 1995 the development draw membership stood at 1,275 and the sports club membership was 3,668. By 1997, the Garda Recreation Club had reduced its borrowing requirement due to increased revenues generated by the increased numbers joining the development draw, in addition to a fantastic year of activity in both Harrington Street and the clubhouse.

Seeing that the clubhouse with all its associated clubs was not exclusively for the use of Garda personnel, it was possible to market the premises as a community resource for West Dublin. The Dublin 15 area, in which Westmanstown is located, became one of the fastest-growing suburbs during the Celtic Tiger and, as there was a dearth of sports facilities in the area, Westmanstown filled the vacuum. It became a widely used facility not alone for sport but for recreation too. Many functions, meetings and community fundraising activities were accommodated in the clubhouse and the number continued to soar during the 2000s. For all the clubs gathered under its umbrella, all were open to civilians to join. The football pitches were and continue to be widely used by local teams for matches, while it was and is the venue chosen by the governing bodies of the respective codes for the playing of important fixtures. Continuing efforts were made to augment membership at Westmanstown by producing club brochures and promotional videos showing the benefits of club membership, which undoubtedly bore fruit.

From 1993, the position of treasurer during much of the development at Westmanstown was held by Derek Byrne. With absolute dedication and great skill, he led the fundraising initiatives. Today the Garda Recreation Club owes Derek a deep debt of gratitude for the manner in which he conducted club business to realise the dream of Westmanstown. His tenure as treasurer will be remembered as one of the most effective and successful in the history of the club.

Fundraising continued to be foremost in the thoughts of Jim Murphy and his committee after the opening of Westmanstown. By 2001, the club had a £10 million loan with AIB. The introduction of the euro in January 2002 saw the membership subscription for the Garda Recreation Club rounded off to £2.50 per week. Despite local efforts at raising money through members' draws and increasing club membership fees, the belief was there that some form of government funding might be obtained. Over the years, meetings were held and applications made to several public bodies and government departments, such as the National Lottery, Department of the Environment, and the European Community Regional Fund, often to little avail. However, a National Lottery grant of £40,000 under the sports facilities category was awarded in 1991, which went some way towards defraying development costs.

Raising the money

I was in Carrick-on-Shannon in County Leitrim when my mobile phone rang one day in summer 1993. 'Hello, Jim Murphy, chairman of the Garda Club here...'

I knew who Jim was as I had been introduced to him by Martin Callinan, then vice captain of Westmanstown Golf Club, some time previously in 1992. At that time, I had been organising a corporate golf day and had requested a flagpole to be erected to fly the corporate flag on the day, so to speak. Jim had come over to the bar to tell me in his own inimitable way that a flagpole was not a priority as the new 43,000-sq-ft clubhouse was without curtains and the car park without tarmacadam!

Now, since I had joined Westmanstown Golf Club and given my many years in the business sector, I had a pretty good grasp on how to get things done when there were so many competing forces for very scarce resources. I also knew of Jim Murphy's reputation. I told him that if he erected a flagpole, I would get the company to sponsor it. This is the language that Jim Murphy understands very well, as he is a master of extracting funds from any and all sources, and makes things happen out of apparently nothing. The fact that I had the contact details with me to give him and also the fact that the flagpole supplier was a fellow Mayo man helped expedite matters. The upshot was that not one but four state-of-the-art flagpoles adorned the entrance to the clubhouse that would not look out of place at the European Parliament Building in Brussels! I got to fly the corporate flag on a very successful golf day and Jim got the poles.

Hence the phone call from Jim inviting me to join a development subcommittee with a focus on fundraising, to which I readily agreed. This subcommittee, chaired by Jim Murphy, comprised both Garda and civilian members active in their respective clubs based at Westmanstown: golf (including the ladies), rugby, Gaelic, soccer, bowling and tennis, as well as management staff based at the centre. Within a relatively short timeframe we were recruiting people to join as social members.

The main attraction was to be a monthly members' draw. This featured attractive prizes and would be part of the first Saturday of each month's entertainment schedule, which included live music in the main bar. The line-up of monthly prizes included sun holidays, TVs and audio entertainment units, vouchers for main shops, weekend breaks, etc., with a special Christmas draw featuring a Ford Escort car. Despite the initial reluctance of some target members of having to pay €52 per year to join the draw, the draw went ahead.

Signing up their respective station colleagues in the DMA for the members' monthly draw was the task of the district representatives. At the time there were 3,500 Garda members and their weekly subscription formed the backbone and cash flow that made everything possible in the first place. Recognising that Garda members had little experience of the commercial world, many of the affiliated clubs opened their clubs to civilian members as associate non-voting members. The associate status of civilian members had no negative impact on the efficacy of the day-to-day operation of their particular club. In so far as it was possible under the mother club and affiliated clubs' constitution, in practice everybody enjoyed parity of esteem. The constitution of the mother club as set up under Ned Garvey was designed to protect the equal and absolute right of its membership to ownership of and access to all the facilities provided by the club.

In the recruitment of sponsors of the centre, it was extremely important that the right balance was struck in relation to the Garda Club as a separate but related body to the State's national police force, and the risk of any form of preferential treatment to participating sponsors engaged in the supply of goods and services to An Garda Síochána. In this regard, a carefully thought-out proposal was prepared and presented to a number of potential sponsors. These sponsors were divided into two groups: first the major sponsors for the premier prizes such as cars, foreign holidays and entertainment equipment and, secondly, minor sponsors for weekend breaks, shopping vouchers and restaurants.

The fact that the centre was located within the fastest-growing part of Europe was also exploited with regard to both personal and corporate populations within the centre's catchment area. Furthermore, we wished to capture a major sponsor that would be with us over a sustained period. This led to engaging with the then marketing director of Ford Ireland, Eddie Murphy, with a view to them becoming the main sponsor for the development of the new sports centre. After initial meetings, a deal was reached with Ford Ireland to provide a free Escort car with associated promotional support.

The relationship with Ford was always very strong with Westmanstown and the senior officers of the club, as indeed with the force, given they were major suppliers of Garda vehicles over many years. The interaction was consistently positive, professional and courteous, even when the sponsorship benefit to Ford was hard to measure. Notwithstanding this, the agreement was initially for one year. This was rolled over for the duration of the monthly members' draw, which turned out to extend to a period of five years.

The contribution that the fundraising campaigns made to the financing of the new sports centre was very important in cash-generating activities directly, such as the draw and through bar and function sales. Suffice to say, no other similar organisation in the world boasts the achievement of the club manifest in Westmanstown Sports and Leisure Centre today. And the story continues...

Conor McGuinness

Above top: Garda Representative Association personnel present an oil painting to Westmanstown.
Above: Chairman Jim Murphy accepting a presentation from Aidan O'Murchú of St Raphael's Garda Credit Union.

***Above:* 18th Green, Westmanstown Golf Club**

Westmanstown Sports and Leisure Centre

During the 1990s, it became increasingly apparent that the existing sports centre was inadequate to meet the needs of the members. That and the fact that the committee never abandoned its original objective of providing full sports facilities meant that things would not stay static for long. The decision to erect a new sports and leisure centre at Westmanstown would in time bring the Garda Recreation Club into an entirely new league. It would surpass by far what was currently available for members and their families in the line of sport and recreation.

As the cash-flow situation at Westmanstown became more manageable, serious focus was directed at the planning stages of the new sports facility. The gym facilities in particular, though limited, were in high demand at Westmanstown. It followed then that a new gym would be a key aspect of the proposed new sports building. In March 1993, St Raphael's Credit Union contributed £9,500 towards the Westmanstown Development for the gym equipment in particular. Work also began on the three tennis courts and one basketball court in March 1993, while the committee looked into the possibility of providing a lawn bowling green should there be sufficient demand for it.

Where certain sports were concerned, the committee undertook feasibility studies. For example, the Garda Handball Club and the Garda Swimming and Life-saving Club were just two clubs in particular in dire need of their own facilities. The swimming club had made representations to the Garda Recreation Club over the years but with the advance of the sports centre in 1993, Mick Feehan, on behalf of the swimming club, renewed their appeal for facilities to be incorporated into the new building. After some consideration and much discussion, sanction was finally given to commission a feasibility study at a cost of £7,000. This contract was eventually awarded to Ove Arup, a highly regarded company of consulting engineers. When the report was completed and presented to the committee in 1995, it strongly recommended the need for this facility in the Westmanstown area, and was positive about its future success. Research and discussion continued. Committee members led by chairman Jim Murphy visited almost every sports club in the country that had the type of facilities envisaged by the Garda Recreation Club. A certain amount of groundwork had also been done a decade earlier, well before the sports and leisure centre had got off the ground. In November 1986, the land subcommittee had paid a visit to the Aer Lingus Sports and Social and Athletic Association (ALSSAA) premises near Dublin Airport. This high-tech ultramodern centre had been providing a vast array of sports and leisure activities for many years to airport employees. Indeed it was the then chairman Brian Prendergast's cherished dream to provide a social and recreational complex along the lines of the ALSSAA project. The visit had afforded the committee first-hand knowledge of how a centre could operate successfully.

The development plan for the sports complex at Westmanstown was officially launched in 1995. The question of who would design and operate it was another hurdle that the committee had to surmount. A lucky break in the search came when

Tennis Club chairman Gabriel McIntyre met and discussed the matter with Prof Frank Boland, a lecturer in engineering at Trinity College, Dublin. Prof Boland knew the type of project the Garda Recreation Club had in mind and was able to point the club towards the man he felt would be up to the challenge. He strongly recommended Robbie Dolan, who acted for International Leisure Group, and who was the driving force behind Crunch Fitness, a chain of luxury health and fitness gyms. This was a fortuitous break as it enabled the chairman and his committee to visit and inspect these gyms, located at UCD, UCG, Dún Laoghaire and Aston Quay in Dublin at the time. Those inspecting the premises on behalf of the Garda Recreation Club were very impressed by the standard and the efficiency of their operation.

Robbie Dolan was very familiar with the fitness and leisure industry and was a successful operator and developer in the area. He had a lifetime's experience in design and business management. Born and reared in Dublin, he had been a promising young tennis player who attended Oatland's College in Mount Merrion. From there he won a tennis sporting scholarship to the University of Hawaii, where he graduated with a degree in business and marketing. He continued to play tennis at the highest level and represented Ireland on the Davis Cup team of 1990.

After a series of preliminary meetings with Robbie, Jim Murphy briefed the club committee and was satisfied that he had found the man that could make things happen. A further meeting between the executive committee and Robbie was arranged and matters discussed in greater detail. Design, build-time and cost were fully explored and all those present left the meeting fully satisfied that Robbie Dolan was capable of surmounting any difficulties that might lie ahead. With an awe-inspiring degree of enthusiasm and commitment, Robbie set about his task. The committee, after some long and hard bargaining, finally charged Robbie with the job of building and operating the leisure centre according to his design. The entire centre was designed jointly by him, acting for International Leisure Group, and by McDonnell & Dixon Architects. By 2001, the design had been accepted and all planning hurdles cleared. It was constructed by Manley Construction at a total cost of €7.1 million with expected annual running costs of £450,000. All specialist materials, including marble from Italy, was sourced personally and imported by Robbie. The centre was designed to cater for indoor football, tennis, badminton, basketball, handball, boxing and indoor bowling. It was to be equipped with a twenty-station gymnasium and the facilities would be complemented by a solarium, sauna, steam room and plunge pool.

It was a long arduous process bringing the plan to completion, ensuring the design, planning and construction conformed to the highest standards and securing the necessary funding. Fingal County Council, formed in 1993 under reformed local government, was consulted widely, having originally deemed the land at Westmanstown a 'priority landscape area'. Certainly, having the centre at the heart of local communities was one incentive for the club to apply to Fingal County Council for funding in 2000 to ease the financial burden of the development. The cost of the development was colossal by the standards of the day. Indeed, the entire

Westmanstown project and the numbers frequenting it were on the scale of a large village. Its reliance on the national electricity grid was considerable. Such was the extent of its operation that it invested in a generator in 1999, at a cost of £20,000.

Where Garda clubs could not be facilitated at Westmanstown, the Garda Club continued to support them through their grants system. On some occasions, it was possible to meet their needs. For example, permission was granted to the Garda Sub-Aqua Club in 1999 to build a boat and equipment house at Westmanstown, which was financed by themselves. This was on a site beside the golf shed and was officially opened on 21 April 2000.

On 10 April 2002, the then Taoiseach Mr Bertie Ahern TD laid the cornerstone of the partly constructed sports centre. He paid tribute to the Garda Recreation Club for providing a club that many people from the local community would benefit from and which was open to members and non-members alike. To mark the occasion, he was presented with a special golden trowel by Gabriel Manley of Manley Construction. The Taoiseach returned the following year on 3 February 2003 to officially open the sports club, to much fanfare. The 50,000-sq-ft centre could now boast a multi-sports complex second to none. It featured a 15,000-sq-ft gymnasium with 200 pieces of equipment with computerised fitness training programmes; a 25-metre, six-lane swimming pool with children's pool, incorporating a 35-foot cinematic screen and tropical palms. In addition, it had the unique feature of a 200-metre indoor running track overlooking the golf course.

The main sports hall could facilitate basketball, badminton, handball, indoor soccer, judo, children's gymnastics, yoga, Pilates, dance aerobics, hip-hop, spinning, step aerobics, martial arts, circuit training and a range of activities of the modern age. The changing rooms alone provided for 400 lockers, with both ladies' and gents' locker facilities with their own spa featuring jacuzzi, sauna, power showers, solarium and steam rooms. Keeping pace with the times, Peacock Beauty Salon for both men and women could offer various therapies such as spa body treatments, massage and day spas onsite. Adjoining the building were four championship floodlit grass tennis courts, where the Garda Tennis Club could provide a range of tennis programmes, tournaments and coaching for adults and children.

The final cost of the sports and leisure centre was over £10 million. With his trademark energy and efficiency, Robbie Dolan started to run the facility in 2002 on a franchise basis as Crunch Fitness. The decision was a fortuitous one for the Garda Recreation Club and it has been an unqualified success to this day.

After the opening, the drive to recruit new members for the gym got into full swing. Robbie's marketing expertise proved fruitful and in a short time he had the centre operating to full capacity. As part of the management–customer feedback policy, it was discovered that the centre lacked a family changing room. Following a number of complaints from parents, the Divisional Committee acted quickly and within a short period a family changing room was provided.

As time progressed, more and more people applied to join Crunch Fitness.

The efficiency and thorough cleanliness of the centre were impressive to many. When asked how he managed to achieve such results, Robbie replied: 'I operate all my centres on seventeen separate manuals, which represent seventeen separate systems. By doing it this way good results are always achieved.' The leisure centre continues to go from strength to strength and thankfully has not to date succumbed to recessionary pressures.

Garda Club staff: an appreciation

Down through the years the Garda Club has been very fortunate in its choice of staff. The bar staff and office staff at both Harrington Street and Westmanstown have and continue to show unfailing courtesy and cooperation in carrying out their duties. Too many to name individually, they have each contributed to making the Garda Club a home from home and ensuring a sense of conviviality prevails. A warm and heartfelt thank you is extended to them all.

'A mother to us all'

All our actions and transactions at Westmanstown were monitored and filed away by our manager at Harrington Street, Helen Corrigan. Helen was like a mother to us all and to our families. She kept us all together when there was a bit of infighting. Over the years she solved many a problem for the Recreation Club and was known to everyone.

Bosco Muldoon

Entrance to Westmanstown clubhouse

Left: Taoiseach Bertie Ahern *(second left)* officially opening the Sports and Leisure Centre in 1994 with Jim Murphy *(left)*, Mick Feehan and Brian Prendergast

Right: Mr Brian Lenihan TD *(left)* with Mick Feehan and Deputy Commissioner Nacie Rice at the opening of the Sports and Leisure Centre

Above: Attending the official opening of the Sports and Leisure Centre in 1994 were *(left to right)* Robbie Dolan, Bosco Muldoon, Dominic Power, Colm Church, Kieron McEneaney and Gary Kelly

Below: **In good spirits – members attending the official opening of the Sports and Leisure Centre in 1994: *(from left)* Jerome Twomey, John Joyce and Brian Moran**

Above: **Ladies of Westmanstown with Taoiseach Bertie Ahern: *(from left)* Deirdre Byrne, Tracy McGrath, Sinéad Cashell and Helen Corrigan in 1994**

Above: **Staff of Crunch Fitness, 2010**

Above: **Taoiseach Bertie Ahern TD officially opens Crunch Fitness at Westmanstown on 3 February 2003. (*Pictured from left*) Jim Murphy, Mick Feehan (chairman), Taoiseach Bertie Ahern, Peter Fitzgerald, Christy McCarthy and Seán Murphy**

Mick Feehan – a swimmingly good chairman

Michael (Mick) Feehan's tenure as chairman began in 2001, with Jim Murphy's retirement from the force. Mick too left an indelible mark on the Garda Recreation Club and contributed enormously to its development. Over the years he was deeply committed to furthering the membership and served on several subcommittees to that end. For example, he successfully helped to recruit members from the Garda College, Templemore and later the Dublin Metropolitan Region headquarters at Harcourt Square. In addition, he chaired at one time the membership committee of the L to W Districts, CDU & Depot.

The development of Westmanstown Sports and Leisure Centre as an ultramodern facility was central to Mick Feehan's vision. An accomplished swimmer himself, Mick was a long-standing member of the Garda Swimming and Lifesaving Club and brought great distinction to the club. He took a keen interest in developing superior sporting facilities at Westmanstown, in particular swimming amenities given the dearth available to the club. His extensive knowledge of all matters swimming proved very valuable to the Garda Recreation Club. As a result, he was instrumental in promoting the need for a feasibility study. This was eventually undertaken by consulting engineers Ove Arup and completed in 1995, giving a favourable response to the proposal.

Recognition of his dedication and capability came in 1998 when Mick was elected vice chairman of the Garda Recreation Club and subsequently chairman in 2001. The realisation of his sporting dreams soon began to take shape. His sterling efforts bore fruit on 3 February 2003, when the then Taoiseach Bertie Ahern TD officially opened Crunch Fitness at Westmanstown Sports and Leisure Centre, boasting a 25-metre, six-lane swimming pool with children's pool. The following year, on 22 November 2004, Taoiseach Ahern returned to officially reopen the considerably enhanced Westmanstown Sports and Conference Centre. It was a great and gratifying day for Mick Feehan as chairman and the Garda Recreation Club as a whole. In 2008, his tenure came to an end and he proudly passed the baton to Dave Dowling.

Banking on Westmanstown

In April 1985, I took a phone call from Mrs Helen Corrigan, administrative manager, seeking a meeting on behalf of chairman Jim Murphy, secretary Cyril Doyle and treasurer Ray McEneaney. Helen told me that they would be 'seeking to borrow a lot of money but not to worry as it will be paid back!' In my role as senior deputy manager of the branch, I managed *inter alia* a portfolio of accounts, including the Garda Recreation Club under the title of the Trustees of the Dublin Metropolitan Garda Recreation Club (DMGRC). In addition, there were the sixteen sporting clubs, all of which were allied to the umbrella organisation, namely the Garda Recreation Club, whose members contributed £1 per week from their salaries.

Helen and I arranged the meeting with Jim, Cyril and Ray for the following day. I recall the day vividly when they all arrived in, armed with a set of management accounts for 1984 and a map. The latter amused me for when Jim opened it up, it covered the entire desk in my office. It was a map of the lands encompassing Westmanstown, where they proposed to purchase lands piecemeal for the various clubs within the Garda Síochána, namely the GAA, rugby, soccer and a nine-hole pitch and putt course. Jim began by saying that they had agreed the purchase price for 48.2 acres at £240,000 and wished to borrow £200,000, in part through bridging finance and a three-year term loan, as they had £40,000 on deposit themselves with St Raphael's Garda Credit Union.

When seeking the facilities of £200,000+, we noted in our application to head office that 'we were very impressed with the executive', namely Jim, Cyril and Ray. In 1988, the next plot of land became available to Jim Murphy and colleagues, some of whom would later move on from their post as club officers. But Jim was like the Chinese leaders, he simply went on forever. This, in fact, suited the bank very much as we were always anxious to see a continuation in any organisation so that the various parts were held together and all transitions were seamless. In February 1988, they had negotiated the purchase of a further 30.5 acres for £160,000. At this juncture they had £60,000 on deposit and £100,000 over two years at £4,460 a month.

The club having 4,300 members was central to any borrowing and repayment, as members paid £1 per week deducted from their salaries at source and it was paid directly by the Department of Justice to DMGRC. It was the total source of a bank borrowing repayment and constituted planned taking rather than planned giving. It meant that the club could repay the previous £200,000 ahead of time. The initial plans drawn up were for a spend of £2.37 million by way of two/three project stages of £1 million each. These project stages envisioned an extensive sports centre on the lands, which were

Dublin Metropolitan Garda Recreation Club
8 - 10 Harrington Street, Dublin 8.

Telephone : 4756028 / 4781505 / 4753764
Fax : 4750420

17th, September 2001.

Mr Liam O'Brien,
Manager,
AIB Bank,
Dame Street,
Dublin 2.

Re : Loan for Development of Westmanstown Sports Centre.

Dear Liam,

I outline hereunder a certified copy of the minutes of the meeting of the Divisional Committee of the Garda Recreation Club, held on the 13th, September 2001, at which a quorum was present.

The Chairman Jim Murphy proposed that we obtain a loan from Allied Irish Bank, Dame Street, of £10M for the purpose of developing our leisure/sports centre at Westmanstown, at the terms agreed with the bank as follows – The interest rate charged will be the EURIBOR rate plus 1%, repayable over 25 years at the following monthly repayments. From 2003 to 2006 @ £54,000. From 2006 to 2028 @ £63,139 per month.

The proposal which was seconded by the Treasurer Derek Byrne was unanimously carried by the meeting.

I trust that the above is sufficient for your records.

Yours sincerely,

Christy McCarthy
Hon Secretary.

close to the M50 and M4. The Garda Club executive was confident of the land acquisition and no more of it was being made. At the time, the economy was in a poor state with high interest rates (12 per cent for a three-year term loan), high inflation and high unemployment, with the brain drain being our biggest export at the time. Hence, there was no appetite for either bank borrowing by the customers or lending by the banks, despite the latter being our bread and butter. Therefore, the Garda loan repayment was very welcome. Ironically, there is a bank philosophy that says 'a lender should be more cautious in good times and more risk-orientated in bad times'. It is a pity this school of thought has not been followed in the recent past.

At the time of the latest request, the Garda Club had a small profit of £65,000 for the six months to September 1987 and an increased projected £120,000 profit for the twelve months to April 1988. This was very considerable when seeking funds to purchase a capital asset, especially land. The application to head office carried my strongest recommendation on behalf of the branch for several reasons: the excellent account history since 1961; our confidence in the management of the trustees, officers and committee members; the repayment capacity clearly evident through the 'planned taking system'; and the substantial collateral advantages of the now eighteen other connected accounts, i.e. the various other Garda sporting bodies that banked with AIB.

At the branch level, we were now laying the foundations for large proposals to come our way as the sports centre project, while not 'shovel ready', was on its way in terms of architects, plans, designs and so forth. In May 1988, a further 7.4 acres was purchased and plans were being committed to paper to allow for a 9/18 hole pitch and putt course, five playing pitches, bowling, tennis grounds and a car park. Within twelve months, by May 1989, 129 acres in total were purchased; £250,000 had been spent on 8/9/10 Harrington Street; plans for a leisure centre comprising 3,440 square metres costing £2.75 million had been approved by the club members. An application to the National Lottery for £400,000 was made and £40,000 was subsequently received. In addition, an increase in member subscriptions per week of £2 was sought. In April 1989, a facility was sought of £360,000, which was sanctioned by the bank for the purchase of 43 acres and the refurbishment of Harrington Street over seven years at £6,210 per month.

To appreciate the effect of the high interest rates obtaining in Ireland at the time, we wrote to the Garda Club in April 1990 advising that when considering the various levels of repayments against a borrowing level of £1.07m, £2.07m, £2.5m, they should do so against an existing interest rate of 15 per cent as there was a strong likelihood of rates remaining high for some period. At the time the Deutsche mark interest rate was 10.25 per cent.

Also in March 1991, the bank, armed with all the information required, sanctioned a facility of £2.5 million over twenty-five years, with repayment of £27,750 per month. Central to the sanction of the facility was that, firstly, for the lands acquired and developed to a total cost of £1.3 million, it had been totally funded by the members themselves over the period 1985–1991, and that 3,400 members had contributed £1.50 per week, thus contributing £265,000 per annum.

In March 1992, when figures were finally tied down, the bank sanctioned £3.07 million over twenty-five years at prime (Central Bank) rate plus 0.75 per cent. At this time 12.5 per cent was subject to repayment of £30,965 per month, which was £1,000 per day for the next twenty-five years. In sanctioning the facility at the time, the bank wondered about the ability to realise the security if it became necessary. At branch level we conceded the overall project would be well managed and controlled with 'reasonable men at the helm'. Thus, the project got under way with the funding in place, which *inter alia* included a bar measuring 120 feet in length. When completed during the 1990s, the entire building project comprising all it was intended to encompass was indeed very impressive and an absolute credit to all involved.

While continuing to generate good profits in both Harrington Street and Westmanstown, the Garda Club in the late 1990s borrowed a further £600,000 to refurbish Harrington Street. This was an easy decision for the bank given falling interest rates, and with loan repayments remaining as initially set out, there only remained £700,00 ahead in repayments – every bank's dream when seeking additional facilities.

With Jim Murphy as chairman and Derek Byrne as the very active treasurer, it was to be expected that they would not rest on their laurels for too long. Thus it was that the largest sporting complex was committed to a drawing in 2001 costing in total £10 million, which would be the culmination of Westmanstown for the Garda Club members and their families. The putting in place of the £10 million in total resulted in many meetings between Jim, Derek, Michael, Christy and the bank through myself in the branch and my colleagues in the bank centre, all of whom were very helpful in the process. It was to allow the project to precede a total facility of €12.7 million, which was sanctioned in January 2003, and had to be repaid over thirty years at the rate of €67,000 per month.

When I retired from the bank in June 2005, the project had been completed, was up and running and everything was going according to plan. Suffice to say I was delighted to have been a part of it from 1985 to 2005.

Liam O'Brien, Allied Irish Bank

Sporting success

Not only did the chairmen and committees see the realisation of the buildings, pitches and golf course but also sporting success. Within a short period, the Garda AFC was promoted to playing the Leinster Senior League; the GAA Senior team joined the ranks of Dublin League champions, while the Garda RFC came close to achieving senior status. On completion of the building work in 2003, Westmanstown became an attractive venue at international level. The first such group to avail of the facilities was the Irish athletes taking part in the Special Olympics World Summer Games hosted in Ireland in 2003. The facilities at Westmanstown were made available to these Irish athletes in the run-up to the games and all fees were waived. In November 2008, the All-Blacks used the rugby facilities at Westmanstown for training sessions in the European leg of their autumn tour to great satisfaction. It was truly a coming-of-age for the splendid grounds and facilities. To the present day Westmanstown continues to serve the sporting needs of not just members of An Garda Síochána but also builds a bond of unity between Garda members and the local communities in West Dublin, as well as nationally and internationally.

A chairman to remember: Jim Murphy

Successful leaders share three abilities. The first is the ability to get along with others and build teams. Another is the ability to make sound and timely decisions. And the third is the ability to get things done. Such were the attributes that Jim Murphy brought to his role as chairman of the Garda Recreation Club committee from 1987 to 2001.

In 1964, Jim joined An Garda Síochána as part of the recruitment campaign of the 1960s. Previously, he had sharpened his bartering and bargaining skills in the highways and byways of Mayo, while manning a travelling shop that supplied families with vital weekly provisions. As a keen Gaelic footballer, Jim also had won a west Mayo title in 1960 with his club, Ballintubber. But his entry to the force saw him transfer his allegiance to the Garda GAA Club. His association with the GAA has been a huge influence in what later became an all-consuming ambition to see sporting facilities provided for members of An Garda Síochána.

During the 1970s, Jim participated in helping out at bingo sessions, the Saturday night cabaret and other functions in the Garda Recreation Club. With his eye on an administrative role, he succeeded in being elected to the committee as a district representative for E District in 1979. In his new role, Jim threw himself into fundraising and became an active member of the bingo group. He was also part of a subcommittee responsible for running the dances at Harrington Street. The Thursday night 'Big Band' dances were especially famous and Jim met and negotiated with many well-known bands of the day, who drew huge crowds to Harrington Street. This resulted in considerable money being saved with a view to purchasing suitable land when it became available. In 1983, Jim became vice chairman of the committee. This was at a time when the club was picking itself up after the traumatic period of 'the Garvey Affair'. As vice chairman between 1983 and 1987, Jim played an important role in helping to resolve and bring about a win-win outcome in the impasse surrounding Ned Garvey's litigation case against the Garda Club. It was all achieved through Jim's trademark skills of negotiation, consultation and compromise.

With all eyes then looking to the future, the goal was to buy suitable land to further the sporting aims of the force. Jim knew at first hand the importance of the Garda GAA Club having their own playing pitch if they were ever to take their place seriously in the competitive scene. Years of being boarded out had not helped any of the field sports within the club. On 28 January 1987, Brian Prendergast stepped down as chair of the committee and Jim assumed the position.

When the 48.2 acres of land came up for sale at Westmanstown that year, Jim, along with the other officers of the committee, went to the bank to seek the very best terms to borrow money. For the first time years of planning, negotiating and hard work were coming to fruition. Jim was as ever totally committed and even interrupted his time in the GAA tour in America to look up Gerry Flynn in New York, one of the brothers subsequently selling more Westmanstown land. Jim, as it turned out, was instrumental in getting an extra bit of land and at a more favourable price too. He truly never lost an opportunity to fight for and put forward the needs of the club on all occasions.

As chairman from 1987 to 2001 – years coinciding with incredible growth in the Irish economy – Jim oversaw the planning, financing, building and establishing the direction of the Westmanstown complex. Having set up various subcommittees, he succeeded in motivating and inspiring, while at the same time establishing a climate where strong committee members pooled their expertise in the achievement of their goals. Highly committed, Jim would let nothing get in the way of achieving the aims of the Garda Club committee. His meetings with the design teams for the Westmanstown projects, builders, suppliers and, in particular, bankers were legendary – and much feared by those who did not have their homework done or were not up-to-date with their answers!

The influence on sport and provision of sporting facilities that Jim wields is also reflected in his support of the annual challenge match in Gaelic football between An Garda Síochána and the PSNI for the Thomas St George McCarthy Cup. His talents were recognised in 1987, when he was presented with a Coiste Siamsa Silver Jubilee Award for Gaelic football. Working tirelessly to provide sporting facilities, he was again honoured by Coiste Siamsa in 1998 with a sports administrator award. In conclusion, Jim's contribution to the Garda Recreation Club will be forever associated with Westmanstown, and his dedication to the provision of facilities for the Garda members will be long remembered.

Above: Officers and committee members unveiling a portrait of chairman Jim Murphy by artist Pat Phelan in 1997

Tribute to Jim Murphy

The chairman Mick Feehan paid a glowing tribute to the outgoing chairman, Jim Murphy. He stated that Jim had single-handedly driven the Westmanstown project and brought it to what it is today. He said that all members of the force present and future owe him a great debt of gratitude for the work done over a long number of years on behalf of the club.

Minutes of annual general meeting, Dublin Metropolitan Garda Recreation Club, 15 October 2001

Above: Taoiseach Bertie Ahern *(right)* officially reopening Westmanstown Sports and Conference Centre on 22 November 2004, accompanied by club chairman Mick Feehan

This Sporting Life

Sports Clubs at Westmanstown

Chapter

8

Sport is human life in microcosm.

Chapter 8
This Sporting Life

THE Garda Club dream of catering to a host of different sports became a reality with the advent of Westmanstown. What initially began as a home for sports such as golf, GAA, rugby and soccer soon burgeoned to include tennis, bowls, basketball and swimming. Other leisure pursuits such as bridge and general fitness also met the needs of the ever-growing community in the catchment area. Year after year the clubs went from strength to strength with their achievements gaining recognition and praise. Today the Westmanstown Sports Complex is regarded as one of the best in the country, catering for all major sports. Here some of the clubs chronicle their proud association with Westmanstown.

Garda GAA Club

The Garda GAA Club has had an illustrious history within the wider story of the Gaelic Athletic Association. Its origins go back to the foundation of the State and that of An Garda Síochána. Fuelled by the extraordinary zeal, patriotism and love of sports of Commissioner Eoin O'Duffy when he took over the force in September 1922, Gaelic games became an integral part of Garda life. Through his influence and efforts, to ensure that good footballers joined An Garda Síochána and were attached to stations in Dublin and could play for the Garda team, the club grew strong. The 1920s are best remembered for being the golden years of Garda hurling in Dublin. In the twentieth century, the Garda GAA Club was the only club to win five senior championships in a row, from 1925 to 1929 and also had a memorable win in 1931.

For many decades since 1923, long before Westmanstown was ever conceived, the home ground for the Garda GAA Club was a pitch in the Phoenix Park. Indeed for a period, since the reorganisation of the club, the pitch was shared with the Garda soccer and rugby clubs, a unique occurrence in GAA circles! Despite the cordial relationships between the clubs, it was not uncommon for players to turn out for games on Sunday mornings only to find the soccer pitch badly dug up and, of course, the reverse also often happened. Consequently, the GAA Club desperately yearned for a ground of its own. Over the years, the GAA committee made two failed attempts, one beside the Foxhunter Pub in Lucan and the other to the rear of the Halfway House, to purchase a suitable site for the purpose of developing its own exclusive pitches. For one reason or another, none of these efforts bore fruit. In 1985, however, club activist and later chairman PJ Gallagher noticed fifty acres of land for sale at Westmanstown, Clonsilla. This was on the back road between Clonsilla and Lucan and in a quiet agricultural area. It certainly appeared to be suitable for the needs of a developing GAA Club. With fellow committee member George Heneghan, PJ approached the auctioneers with a view to acquiring sufficient acreage for the needs of the club. There was an initial reluctance on the part of the vendor to divide the land, but eventually the auctioneers offered the Gardaí sixteen acres for an asking price of £86,000. An exorbitant sum of money in the mid-1980s!

At the same time the Dublin Metropolitan Garda Recreation Club at Harrington Street was looking for land to build a sports club. It so happened that their vice chairman, Jim Murphy, was also chairman of the GAA Club, so it was not too surprising that both committees got together and went to view the land at Westmanstown. After some discussion, the Garda GAA Club withdrew its proposal to buy and the full fifty acres were purchased subsequently by the Recreation Club. In return, as outlined in the previous chapter, three smaller lots were sold on: one to the GAA Club, one to the Soccer Club and one to the Rugby Club. Initially there were many long, sometimes heated, meetings between the parent body, chaired by Brian Prendergast, and the three clubs. Jim Murphy, George Heneghan and PJ battled for the GAA Club, Gus Keating and the late Paddy Coffey for the Soccer Club, and Gabriel Bradley and the late George Trenier for the Rugby Club, and indeed many others as well. Despite one or two sceptics talking about the 'white elephants in the middle of nowhere', goodwill won out and Westmanstown Sports Complex was born. The GAA Club purchased nine acres and developed two pitches of the highest standard with a substantial drainage programme undertaken from the beginning. The first match played at the grounds was against Synge Street on 2 October 1988. It was a memorable and joyous occasion, not least because the Garda GAA Club emerged victorious with a score of 1-9 to 1-4.

The club has certainly been fortunate in its choice of groundsmen, first, George Heneghan, who was there from the start. A proud and likeable Mayo man, he was a great loss to the club when he decided to emigrate to Australia with his family in 1991. George served the club with distinction through many years as a player, trainer, mentor, linesman and umpire. He is greatly missed to this day. Since his departure, the position has been filled by Jerome Twomey from Cork, who has kept the grounds in pristine condition with much care and dedication. The club is very lucky to have had two dedicated men to perform such a demanding task.

On 21 May 1998, Commissioner MP Byrne unveiled a plaque at the grounds to mark the seventy-fifth anniversary of the very first football championship match in which the Garda Club took part. This had been played in May 1923 against Milltown Emmets. On the anniversary, the grounds were blessed by Fr Hilarian Cleary CP, chaplain to An Garda Síochána. A challenge game was staged, appropriately against St Vincent's, the Garda Club's great rivals.

The Garda GAA Club has benefited greatly from the move to Westmanstown. It is now fielding five adult teams: three men's teams and two ladies' teams. The ladies' section was formed in December 1997. In 2004, Westmanstown Gaels – the juvenile section of the club – was formed under the chairmanship of George Kyne, assisted by Grace O'Boyle and Brian Keville. This is certainly the way forward for the club's future, drawing children from the West Dublin area and members' children from around the city.

Further plans for the ground are already in place to add to its established reputation and make it an even greater source of pride for the GAA Club and, indeed, for every member of the force. The club was successful in obtaining a grant from the 2007 Sports Capital Programme towards a synthetic all-weather training pitch and flood lighting. It was officially opened by Minister for Finance Mr Brian Lenihan TD in December 2008. This feature is available to all members as well as club members. In the long term, the local community, through the club's commitment to Westmanstown Gaels, will use the facilities. The year 2009 was also a memorable one for the GAA Club at Westmanstown. It celebrated the 125th anniversary of the GAA with a special Mass, in which the Westmanstown Gaels played a unique part. Today the magnificent complex is a credit to all those who have given their time and energy to its growth since 1985.

PJ Gallagher

Above: Chairman of Garda GAA Club, Michael O'Connor presenting the Tom Langan Memorial Cup to Commissioner Edmund Garvey, flanked by Jim Murphy *(left)*, Assistant Commissioner Enright and W McGee *(right)*

Above: **Garda GAA Dublin Metropolitan Area team in the 1970s**

Above: **Bobby Howick of Guinness Ireland (*second right*) making a presentation to the winners and runners-up of the Garda/Guinness Tournament, flanked by Garda Club chairman Edmund Garvey (*right*)**

A PRO to remember: Jim Dunne

Reflecting on the history of the Garda Club also means thinking of those who offered support and friendship in those early years, helping the club to grow and develop. Jim Dunne, sadly now passed away, was one such figure. An *Irish Times* journalist, originally from County Tipperary, Jim began his career with the *Irish Press* and later became editor of *Business & Finance* magazine. It was during these years that he struck up enduring friendships with several members of the Gardaí.

He played his part in one of the most noteworthy ventures the club embarked upon over three decades – the Garda/Guinness tournament in Gaelic football, which was organised from 1977 to 1986. The idea of the tournament originated from lively talk, often over a pint or two in Bowes of Fleet Street. But the decision to actually organise the tournament and get it off the ground soon followed. At this period in the club's history the football team had not been having the best of fortune and some of the officials felt it would be a major boost to morale if the team was pitted against some of the best clubs in the country. Jim Dunne joined the organising committee along with Michael Enright, then chairman of the Garda Club, and later chairman Jim Murphy, who filled the position of committee secretary as the competition launched in August 1977. Some years ago Jim Dunne recalled his sourcing of the pivotal sponsor for the competition.

'I used to meet the detectives from Pearse Street in Bowes and through *Business & Finance* I had business contacts, so when the decision was made I found the club a sponsor,' he said. 'The first port of call was to Guinness and I discovered that Guinness were delighted to become involved with the Garda and the GAA. As far as I can remember the first sponsorship was £5,000, which was substantial at the time, and the winning team got a set of Omega watches.'

It had been the wish of the club to project a favourable image of An Garda Síochána through its activities and the committee believed it achieved this in great measure with the successful football tournament. Initially, eight clubs were involved in the competition but by 1979, this had doubled to sixteen. Indeed, the tournament filled an important void in the football calendar throughout the late 1970s and early 1980s. Difficulties and confusion surrounding sponsorship from alcohol companies eventually spelt the demise of the tournament. However, there was some later additional success in the sponsorship stakes with the backing of the club by CMI, a forerunner to Chorus.

Jim's interest in and support for the club and expanding plans for Westmanstown continued and he remained unofficial PRO for the Garda GAA Club for many years.

Clare Murphy

Above: **PSNI and Garda GAA battle it out for the Thomas St George McCarthy Cup in 2009**

Above: **Phil Markey, chairman of the Dublin County Board, presenting the Dublin Division 1 League cup surrounded by a victorious Garda GAA team**

THE GARDA SÍOCHÁNA FLAG FLYING BESIDE THE PSNI (PHOTO:PHOTOCALL IRELAND)

(L-R) THE GARDA SÍOCHÁNA COMMISSIONER PAT BYRNE, GARDA PLAYER JOHN KEANE, REF SEAN FINNUCANE, PSNI GAA PLAYER DAMIAN TURKER AND PSNI CHIEF CONSTABLE (PHOTO:PHOTOCALL IRELAND)

GARDA COMMISSIONER PAT BYRNE RECEIVES THE MCCARTHY CUP FROM CHIEF CONSTABLE HUGH ORDE. (PHOTO: PHOTOCALL IRELAND)

HISTORIC AND SYMBOLIC GAA MATCH

GAA history was made on October 30th 2002, when a Garda GAA team played an inaugural Gaelic football match against the Police Service of Northern Ireland GAA team. The game was played at Westmanstown on the outskirts of Dublin. This is the first match of its kind since the abolition of Rule 21 by the Gaelic Athletic Association - which had banned members of the security forces in Northern Ireland from playing the game. This rule was abolished in November last year after campaigning by reformers, and the signing of the Good Friday Agreement.

The game was watched by Commissioner Pat Byrne, PSNI Chief Constable Hugh Orde and officers from both police services, but was not generally open to the public, as PSNI officers had expressed reservations about their safety. The Minister for Justice, Mr Michael McDowell was also in attendance, sporting a pair of shiny green wellies. The PSNI team was not named, there was no team picture and the media were asked to refrain from taking pictures during the game. Though some pictures of players entering the field were published in the national press - defeating the object of the media blackout on the field of play.

The match was symbolic of the close relationship between the two forces. Garda leaked an early goal, but were soon scoring at will; ending the first half with a considerable lead. However, this lead was whittled away in the second-half, until the PSNI team were back into the game, especially when they scored their second goal - the result of a muddy goalmouth scramble. Garda then pulled clear again, scoring the final four points without reply.

GARDA Síochána 1-18 PSNI 2-8

At the press conference afterwards, Commissioner Pat Byrne admitted that he did get the jitters in the second half as the PSNI team began to catch up, and the Chief Constable started to smile. There were also some doubts about the impartiality of the referee - a member of the Gardai. Commissioner Byrne quipped (tongue in cheek) that this could be a matter for the Garda Complaints Board.

Chief Constable Hugh Orde said, "This is a symbolic step forward. Because of attacks on officers from the catholic community - the game was played 'behind closed doors' to reflect some of their concerns. There are sensitivities because of some of the lads' welfare.

"The reality is, it will take time to become fully integrated. The most important thing is that the team was here, and they played. It is yet another step forward in the peace process.

"I believe that, in time, this game will have a significance far beyond its sporting context. Today's match continues a long tradition of friendly rivalry between our two police services."

Chief Constable Hugh Orde presented Commissioner Pat Byrne with the McCarthy Cup. George McCarthy, a member of the Royal Irish Constabulary, was one of the founder members of the GAA movement.

Above: **The *Garda Review* records the historic Gaelic football match between Garda GAA and the PSNI in 2002**

Above: **Garda GAA Club, winners of the Intermediate Championship in 1986, pictured in 2011**

Above: **Garda GAA Club, 2011**

Above: **Garda GAA Ladies team, 2011**

Westmanstown Gaels

Since the Garda GAA Club's move to Westmanstown in 1988, the formation of a juvenile section had been suggested several times. The notion of a juvenile section was motivated by a number of factors, including the desire that the club should develop the Gaelic Athletic Association in West Dublin. At the time many Garda members were living in Lucan, Clonsilla and nearby areas, and it was felt that the GAA Club could provide Gaelic games for their children together with children from the local community.

It was also a fact of life that a large number of the club's players had become involved with other clubs (including clubs within the GAA Club's own locality) after their playing days were over. This was largely because the club had no juvenile section and, consequently, they became involved with other clubs with their children. It meant that the club was losing most of its people when they finished playing. This was reflected at committee level especially, where it was always difficult to get people who had completed their playing days to stay on with the club. Indeed it became impossible to fill the committee without asking players to become involved.

A further issue that was obvious to the officers of the club was the usage of the grounds by its teams. The club is very proud of its facilities in Westmanstown but alas they were not being utilised to their optimum. The two full-size pitches saw teams playing on average about thirty-five to forty matches a year, which did not equate to one game a week on one pitch. The club felt strongly that the local community could use the facilities, and in the process expand the club and Gaelic games. Between 2002 and 2005, George Kyne was chairman of the club and in 2003 he produced a document on this matter. It was discussed at a special meeting of the club committee in September of that year, where the committee agreed to start a juvenile section and submit a proposal to the AGM. At this meeting, the following December, a proposal to start a juvenile section was proposed by George Kyne and seconded by John Kane. The proposal was unanimously adopted by the membership and the juvenile section came into being.

The committee then turned its attention to the naming of the juvenile section. It was agreed by all present that it should not be called Garda for obvious reasons. After much discussion, the meeting agreed with the suggestion by John O'Mahoney that the new club should be attached to the Westmanstown complex in some way, and thus 'Westmanstown Gaels' was born. The new section was duly registered with Dublin County Board, who met with club officials and allocated the club its catchment area. A number of people in the Garda GAA Club offered their services to this new section: George Kyne took on the role of chairman, Grace O'Boyle became secretary and Enda Mulryan treasurer.

The officers got down to work in earnest in 2004 to develop the fledgling club. Help was on hand from Gerard O'Connor on the county board, who gave the Gaels a number of coaches to run a summer camp. The new club was advertised during the summer that year and its first summer camp held from 9 to 13 August. Co-ordinated by Mary Galvin, the camp was a great success, with fifty-seven children in attendance. From this group, members were recruited. The first day of the club proper was Saturday, 11 September, when thirty-four children came and joined Westmanstown Gaels. As everyone involved with Westmanstown Gaels was new to running a juvenile section, it employed Mary Galvin to oversee the running of its training sessions on Saturday mornings. Having access to the hall in Crunch Fitness was an added boon, as it could cater for the nursery section every Saturday morning.

Within a short space of time the club was fielding a team. On November 2004, its under-8 boys had their first challenge match against Lucan Sarsfields. On the day, Sean Egan had the distinction of becoming Westmanstown Gaels' first scorer, when he put over a point. The following week the girls had their first challenge against St Peregrine's of Clonsilla. Towards the end of November that year the club was allocated funding from the county board, as part of the schools coaching programme, to send a coach into the local schools to recruit children into the new section. Ciara Lowry was the club's first coach and her appointment proved very successful with a significant increase in numbers.

In January 2005, the club held its first annual general meeting with about thirty parents in attendance. A committee was elected and the previous officers re-elected: George Kyne as chairman, Grace O'Boyle as secretary and Enda Mulryan as treasurer. Over the following months, the section consolidated even more when its numbers increased to approximately seventy-five children. This allowed the club to enter a team in the juvenile leagues in Dublin at under-9 with the boys and at under-12 with the girls. On Saturday, 5 March 2005, Westmanstown Gaels' under-8 boys took to the field for the first time against Lucan Sarsfields in the GAA's Go Games. While they went on to lose that match, this panel of boys nonetheless went from strength to strength. They had a very good first season and a promising future ahead. Meanwhile, the under-10 girls started their league campaign on 9 April 2005 at home to Templeogue Synge Street. They had a very mixed season but the players all showed improvement and displayed great team spirit when they were together. Two of the older girls, Robyn Swan and Larissa Stanciu, made the Dublin under-12 Development Squad that year, a huge achievement for two girls who had never played football before.

By 2005, membership of the club was at the 100 mark with only six children having been with a previous club. On 28 June 2005, the official launch of the club took place at Westmanstown. It was attended by the GAA president, Mr Sean Kelly; the Garda Commissioner, Mr Noel Conroy; chairman of St Raphael's Credit

Officials from the Garda GAA Club and children of Westmanstown Gaels at the opening of its all-weather pitch in 2008. Also pictured are former Minister for Finance Mr Brian Lenihan TD, who performed the official opening, and former Garda Commissioner Fachtna Murphy

Above: Fr Joe Kennedy *(third from right)* blessing the new all-weather pitch in 2008, accompanied by *(left to right)* Jim Murphy, George Kyne, Nacie Rice, Frank White, Brian Keville, Revd Andrew Orr and *(on left of Fr Kennedy)* Gerry Harrington and Garda Commissioner Fachtna Murphy

Westmanstown Gaels chairman George Kyne *(right)* presenting a prize to Padraic Brogan. Also pictured are *(back row, left to right)* John Stenston, Eddie Martin and Brian Keville with Grace O'Boyle and Geraldine Culloty in the foreground

Union, Mr Dermot Hobbs; Dublin County Board delegates; and the Sam Maguire Cup. At the launch, Dermot Hobbs of St Raphael's Credit Union announced their sponsorship of Westmanstown Gaels, much to the gratitude of the club. Indeed this section is now very successful with a membership in excess of 150 children playing for Westmanstown Gaels. The club today fields boys' teams at under-8, under-9 and under-10, and a girls team at under-12.

The club is fortunate to have a vibrant committee that run clubs affairs. Geraldine Culloty is the child liaison officer and oversees the implementation of the Code of Best Practice for Youth Sport, now a requirement of the GAA. Brian Keville has taken over the job of treasurer and John Stenson is the vice chairman. The committee produces a quarterly newsletter replete with news and information for parents and interested parties. Fundraising too has become an integral part of club activities. In particular, a fundraiser in Harold's Cross Greyhound Stadium is run each year to raise funds for the section. In the space of seven years the progress of the club has been remarkable. And provision has also been made to hold on to such talented young people when they come of age. The constitution of the Garda GAA Club has been amended to reflect the new section, with children from Westmanstown Gaels feeding naturally into the adult club when they become eighteen.

The section has certainly fulfilled its purpose of providing Gaelic games to children and members of An Garda Síochána living in this locality. Its future is very secure in the hands of these fine young people.

George Kyne

Garda Rugby Football Club (RFC)

Though rugby is a sport long associated with An Garda Síochána and the Dublin Metropolitan Police, it was only in 1965 that the Garda Rugby Football Club was founded. Back in 1965 it so happened that a number of Garda members, better known as rugby enthusiasts, felt there was sufficient young rugby material within the force stationed in the Dublin Metropolitan Division to form a rugby club. A meeting was held in Pearse Street Station with a reasonable attendance of all ranks, and the first rugby committee was elected to steer the club's future activities. The members of that committee included its first president William Halloran, vice president Dave Devaney and honorary secretary Pat O'Shea.

Application was made to the Leinster Branch and with the help of the late Judge Conroy the club was affiliated in September 1965. The first friendly game ever held was against a team from Bective Rangers and played in the Army Grounds in the Phoenix Park – the reason being that there were no showers in the Garda Grounds at the time. The match resulted in a draw but it is worth noting that the game was played on the full Gaelic pitch (how times have changed!). In the 1966/67 season, the club played junior competitive rugby for the first time and won their section of the league.

Deputy Commissioner Eamonn Doherty *(centre)*
leading the Garda RFC on a tour of the Far East in 1982

Check-in Area 1
Desk 9
Aer Lingus
Desk 10
Aer Lingus
Aer Lingus
Aer Lingus
Aer Lingus

The club was based in the Garda Grounds in the Phoenix Park for many years and great credit is owed to the enthusiasm of the players of the time, as the goalposts had to be erected before each game and taken down afterwards. In those early days the club was coached by the late great Gordon Wood, who propped for Ireland and the Lions and father to the legendary Keith Wood. In the mid-1970s, Gordon put up a trophy that is played for between the Garda and the Defence Forces each year and is attended by a member of the Wood family. From the Phoenix Park, the club moved to Blackhall Place, from where it was coached for a number of years by the late Ian Cairnduff. Then it was on to Armagh Road where the pitch was located behind the convent schools. There the club was blessed with many happy days and good memories, before moving to its present home at Westmanstown.

The club quickly became widely known, not alone locally but particularly by other police forces in England, Scotland, Wales and France as well as the then RUC, who were all seeking invitations for games. The club's first game outside Leinster was at the invitation of Dave Davidson (father of Jeremy Davidson, Ulster and Ireland lock), who was the PT instructor at the RUC Training Depot in Enniskillen. The fixture continued for many years but was set aside during the Troubles, though it was revived in 1994 and continues to this day with the PSNI. It is worth noting that over the past few years a combined Garda/PSNI team has been established and played their first match against the Leinster Juniors. They went on to enter the Cyprus International 10s and won the competition twice. Other annual trophies played include the Jim Doyle Trophy, the Crowley Cup and the Travaskis Cup.

Since that first venture to Enniskillen, the club has toured widely in England, Scotland and Wales, and competed a number of occasions in the Bill Marshall Police 7s in Edinburgh, reaching the finals four times and winning in the third year. In 1982, fifty-three members of the club undertook a three-week tour of the Far East, including Hong Kong, Singapore and Thailand. It was highly successful as they won all five matches. The club also toured in the USA, visiting Boston, Chicago and New York, then to Trinidad and Tobago in 1990 and three years later to Argentina.

On the home front, the club has had mixed fortunes over the years; its first trophy was the O'Connell Cup in 1968. In the late 1980s, the club was coached by Jim Lowrey and in 1986, for the first time in the history of the club, it was invited to play senior rugby in the Leinster Cup. Thus, on 29 March 1986 it played Old Wesley at Donnybrook. The most successful years were the early 1990s when the club won the Spencer Cup four years in a row from 1990 to 1993 and again in 2001 and 2004. Since the start of the Leinster League, with the exception of two seasons, the club has been in Division 1.

In 2005, there was a most welcome addition to the club – a ladies team commenced playing under the banner of the Garda RFC. They had a good start to their season, which they built on in subsequent seasons. Annual fixtures have also been arranged against the PSNI and the Defence Forces to coincide with the male games. The club is fundamentally an open club for both male and female teams, but on the occasion of games against other police forces or the annual game against the Defence Forces, then an all-Garda team is selected.

For many a year, the club has been honoured by the selection of a number of players on the junior interprovincial team and have contributed to the selection committee. Down through the years, members have also been active in the Referees Association, and the junior secretary of the Leinster Branch for several years was Ray Campion, a founder member of the club. Today the facilities at Westmanstown are state-of-the-art and improving each year. Such is the high standard, they have been used in recent years by the Leinster Branch for Senior and Junior Schools Games for the Leinster junior interprovincial squad-training and, more recently, by the New Zealand All Blacks touring team.

The club had a very successful season in 2011. The first XV won the Leinster League Division 1B title and thus gained promotion to Division 1A. The second XV also moved up to a higher division as a result. The women's team did the club proud by winning the Leinster League Division 3 title and were promoted to represent Garda Rugby in Division 2 North of the Women's All Ireland League.

The marvellous condition of the pitches over the years can be attributed to one man, the late George Trenier, who was a veritable legend in his own time. Apart from his work on the playing surface, his contribution to the administration of the club could not be quantified. He is sadly missed by all who knew him.

With the promised enlargement of the force, the club hopes to attract more players and looks forward to a bright future of continued success to it and its brother footballing clubs at Westmanstown. Finally, the club owes a deep debt of gratitude to the Westmanstown committee for their hard work and dedication to maintaining the high standards that have been set from the opening of the facility in 1985, and for which the club is forever grateful.

Ray Campion

George Trenier

The late George Trenier was certainly a force to be reckoned with. As a committee member and as an active member of the Garda Rugby Club, George kept his finger on the pulse of creating a first-class sports facility for the members. He was always supportive of the executive and added flavour to committee meetings with his frequent questioning of discussions.

When the land at Westmanstown was acquired, George spent all of his spare time working very hard there. On one occasion, he came along to find a man cutting down one of two big trees behind what is now the clubhouse. He nearly went berserk he was so infuriated. The remaining big tree in that area is now a feature of the golf course design and at Christmas time is always lit up. It constantly reminds us of George and is referred to as 'George's Tree'.

George knew every square foot of the land at Westmanstown and looked after it as if it were his own. He could be found in his spare time planting hedging or clearing ground. When he retired from An Garda Síochána, he took up a position at the club where he looked after the general maintenance of both the grounds and the clubhouse and saw to it that everything was kept in good order.

Yes, George was a force to be reckoned with. He was funny, loyal, hard-working and above all a proud member who saw the dream realised at Westmanstown. Today, a plaque on a finely carved wooden bench fronting the clubhouse commemorates his wonderful association with Westmanstown. Likewise, the George Trenier Memorial Cup was instituted in 2009 by the Garda RFC in his honour.

He is very much missed. Rest in peace.

Helen Corrigan

Right: George Trenier bench

Above: Garda RFC v Irish Army, 1992

Above: George Trenier *(far left)* with members and guests of the Garda Rugby Club at the opening of the clubhouse in 1992

bove: The All Blacks train at Westmanstown during their World Tour in 2008

Above: Club president Ray Campion presenting All Blacks captain Richie McCaw with a Garda Rugby Club plaque after a training session at Westmanstown in November 2008

Above: Garda RFC in action in 2009

Above: Garda RFC in November 2009

Above: The George Trenier Memorial Cup 2009, proudly presented by Irene Trenier and her son Craig and daughter Caroline

Unifying force of rugby

The establishment of the Police Service of Northern Ireland (PSNI) in 2001 and its excellent relationship with An Garda Síochána ushered in a new era in All-Ireland sporting initiatives. Chief among them was the Ireland Police Rugby team in 2003, made up of serving police officers from both forces, and very much the brainchild of Det Supt Eamon O'Grady of An Garda Síochána and Supt Alan Mains of the PSNI. The team played its first game against the Leinster Junior XV in March 2003 and since then has gone from strength to strength. It has played matches against visiting police teams, including the Australian Police, and also Irish and British Fire Services rugby teams. On two occasions Ireland Police won the Cyprus Tens tournament and has also travelled to Boston and the United Kingdom.

On 15 May 2009, the Ireland Police Rugby team memorably took on the British Police Rugby team at Donnybrook in Dublin. The game was refereed by Alain Rolland, the Irish International referee, and a reception was hosted afterwards by President Mary McAleese at Áras an Uachtaráin.

In September 2011, a major development took place. Building on the deepening goodwill, the Garda RFC and the PSNI formed a rebranded rugby team to line out in emerald green jerseys. The combined teams play under a new emblem taken from the crests of the two police forces. The badge incorporates the four rugby provinces, with the surrounds from the Garda crest on the inside and the PSNI crest on the outside. Their first match was held on 2 November 2011 against a British Police Select Team at Newforge, Belfast – their third fixture against the British Police to date. Despite valiant efforts, Ireland Police were defeated on a scoreline of 24-18.

The structure of Ireland Police Rugby is not without precedent and is constituted on the model of the Irish Rugby Football Union. It also reflects the vibrant cooperation and friendship between the two police organisations on the island of Ireland.

IRELAND POLICE RUGBY

Above: **Garda RFC Metropolitan Cup Final in 2010**

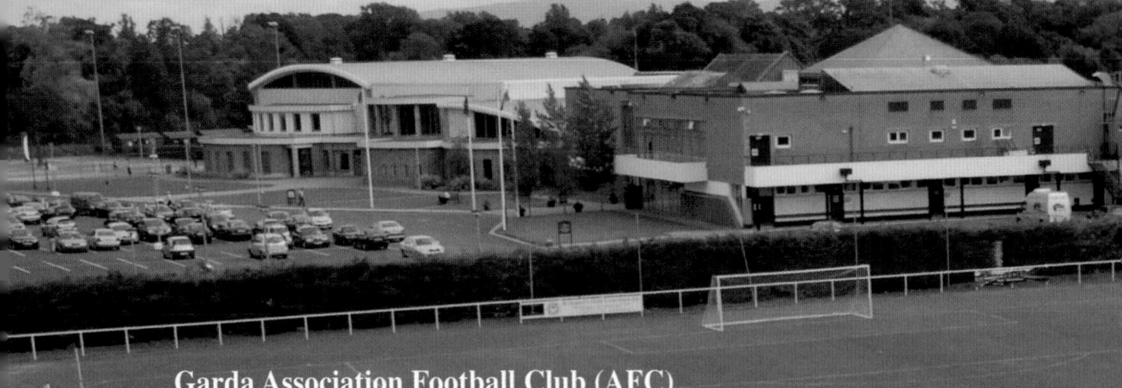

Garda Association Football Club (AFC)

The Garda Soccer Club was formed in 1960 when five members, managed by Dave Walshe, entered a five-a-side tournament in Dublin's O'Devanney Gardens. The team, which included Sean Ferriter, Paddy Coffey, Denis Naughton, Tom Reeves and Joe Coggins, was beaten in the final, but more significantly the Garda AFC was born. The club subsequently entered the Dublin Amateur League and largely through the efforts of Paddy Prendergast secured a home ground at the Garda Grounds, Phoenix Park. In that first season, Garda AFC won the Civil Service Cup, which at the time was a very prestigious competition.

The Garda AFC continued in the Amateur League for a number of seasons before joining the Athletic Union League (AUL) under the guidance of John O'Brien. Garda AFC enjoyed many fine seasons in the AUL before taking the decision in 1983 to apply for the Leinster Senior League (LSL). The club played its first game in this league in August 1983. As the rules of the LSL stated that senior clubs must have an enclosed ground, Garda AFC were forced to rent the Belvedere College grounds on the Navan Road, and continued to play there for the following three seasons.

One of the high points of the early years was in 1986 when Garda AFC qualified for the FAI Senior Cup and drew Derry City. The match was memorably played in the Brandywell before 14,000 spectators. Garda were beaten 5-0 but battled

Above: **Presentation by Motorola to Garda AFC prior to the FAI Cup game against Derry City in 1986.** ***Left to right:*** **Garda Commissioner Eamonn Doherty, Motorola representative, John Downey and Mick Leech**

Above: **Garda AFC v Shelbourne in the 1989 FAI Cup at Tolka Park.** ***Back row, from left:*** **P Hartnett, M Hennebry, D Edmunds, R Durrad, C Flynn.** ***Middle row, from left:*** **J Moore (physio), T Kinsella, R Smyth, J Dunne, J Sheedy, T Lavery (coach).** ***Front row, from left:*** **D Schutte, P Wilkins, G Keating (manager), D Kavanagh, L Dempsey**

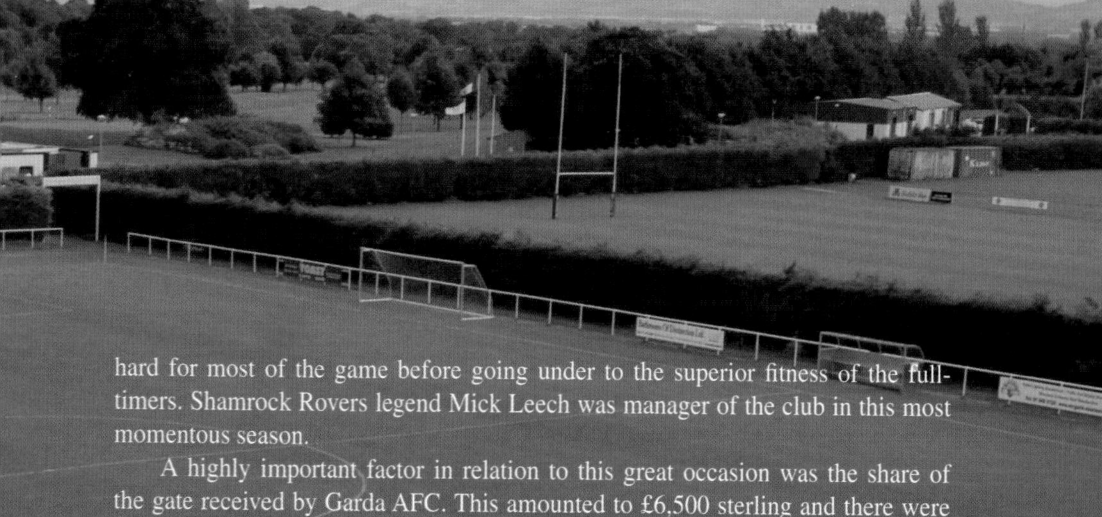

hard for most of the game before going under to the superior fitness of the full-timers. Shamrock Rovers legend Mick Leech was manager of the club in this most momentous season.

A highly important factor in relation to this great occasion was the share of the gate received by Garda AFC. This amounted to £6,500 sterling and there were immediate plans for it, as the club was in negotiations with the Garda Recreation Club concerning the purchase of pitches at Westmanstown. The club had agreed to buy two pitches initially and indeed developed what are now the soccer pitch and the main rugby pitch. Jim Murphy was the main negotiator on behalf of Harrington Street, while Vinny Hyland, Gus Keating, John Downey and Joe Dempsey were fighting for the Soccer Club. A request was made to the club to forego one of the pitches to facilitate the construction of a nine hole golf course. This was agreed and Garda AFC subsequently purchased the pitch. So at last the club had a home ground of which it could be proud.

The ground was officially opened on Wednesday, 11 May 1988 by Garda Commissioner Eamonn Doherty and blessed by Fr Brian Darcy in the presence of Garda AFC chairman Dave Walshe, secretary John Downey, PRO Larry Coady and the proud members of the committee. In September 2008, the Provincial Inter-Leagues Competition was held in Westmanstown and won by the Munster Senior League.

***Above:* Garda AFC committee in 2008 *(left to right):* Brendan O'Byrne, Paudge Hearne, Mark Hearne, Conor Flynn (manager), Terry Butler (coach), Robert Blake, Keith Rothery, Richard Garvey, Paul Cullen**

Since 1988 the Garda AFC has been involved in several memorable games in Westmanstown. These include FAI Senior Cup matches against Cobh Ramblers and Drogheda Utd; FAI intermediate cup matches against opposition from the four provinces; Metropolitan Cup victories over clubs such as St James's Gate, St Francis and Wayside Celtic. These clubs have all come to Westmanstown and enjoyed the excellent facilities and continue to do so. In addition, the National Garda team defeated Switzerland 7-2 in the qualifier for the European Police Finals at Westmanstown in 2006. The Garda AFC went all the way to the semi-final, where they were defeated 2-1 by Germany at the Borussia Dortmund stadium. The reaction of the Swiss delegation to the facilities on offer in Westmanstown was one of awe. In September 2008, the Provincial Inter-Leagues Competition was held in Westmanstown and won by the Munster Senior League.

For many years, the club has been sponsored by St Raphael's Garda Credit Union and has called the ground St Raphael's Park in recognition of their tremendous support to the club. A new committee took over in September 2008, comprising Mark Hearne, president; Paul Cullen, chairman; Richie Garvey, secretary; Bobby Blake, treasurer; and the following committee members: Paudge Hearne, Keith Rothery, Brendan O'Byrne, Mark Hearne, John Dunne and Ciarán Barry. Today there are three teams attached to the club. These are the Leinster Senior League Division 1B team managed by Conor Flynn and coached by Terry Buttler; the Senior League Division 1D team managed by Ciarán Barry and coached by Brendan O'Byrne; and the Leinster Ladies Division 1 team, which was beaten in the 2009 Cup final.

The current committee has worked hard developing the pitch to a high standard, which has paid dividends. The FAI's U-17s, U-18s and U-19s have used the facilities at Westmanstown for training, as has the Italian Senior Ladies team. Furthermore, planning permission was granted for floodlights on the pitch, which were installed in early 2010. In 2009, the club took over the DMR League, which was a huge success with great interest shown by most district teams. The national side, managed by Paudge Hearne, has brought great distinction to the club, having qualified for the European Police Championships following their defeat of Italy, 3-0, in Westmanstown and the Czech Republic, 2-0, in Prague. The event was held in Athens, Greece, in May 2010 and France emerged victorious. The year 2010 also held special significance for the club. It marked its fiftieth anniversary and all its many achievements since its birth were celebrated in Westmanstown during the year.

Gus Keating and Richie Garvey

Above: **Ladies and Mens Garda AFC in 2009**

Above: **Garda National Team after beating Italy in the European Qualfiers in 2009**

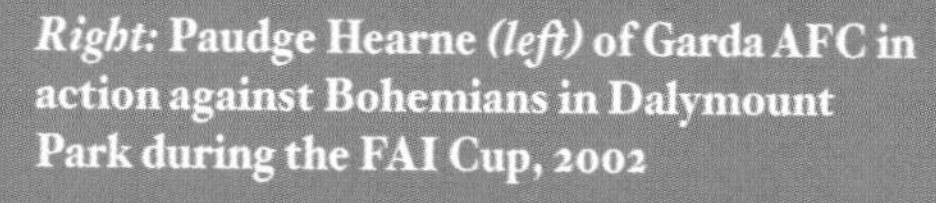

Right: **Paudge Hearne *(left)* of Garda AFC in action against Bohemians in Dalymount Park during the FAI Cup, 2002**

Westmanstown Golf Club

Great things can emerge from conflict and division and that was truly the case with Westmanstown Golf Club. One of its founder members and a past captain, Majella Ryan, recounts the days when a golf course at Westmanstown was just a flicker in the imagination, if not a source of ridicule:

> *Over the years, the Garda Club has been the venue for many meetings, both vocal and volatile. Yet again, it proved to be the gathering point for discussion and argument in the context of Westmanstown Golf Club. During the early part of 1987, a number of persons – all involved in the Garda Club – discussed, debated and argued about the possibility of establishing a second Garda golf club. Those involved were aware that a landbank had been purchased at Westmanstown by the Garda Club committee to accommodate the Garda GAA, rugby and soccer clubs. It should be borne in mind that at this time Stackstown Golf Club had been established at Rathfarnham as a Garda golf club. So the introduction of a second Garda golf club looked to be somewhat ridiculous.*

Majella Ryan and Bosco Muldoon were certainly the early pioneers of the club. They were undaunted in the face of the aforementioned opposition, and displayed an unquenchable thirst for success. Majella was stationed at the Crime Branch in Garda Headquarters, while Bosco was stationed at Finglas and also on the Garda Club committee at the time. In fact, Bosco recalls that Majella, a keen golfer, pestered him every week when they were working at the fundraising dances in Harrington Street where all the top Irish showbands played. It was they who ultimately set the wheels in motion for a second golf club. They became part of a group of five, who were essentially the 'founders' of Westmanstown Golf Club. The others included Cyril Doyle, stationed at Pearse Street and also secretary of the Garda Club at the time; Garda Club chairman Jim Murphy, detective inspector attached to the old CDU in Harcourt Square; and Jim Tymond, a detective attached to the Fingerprints Section at Garda Headquarters.

The idea of a pitch and putt course was envisaged initially by the Garda Club committee but the possibility of funding the purchase of additional lands at Westmanstown to accommodate golf was discussed over many evenings at Harrington Street. It was a decided advantage that those members involved at this time occupied key positions on the Garda Club committee. Eventually, a business plan for the establishment of Westmanstown Golf Club was compiled and submitted to chairman Jim Murphy and the Garda Club committee. The plan proposed the purchase of land adjoining the existing landbank at Westmanstown and to establish a nine hole golf course. Costings for course construction, machinery and portacabins were all set down, as well as membership details and the potential future revenue generated within the Westmanstown clubhouse by golfers. The plan was positively received by the committee and resulted in the setting up of an informal golf committee to advance the project.

This first committee comprised Cyril Doyle, captain; Majella Ryan, vice captain; Jim Tymond, secretary; and members Jim Murphy, John Murphy, Martin Callinan, Peter Hughes, PJ Browne, Willie McGee, Michael Dunne, Dick McDonnell, Jim Muldoon and Christy McCarthy. Cyril Doyle's workload as captain was enormous but he showed unswerving loyalty and dedication to getting the club up and running. There was a huge range of tasks to be undertaken by this dedicated group and everyone contributed in their own unique way. Membership of the club was opened and a serious drive made to enrol Garda members at the princely sum of £300. Though many responded well to the idea of a second golf club, others felt the Garda Club was wasting its time. Nonetheless, the committee decided the project should go ahead and set out to collect some money. The first person encouraged to part with his money was Peter Synnott, according to Bosco Muldoon:

> *During the late 1980s I met Peter Synnott of SDU, who asked me how many members we had got for golf. I duly informed him about thirty to forty and that it was on a first-come basis. Without hesitation, Peter told me that he would give me £300 the following weekend. Therefore, it was on 25 May 1988 that I issued Peter with receipt number one. Gazing at his ticket in disbelief, Peter tore into me about where were the other thirty or forty members. I smiled and told him that they were waiting on St Raphael's Credit Union!*

Clearly, Muldoon and Ryan were a persuasive double act. A former mens captain, Eddie MacBride, recalls his first introduction to Westmanstown, when Majella Ryan rang him in 1988: 'He asked me would I consider joining the new Garda golf club at Westmanstown and did I have £300, which was the joining fee. Well, I didn't have any spare money then, but Majella convinced me it was an offer I could not refuse – and I haven't looked back since!'

Despite their best efforts, the substantial Garda membership for Westmanstown did not materialise and this placed a degree of difficulty and pressure on a business plan envisaging full membership. Admittedly, there was a level of suspicion from many quarters that the landbank purchased to establish nine holes of golf was far too small and could never amount to a challenging golf course. On the other hand, Bosco Muldoon felt the potential Garda membership was sitting on the fence waiting for the course to be constructed so they could see what it was like prior to joining. According to chairman Jim Murphy, this stance was not feasible as money was needed urgently. A decision was therefore made in September 1988 to seek civilian members, i.e. non-Garda members. However, priority would be given to ex-members of the force, members' sons and daughters, and so forth. Notice of the proposed golf club was circulated by word of mouth in all the local areas and the response was nothing short of phenomenal. Membership interviews were duly arranged at the Garda Club in

Harrington Street. There were so many applications that the committee had to set out three separate weekends, both Saturdays and Sundays, and also some evenings for interviewing these applicants.

There were at least 1,000 applicants but only 200 people were needed to pay the £1,000 upfront plus the same annual fee. The reason being that the club was prohibited from taking in any more seven-day or five-day members because the Garda membership had to be greater than the civilian membership. The club also took in at least five life members at £6,000/£7,000 each. Granted, it was expensive at the time but great value today if you still hold membership. Leading businessman Ben Dunne was just one of those life members. Though he only occasionally played golf at Westmanstown, he did sponsor its first Pro-Am. As he had no desire for any publicity, the event was called the Paddy Skerritt Westmanstown Pro-Am, after the renowned Irish professional golfer. The event yielded a considerable amount of money for the club as well as putting it on the golfing map.

Sometime later, an approach was made by Luttrellstown Castle for corporate membership. Nick Bielenberg, who ran Luttrellstown, thought it a good idea that his hotel guests could play a round of golf so near the castle. Subject to various conditions, his application was accepted at £20,000 for a limited number of green fees per year. This removed the financial hardship somewhat and allowed the development of the club to proceed. Bosco Muldoon recalls that Luttrellstown also supplied the club with the best slurry available, 'if you were to judge by the smell', which was used to fertilise the fairways. Within a few years, however, Nick Bielenberg decided to build his own golf course at Luttrellstown with a fabulous wooden clubhouse imported from Norway. Golf Classics and race nights were also organised to fundraise for the fledgling club at Westmanstown. In 1989, the first classic raised in the region of £10,000 and hence became an annual event.

One of Europe's most distinguished golf course architects, Eddie Hackett, was responsible for the original design of the course. Eddie quickly displayed a sense of determination and spent endless time onsite. He drew on his considerable experience and produced the original nine holes. The contractors for the first phase of building were Tom Bryan and Tom Carroll, who had constructed many golf courses and were reliable, professional and very well regarded. Around this time Eddie was aware that the club needed a greenkeeper onsite and suggested a young novice, Gerry Byrne, who had completed his greenkeeper course at the Botanic Gardens in Dublin. Gerry was Westmanstown's first greenkeeper, who, according to Bosco Muldoon, was 'a great man with a sledge'. Gerry was also ably assisted by Johnny Gannon and workers from FÁS.

By October 1988, the Golfing Union of Ireland had accepted the affiliation of Westmanstown and the necessary guidelines and structures were subsequently put in place. In a Garda Club meeting in October 1988, it was decided that the Garda

Club should retain initial control and influence over the golf club and run it for 1988/89. Officers were elected as follows: Jim Murphy as president, John Murphy as vice president, Cyril Doyle as captain, Majella Ryan as vice captain, James Tymond as honorary secretary, Bosco Muldoon as honorary treasurer. Committee members comprised Christy McCarthy, Richard McDonnell, Peter Hughes, Michael Dunne, Peter Synnott and Brendan Fennell.

Though the facilities in the club in the early years were fairly rudimentary, they did little to detract from the socialising that took place. Eddie MacBride recalls how the course back then was only nine holes and pretty basic. The tee boxes were timber pallets with a heavy-duty mat on top and the clubhouse was a 40-ft container that served the club well. The club's first steward was Gerry Creagh, and his office, as well as the general office and changing rooms, were portacabins purchased by Harrington Street. Social events, such as barbeques, took place in the greenkeeper's shed and many a late night was had by golfers in this shed. It was 'as good as Augusta to all us beginners at that time', according to Eddie. One of Westmanstown's great characters was Ellis Poynton, who was the club's first security man and whose family lived locally for generations. Today he is remembered with great affection by members.

During the early years, golf committees at Westmanstown were always extremely proactive. No detail was too small or insignificant for consideration, whether it was the design of the club crest or the club colours. The club crest was a matter of particular pride. At a loss to decide on a suitable crest, the committee circulated the members for suggestions. There were entries good and bad but it was unanimously agreed that the bird of prey, the kestrel, was by far the best. The winning entry was submitted by Mick Carroll and the crest later superbly designed by Frank McMahon. During the embryonic years of the club, the kestrel nested in the trees adjoining the second hole and the GAA pitch. It made perfect sense that this wild bird would be an appropriate crest. Mick Carroll's prize, according to Bosco Muldoon, was 'an evening picking stones from the fairways! Mick did his fair share of work on tree planting and stone picking.' The original club colour was a mint-green and was worn by all the members. The change of colour to the dark bottle-green of today came about when the manufacturer of the mint-green colour was unable to continue its production. Today there is a range of colours worn but the club colour nonetheless remains the bottle-green.

An informal opening took place on Saturday, 29 October 1988, with golfers playing on temporary greens. Club president Jim Murphy welcomed all present and declared the course open. Cyril Doyle, then captain of the newly formed Westmanstown Golf Club, teed off much to the satisfaction and pleasure of all present. Some competitions had got underway earlier in September with the first-ever President's Day being won by Dermot Dalton on September 2nd and the Captain's Day won by Peter Hughes on September 30th. The club received several letters complimenting Gerry Creagh on his courtesy to other clubs when the club first started entering competitions. By December 1989, the golf club had 314 members of the force, forty-one seven-day members, sixteen five-day members and nine civilian life members. Each captain sought to improve the standards over the years in various ways. Joe Garagher was the member responsible for putting the fountains into the lakes as well as acquiring the generators that now constitute the back-up system in case of a power cut.

By 1991, having acquired an extra 47 acres of land and, by popular demand, the nine hole course was extended to eighteen holes with the addition of many interesting and challenging features. Course designers Declan Brannigan and Mel Flanagan oversaw different stages of redevelopment and enhancement. This proved to be very successful and with the natural spring lakes and the tree planting in the open areas, the course had taken its place among the well-known and established clubs for golf, with the added attraction of the other sports amenities and the very fine leisure centre and overall clubhouse. By 1992, the club moved into its current clubhouse and Westmanstown Golf Club had finally arrived. In 1997, the par-71 golf course was upgraded so that it could boast a golf course second to none.

It was no surprise that at some stage the reputation of Gerry Byrne would result in different golf clubs approaching him and offering him different challenges. In time, Gerry departed Westmanstown for new pastures, first arriving in Luttrellstown Castle Golf Club and then moving on again to the K Club. Michael McFeely arrived to replace Gerry and proved to be an excellent replacement. His input, energy, enthusiasm and skills have resulted in establishing Westmanstown Golf Club in the premier league.

As time went on, the golfing fraternity sought more autonomy in the administration of its own affairs just as the field sports at Westmanstown had become self-sufficient some time before. Advances were made to the Garda Club committee highlighting the intention of the golfing members to seek a lease of the golf course in order to be established in their own right. In April 1990, a subcommittee was set up to progress matters and eventually, in late 1990, a lease was granted to the club to run its own affairs and to regularise matters. Many meetings ensued in the subsequent years to hammer out the finer details, such as the annual rent to be paid. Eventually in May 1995, after putting it to a vote by their respective members, an agreement was reached whereby Westmanstown Golf Club would pay an agreed rent and lease conditions that were renewable at two-yearly intervals. A lease had been drafted to ensure all points discussed by both committees were properly legalised and would protect the general Garda membership. Eoin O'Buachalla and Company was entrusted with the valuation, while the club's solicitors Maurice Veale and Mr T Morgan BL advised on the document. Mr John S Farrell, barrister-at-law, was consulted by Mr Veale and the firm of Donal M Gahan and Company acted for Westmanstown Golf Club. Great credit is due to Conor McGuinness, who was an able mediator in all the negotiations, often in difficult circumstances.

Today not only can members take pride in the fine quality of the golf course and clubhouse but also in the successes enjoyed by the club. It won its first men's competition in 1997 with the Moore Cup. In 2000, the three wise men who had run the Kestrel Cup – Michael Concannon, Des Rogers and the late Billy Ashton – decided to run a Leinster-based competition for gentlemen sixty years and older. This was to be called the Jimmy Carroll Cup, named after Jimmy Carroll, a former member of An Garda Síochána who had become an international golfer and represented Ireland from 1948 to 1962. In addition, he was Irish Close champion in 1950 and 1953 and also won the Irish Senior's Cup with Sutton Golf Club on five occasions. Given such illustrious success, it was decided to celebrate Jimmy Carroll's life by setting up the tournament in his name. Today the link to Jimmy is carried on by his son Tom Carroll, who is currently a member of the club. Westmanstown memorably won the Jimmy Carroll Cup in 2000, and in 2005 the competition was opened up to become an All-Ireland competition, with the finals held at Westmanstown every September.

The club also invested much time and money in the juvenile section of the club, which proved a worthwhile exercise in that the club is now taken seriously in the big competitions, such as the Barton Shield, the Barton Cup and the Senior Cup. Its young players are performing well and playing with a great deal of confidence. In particular, its best player David Reilly won the Kilkenny Senior Scratch Cup in 2008 and the Leinster Youths Championship in 2009 at Headfort Golf Club, as well as the Faldo Series event at Lough Erne in 2009, which put him into the finals in Brazil in October 2009. David featured in the winning Leinster panel for the Inter-Pro Championships 2009 and also competed in the European invitation challenge tour event at Moyvalley Golf Club. The club's current course record-holder is Paul Keogh, who shot an incredible score of 68 gross playing off a handicap of 5 in the Captain's Prize in 2008; Paul also won the Lord Mayor's Trophy at Clontarf Golf Club in 2008.

The current membership of the club stands at 500 gardaí, 200 seven-day members, five five-day members, 200 lady associate members, eight intermediate members and 200 juvenile members. For the first time in the club's history, it recruited a golf professional, Edward Doyle, who previously enjoyed the position of head golf professional at Luttrellstown Golf Club. Westmanstown now looks forward to the great change and standards that Edward will bring to the club.

Majella Ryan, Bosco Muldoon, Cyril Doyle,
Jim Tymond, Ollie Nugent, Eddie MacBride

Year	Presidents	Year	Captains
1989	James Murphy	1989	Cyril Doyle
1990	James Murphy	1990	Majella Ryan
1991	John Murphy	1991	John B Muldoon
1992	John Murphy	1992	James Murphy
1993	John B Muldoon	1993	Tom Sloyan
1994	Brendan Fennell	1994	Martin Callinan
1995	Ted Murphy	1995	Peter Hughes
1996	Cyril Doyle	1996	James Muldoon
1997	Martin Callinan	1997	John Brennan
1998	Peter Hughes	1998	James Tymond
1999	James Muldoon	1999	RA McDonnell
2000	John Brennan	2000	Dan McInerney
2001	James Tymond	2001	Peter Synnott
2002	RA McDonnell	2002	Ronan Monaghan
2003	Michael Concannon	2003	John Joyce
2004	Peter Synnott	2004	Brian Moran
2005	Noel Manton	2005	John Kelly
2006	Dan McInerney	2006	Frank O'Neill
2007	Martin Tarmey	2007	Michael O'Shea
2008	John Kelly	2008	Stephen Crosbie
2009	John Joyce	2009	Eddie McBride
2010	Willie Cooper	2010	Gus Keating
2011	Fergal Keane	2011	John A Doyle

Above: Club Captain 2010, Gus Keating

Above: Club President 2010, Willie Cooper

Above: Westmanstown Golf Club membership sticker, 1988

WESTMANSTOWN GOLF CLUB

PRESIDENT - JIM MURPHY
V. PRESIDENT - JOHN MURPHY

CAPTAIN - CYRIL DOYLE
V. CAPTAIN - MAJELLA G. RYAN

HON. SECRETARY - JAMES P. TYMOND
HON. TREASURER - BOSCO MULDOON

Dear

On behalf of the Committee, I would like to welcome you as a member of Westmanstown Golf Club.

Westmanstown Golf Course will be open for play as and from 12 noon on Saturday 29th October, 1988 on the 9 hole temporary course.

Enclosed please find your Membership Card for 1988 and also a stick-on disc for display on your golf bag.

It is very important to ensure that your stick-on disc is displayed at all times when playing golf in Westmanstown and that your membership card is in your possession for identification purposes as a member of Westmanstown Golf Club.

Many thanks,

James P. Tymond
(JAMES P. TYMOND)
HON. SECRETARY

№ 1. 25th May 1988
Received from Peter Synnott
S.D.4 Harcourt Square
Three Hundred the sum of Pounds.
Re: Westmanstown Golf Club.
£300.00. (Bosco Muldoon)

TERSTON PRODUCT

Above: **Honorary secretary Jim Tymond announces the opening date of Westmanstown Golf Club**

Right: **Peter Synnott's receipt, the first member of Westmanstown Golf Club**

Above: Westmanstown Golf Club president Jim Murphy *(right)* opening the temporary course in 1988

Above: Captain Cyril Doyle teeing off in 1988

Above: Golf presentation in the Roselawn Inn in 1988. *From left to right:* Jim Muldoon, Jim Murphy, John Brennan, Pauline O'Reilly, Paddy O'Reilly, Jim Tymond, Bosco Muldoon and Cyril Doyle (captain)

Above: Captain's Dinner, 1989 *(left to right):* Jim Tymond, Cyril Doyle (captain) and Jim Murphy

Above: Westmanstown's first security man Ellis Poynton with his wife Brigid

Above: Westmanstown's first Pierce Purcell team at Forrest Little Golf Club in May 1990

Above: Westmanstown Golf Club committee in 1992. *Front row, from left:* B Fennell, R McDonnell, T Sloyan, J Murphy (captain), J Murphy (president), B Muldoon, J Muldoon and K Walsh. *Back row, from left:* P Synnott, T Murphy, W McGee, M Callinan, J Tymond, J Brennan, P Hughes and D Dalton

Above: Westmanstown Golf Club committee, 2003

Above: Westmanstown Golf Club Captain's Dinner, c1992. *Left to right:* John Murphy, club president, Ronny Delaney, Michael Carruth, Garda Commissioner Patrick Culligan and Jim Murphy, captain

Above: Greenkeepers at Westmanstown Golf Club, 2010

Above: **Trustees and members of Westmanstown Golf Club, May 2007**

Westmanstown Ladies Golf Club

A unique and historic meeting took place on Monday, 28 November 1988, at the Garda Club, Harrington Street. The first ladies committee of Westmanstown Golf Club was officially endorsed by the parent club. Largely through the efforts and determination of men's captain Cyril Doyle and Garda Club chairman Jim Murphy, the ladies now had an opportunity to swing their clubs and enjoy all that the sport of golf could offer. Charged with the job of getting the club up and running were the officers and committee for 1989: lady president Lucy Nugent, lady captain Hilda McGauley, lady vice captain Bridie Sloyan, secretary Mary Ryan, treasurer Naomi Fennell, social secretary Sara O'Sullivan and handicap secretary Finola McGarrity, as well as committee members Mary Tymond, Teresa Muldoon, Catherine Hynes and Una Cleary.

Though many ladies had expressed an interest in playing golf at Westmanstown, some had never played before, while others such as Lucy Nugent, Hilda McGauley and Bridie Sloyan had considerable experience and were to prove an enormous asset to the club. Indeed it came as a great relief to most of the committee that in the company of these seasoned players the club had a solid foundation of experience, knowledge and a resolute determination to ensure that the ladies of Westmanstown would be a force to contend with in the future. It is a tremendous tribute to these three women that so much was achieved in the early years in so short a time.

From the beginning, lady captain Hilda McGauley and her committee made it a priority to encourage all the ladies to support Ladies Day on Tuesdays, either by playing or just socially for a cup of coffee. Tuesday after Tuesday, it was very rewarding for social secretary Sara O'Sullivan and the committee to see so many arrive and support Ladies Day, a true sign of its success.

Meanwhile, the process of affiliation to the Irish Ladies Golfing Union (ILGU) got underway and proceeded smoothly. The club's application was proposed by its sister club, Stackstown Golf Club, and seconded by its neighbours, Lucan Golf Club, and processed with considerable speed. By 4 April 1988, Westmanstown Golf Club was affiliated to the ILGU.

Back on the greens, the ladies worked hard on improving their game and reducing their handicap. The unenviable task of allocating handicaps to the members fell to the handicap secretary Finola McGarrity. This job required endless hours of checking cards and scores, which she did with great aplomb. A constant source of help too was greenkeeper Gerry Byrne, who with his courteous manner, dealt with all the ladies that descended on his beloved course. Over the years, Cyril Doyle and subsequent men's captains and committees gave unfailing assistance to the ladies and ensured that any problems were dealt with in a manner that spoke volumes for the dedication and commitment of these members to Westmanstown Golf Club. The Garda Club was also the essence of generosity in responding to the club's needs, be it funding money for club pins or the use of their function rooms in Harrington Street.

In the first year, many social events were organised for the members to raise funds or just to meet and get to know one another. These proved very popular, in particular the quiz night held at the Garda Club in Harrington Street on 1 March 1988. Such was its success that it became a yearly event. Considerable help and support was afforded the club by manageress Helen Corrigan, who organised rooms for monthly meetings and quiz nights and handled general enquiries concerning Westmanstown Golf Club. Fundraising was and continues to be an integral part of the club.

As membership grew to sixty, club traditions became established on a firm footing. The Lady Captain's Prize was played on 10 June 1989 and won by Mary Moloney, followed by a marvellous night in the Garda Club. The Lady President's Day was held on 26 August 1989, with a large attendance, and the Lady President's Cup won by Valerie Dalton. This was followed by prizegiving, again in the Garda Club, and a night not easily forgotten by all in attendance. The highlight that year was the Lady Captain's Dinner held in the Garda Club on Friday, 3 November 1989. With a high turnout and an excellent standard of catering from Garda Club caterer Eddie Saul, the night was an outstanding success. By December 1989, the club had grown to 100 lady members.

The club has been blessed with many outstanding captains and presidents in its history to date. Sadly, some are no longer with the club today. In 1992, Mary Tymond became very ill and passed away while serving in her official capacity as lady captain. Naomi Fennell as lady vice captain took over the reins and officially took up the position of lady captain in 1993. Mary, a true Tipperary woman, is honoured every year in a competition called the Mary Tymond Memorial Salver. The club also pays tribute to Deena McKenna, a dear member, friend, past lady captain and past lady president, who died on 7 September 2009. *Ar dheis Dé go raibh a h-anam.*

Over the years, the club has taken part in several competitions. It has also enjoyed many memorable golf outings with its sister club Stackstown. As a result, it instituted the St Raphael's Cup, an annual competition between Westmanstown and Stackstown Golf Club committees. The club has also fielded teams for the Miele Ladies Fourball, Junior Foursomes, the Junior Cup, the CAWS Cup, Irish Mixed, O'Grady Cup, and the Mail On Sunday National Golf Classic. In later years, much help was given to the club in the co-ordination of these teams by Linda Scannell, Carmel Synnott, Mary Kelly, Stasia Connolly, Mary Carroll, Angela Doyle, Bernie Cunnigham, Valerie Dalton, Brian Moran, Betty McDonnell and Brian Daly.

The year 1993 witnessed Hilda McGauley set the first ladies course record with a gross score of 75, while playing off a handicap of 17 in the Lady Captain's

Prize. To date that brilliant record has not been beaten. In 1995, the first cup won for Westmanstown was the Mother and Daughter Tournament Cup: Anita and Margaret Concannon were the proud winners.

The arrival of the twenty-first century saw many more honours at the club. In 2000, the Westmanstown Ladies won the St Raphael's Cup and excelled themselves the following year by repeating it, while in 2002, Mary Boyle and Ethel Mulhern won the All-Ireland Australian Spoons Final. Also in 2002, the Westmanstown Ladies won the ILGU Autumn Teams (fourth team) final under the management of Pearl Monaghan.

In 2003, the Westmanstown winning duo of Stasia Connolly and Betty McDonnell won the All-Ireland Australian Spoons final for 9 for the second year running. In the same year, Kate Leyden – Juvenile (H/C 6) – also won the Duggan Cup for Westmanstown. In 2005, Westmanstown Ladies won the CAWS Cup final in a competition between Corrstown, Ashbourne, Westmanstown and Skerries golf clubs. The winning streak continued in 2009, when Stella Hickey won the LGU Bronze Section and Westmanstown won the Towns Cup, a competition between Hollystown Golf Club and Westmanstown in the format of men's, ladies and mixed team pairings. The CAWS Cup was also won by Westmanstown in 2009.

The year 2003 saw major drainage work carried out on the golf course. Thanks to the foresight of a great men's committee, the club went on to reap the benefits on the fairways and golf course in general. Now after twenty years in existence, the ladies of Westmanstown are firmly established. With unfailing commitment from the members and the high quality of lady captains past and present, the club has grown to maturity and can now compete with the very best of clubs throughout the land.

Lucy Nugent and Carmel Synnott

Above: **Westmanstown Ladies Golf committee, 1988/89**

Above: **CAWS Cup winners, 2005**

Year	Lady Presidents	Year	Lady Captains
1989	Lucy Nugent	1989	Hilda McGauley
1990	Lucy Nugent	1990	Bridie Sloyan
1991	Hilda McGauley	1991	Sarah O'Sullivan
1992	Hilda McGauley	1992	Mary Tymond
1993	Mary Ryan	1993	Naomi Fennell
1994	Mary Kelly	1994	Teresa Muldoon
1995	Nina Boyce	1995	Valerie Dalton
1996	Deena McKenna	1996	Mary Sourke
1997	Pauline O'Reilly	1997	Margaret Boyle
1998	Mary Sourke	1998	Mai Coogan
1999	Anita Concannon	1999	Anne Lawlor
2000	Mary Carroll	2000	Pearl Monaghan
2001	Margaret Boyle	2001	Pauline O'Reilly
2002	Pearl Monaghan	2002	Meryl Coade
2003	Dympna O'Riordan	2003	Eileen Foley
2004	Margaret Reilly	2004	Rosemary Keating
2005	Carmel Synnott	2005	Deirdre Daly
2006	Valerie Dalton	2006	Deena McKenna
2007	Marie Nicholls	2007	Mary Carroll
2008	Angela Doyle	2008	Linda Scannell
2009	Pat McQuaid	2009	Carmel Synnott
2010	Teresa Muldoon	2010	Mary Kelly
2011	Deirdre Daly	2011	Catherine Berry

***Above:* Lady Captain 2010, Mary Kelly**

Hilda McGauley's record-breaking score. *Inset:* Hilda McGauley

Above: **Australian Spoons All-Ireland Winners 2002, Mary Boyle and Ethel Mulhern**

Above: **Anita and Margaret Concannon receiving th Freddy Moran Perpetual Cup at the Mother and Daug Tournament at Donabate Golf Club in 1995**

Above: **CAWS Cup winners, 2009**

Above: Past presidents and captains. *From left to right:* Lucy Nugent (Lady President 1988/89), Pat McQuaid (Lady President 2009), Carmel Synnott (Lady Captain 2009) and Hilda McGauley (Lady Captain 1988/89)

Above: Ladies Committee, 2009: *Back row from left:* Bernie Cunningham (handicap secretary), Darina Curtis, Anna O'Reilly, Mary Higgins, Mairead Keegan, Helen McCole, Linda Scannell. *Front row from left:* Stella Hickey (treasurer), Lady President Pat McQuaid, Lady Captain Carmel Synnott, Lady Vice Captain Mary Kelly and Catherine Berry (secretary)

Westmanstown Bowling Club

In the autumn of 1994, at a Divisional Committee meeting of the Garda Club in Harrington Street, the then chairman, Jim Murphy, asked if anyone present knew anything about lawn bowling. His question took the committee by surprise. By way of explanation, he announced that the Garda Club now had a playable bowling green at Westmanstown but neither club nor players. The green had come about due to the involvement of Jim as well as secretary Christy McCarthy, treasurer Derek Byrne and the builder John Clince.

From an attendance of twenty-three members at that meeting, Dominic Power, the divisional representative at Garda Headquarters, was the only one to have previously stood on a bowling green. He failed to mention, however, that the first time was when he was eighteen and the second time two years later. Nonetheless, Dominic was duly nominated and elected to front a committee to establish a bowling club at Westmanstown. At the first meeting of the club held on 8 December 1994, Dominic was elected president and remained in that position for the next four years. Apart from the great co-operation between Jim Murphy and the executive of the Garda Club and John Clince, records show that Jarleth Connaughton (Traffic) and Ian Gillen (Kill-o-Grange) had been looking for a Garda Bowling Club for a number of years too. Their aspiration was finally realised.

Matters progressed at a rapid rate and, on 7 May 1995, Dominic officiated at the opening of Westmanstown Bowling Club. To launch the event, he rolled the first bowl in a match against the Garda team and a Bowling League of Ireland (BLI) selection. Nobody to this day remembers who won the match. However, at the dinner afterwards the guests were thoroughly entertained by Mr Jim Duff, then president of the BLI, the governing body of bowling in the Republic of Ireland. The assembled guests were also addressed by Jim Murphy, Phyllis Nolan, president of the International Police Association (IPA), and Dominic Power. In his speech, Dominic readily acknowledged the assistance of BLI secretary Jack Burke, as well as of Audie Devlin, secretary of St James's Gate Bowling Club and John Penrose of the same club. The logo of the club came in for special mention. Dominic explained that it incorporated the Westmanstown kestrel on a bowling ball and was designed by Phil O'Reilly (ex-Garda Printing Section) at Dominic's request.

The bowling green is acknowledged as one of the best and biggest natural grass grounds in the country thanks to the dedication of greenkeeper Michael McFeely and his staff. Michael has been with the club since its inception, although Westmanstown Golf Club also assisted with maintenance of the bowling green in the early years.

The first official visiting team to play at Westmanstown was from Lisnagarvey Bowling Club in Newry on 15 July 1995. As Westmanstown Bowling Club progressed it was registered with the Irish Bowling Association – the All-Ireland governing body – in 1998 and has evolved to its present status of being a thriving club with eighty male and sixty female members, ranging in age from ten to eighty-four years of age. The eighty-four-year-old is its only 'honorary' member: Mr Rory O'Hanlon still enjoys a game of bowling and frequently states to one and all that he 'would be dead long ago if not for bowling keeping me going'.

The green hosts the Annual Coiste Siamsa All Ireland Bowling Championships and also the Dublin Metropolitan Region/Garda Headquarters Bowling Championships, when Garda bowlers, both ladies and men, from Dublin, Cork and Donegal 'have it out' every year. A very successful event between An Garda Síochána and the Police Service of Northern Ireland (PSNI) is also played in alternate years at Westmanstown and Newforge PSNI Bowling Club. This competition has been held since the year 2000 and is an eagerly awaited event in the Garda bowlers' calendar.

The range of competitions and leagues that the club participates in continues to expand. The club plays in the Meath Zone Indoor Bowling Winter League and organises a four-day Junior Pairs Competition each August. This draws players from all the bowling clubs in Dublin and surrounding counties. The club and individual members have been successful at national level in BLI competitions. The men won the O'D Cup (Division 3) and the Bowling League of Ireland Cup in 1999 and the Cullen Cup (Division 3) in 2000. Club members Pat O'Looney and Chris Cushen won the Tyler (Pairs) Cup in 1998 and 1999, while Tony Hegarty won the Nassau (Singles) Cup in 2000. In 2008, the men had teams in Division 1, Division 2 and Division 5. In addition, the club has two teams in the Veterans League and have entered for two cup competitions at BLI level.

The ladies have showered themselves in glory over the years as well. The M&F Murphy Fours Cup was won in 1997 by a team comprising Marie Doyle, Kate Padden, Joan O'Looney and Pam Ellis, and also in 2000 with Marie Doyle, Sheila Gordon, Joan O'Looney and Pam Ellis. The WW Robinson Cup (Pairs) was won by Joan O'Looney and Pam Ellis in 1998 and by Anne Reid and Kate Padden in 2001. The McKeon Singles Cup was won by Eileen Foley in 2002 and by Anne Reid in 2004. The ladies have also won the Evening League twice; the M O'Sullivan Cup in 1997, 2000 and 2001, and the Bessie Sharp Memorial Cup in 2002. For the second time, five under-25 club members have been selected to play for BLI at international level. The ladies had teams in Divisions 1 and 2 in 2008 and two teams in the Evening League. In a mark of her outstanding success, Sheila Gordon earned a place on the Ladies International Team in 2007.

The club owes a great debt of gratitude to many other Garda members and civilians. Indeed current members often recall those who formed the first executive committee. Dominic Power was president and BLI delegate, Assistant Commissioner Pat O'Toole was honorary club captain, Paddy Martin was men's captain, Maureen Murray was lady captain, Val Lynn secretary, Andy Hyland treasurer, and the committee consisted of Jim Barber, Joan O'Looney, Christy McCarthy, Jack Horgan, Ian Gillen, Peter Kelly and John Duggan. Club presidents over the years have been

Dominic Power, Brendan Quinn, Michael Griffin, and currently John Walsh. All are serving or retired members of An Garda Síochána, who have given marvellous service and dedication to the club.

Thanks to the foresight of the 'founding fathers', Westmanstown Sports Centre has gained immensely, as has bowling generally in the entire country due to the following club members in particular. John McEvoy and Ricky Byrne, both club members, are competitions secretary and assistant secretary, respectively, of the All-Weather Bowling Association in which the club participates in the Winter League. Michael Griffin was president of the Winter League in 2008. Ricky was also competitions secretary of the BLI in 2008. Both Sheila Gordon and Bernard O'Keefe are registered umpires with the Irish Bowls Umpires Association. A great honour was bestowed on the club in the last couple of years when Sheila Gordon was elected president of the Ladies Bowling League of Ireland (LBLI) and subsequently nominated and elected president of the Ladies Irish Bowling Association. Maureen Murray, the first lady captain, was selected for trials for a place on the Irish International Team. Such is their skill and dedication that Sheila Gordon became a bowls coach, Kate Padden an assistant coach and Noreen McDonnell an emergency committee member of LBLI. In 2008, Dominic Power was nominated and elected as president of the Bowling League of Ireland.

As can be seen, Westmanstown has become a club to be reckoned with. It has hosted many international touring clubs over the years and every visiting team has been amazed at the facilities available at the complex. At BLI meetings, Westmanstown is one of the clubs that is regularly requested by visiting touring teams each year.

The original sponsors of the club continue to support the club, whose assistance is always much appreciated. They are the Garda Club/Westmanstown Sports Club, of course, as well as St Raphael's Garda Credit Union, Garda Depot Canteen and Superquinn Blanchardstown. In 2003, after talks between past president Brendan Quinn and Phyllis Nolan, former president of the International Police Association, the IPA Cup was presented and is played for by club members ever since. The IPA is still actively involved in the sponsorship of this much sought-after cup and sponsors prizes each year. For this, the club is truly thankful.

Finally, the club extends its gratitude to the founders, past and present, members of various executive, bowling and greens committees, the club's invaluable sponsors and all who have assisted in many ways over the years. Westmanstown Bowling Club continues to go from strength to strength!

Brendan Quinn and Dominic Power

Above: **Westmanstown Bowling Club, presidents and captains 1995–1999 *(back row, left to right)*: Dominic Power, Patrick Martin, Christopher Cushen, Bernard O'Keefe and Brendan Quinn. *Front row, left to right*: Maureen Murray, Joan O'Looney, Sheila Gordon and Pam Ellis**

Above: **Dominic Power rolls the first bowl for Westmanstown Bowling Club in 1995**

Westmanstown Bridge Club

The game of bridge, hailed as the greatest card game of all, has always enjoyed great popularity in Ireland, providing immense challenge and lifelong enjoyment. Once the Westmanstown Centre opened its doors in the early 1990s, it was only a question of time when it would cater for all the bridge enthusiasts in the catchment area. Hence, in 1992, John Paul McMahon – then a retired deputy commissioner of An Garda Síochána – assisted by John MacNamara and Ger Walsh, founded Westmanstown Bridge Club. These dedicated men saw bridge as more than just a card game. It was John McMahon's wish that the club would be a friendly, sociable, enjoyable, secure bridge club that would cater for all levels of bridge players. His cherished dream was that bridge players would just love to play in the club. Today you could say his dreams have certainly come true.

The club started with approximately thirty novice members and very quickly became a sizeable club with, at one point, over 200 members. The club continues to be very vibrant with members who span all categories of bridge players. With its affiliation to the Contract Bridge Association of Ireland, it gives players the opportunity to compete and test their skills in the many tournaments held at local, regional and national levels. Today, the club boasts many Master and Grade A players among its membership. Westmanstown has been represented with distinction in many external bridge competitions throughout Ireland.

The first president of the club was John Paul McMahon, followed by Ger Walsh, who both gave distinguished service. The club is now celebrating its eighteenth year in existence and enjoys wonderful support from the Westmanstown Sports and Conference Centre. With all grades catered for, the committee encourages beginners to join. Indeed new members at any level are always welcome. The excellent facilities afforded at Westmanstown means that enthusiasts can play all year round. It is expected that the club will feature prominently over the coming years in the various bridge activities of the newly formed Mid-West Region of the Contract Bridge Society of Ireland.

John MacNamara

Left: John Paul McMahon

Westmanstown Lawn Tennis Club

The inaugural meeting of Westmanstown Lawn Tennis Club took place on 9 February 1994 in Westmanstown Sports Club. On the day the following persons were elected to the committee: Jim Murphy as president, Christy McCarthy as vice president, John Leahy as chairman, Martin Doyle as vice chairman, Jo O'Leary as honorary secretary, Gabriel McIntyre as treasurer, and the following as committee members: Michael Dunne, Jim Blackwell, Karen O'Reilly, John Shannon and Kenneth Harrington. The official opening day of the club took place on 9 April 1994. It was a proud moment when Deputy Commissioner PJ Moran cut the ribbon and opened the courts.

To maximise potential, a development programme was put in place by the club with the assistance of Mr Declan Morgan in October 1995, to good effect. The club first entered both ladies' and men's teams in the Dublin Lawn Tennis Council Leagues in 1996, competing in Class 7 of these leagues. Over the next couple of years the club maintained its growth both in tennis terms and socially. A full and varied programme of events was established for both junior and senior members. Club championships and handicap tournaments for junior and senior members took place on an annual basis along with social events such as barbeques, strawberry-and-cream evenings, fun days, open days, Wimbledon Nights and Club Championships dinners, to mention but a few.

The club enjoyed a commendable amount of success in the various leagues it entered. The year 2002 was the centenary year of the Dublin Lawn Tennis Council; Westmanstown Lawn Tennis Club had both a ladies' and men's team in the finals of the Council's Summer League. The following year, 2003, saw both teams competing in Class 4 of the Council's Summer League. In April 2003, Westmanstown Lawn Tennis Club was integrated into the new state-of-the-art Leisure and Fitness Centre, Crunch Fitness Premier, located within the grounds of Westmanstown Sports Club, and is now known as Crunch Fitness Premier Westmanstown Tennis Club.

Jo O'Leary

Above: Pictured at the opening of the tennis club and courts *(front row, from left):* Christy McCarthy, Jo O'Leary, Kieran Sheehan, Fr Hilarion Cleary, PJ Moran, P O'Toole, Jim Murphy. *Back row, from left:* Gabriel McIntyre, Karen O'Reilly, John Doyle, Pat Doocey, Kenneth Harrington, Martin Doyle, Jim Blackwell and John Shannon

Above: **Anyone for tennis? The official opening of Westmanstown Lawn Tennis Club in April 1994**

Above: **Assistant Commissioner PJ Moran officially opens Westmanstown Lawn Tennis Club in 1994, flanked by Jo O'Leary**

Garda Sub-Aqua Club

The Garda Sub-Aqua Club was formed in 1964 when a small group in the Garda Swimming and Life Saving Club started to experiment with fins, masks and snorkels. Involving eleven members on Whit weekend in 1964, the first trip away was to Achill Island to dive the SS *Aghia Eirini,* a World War II wreck. With no portable compressor or local availability to refill bottles, the diving was limited but very enjoyable.

Throughout the 1960s, the Garda Sub-Aqua Club was inextricably linked with the 'job', with most active members seconded to carry out work-related diving. Nowadays the club is separate to the Garda Water Unit; however, many members of the unit have commenced diving careers with the club. In 1972, formal training courses began at the St John of God Pool, Islandbridge. In 1974, the club purchased a Zodiac Mark II, providing the club with safe, flexible and mobile maritime transport. The first compressor was purchased by the club in 1977, again providing the club with mobility and flexibility.

Membership was limited during the mid-1970s but in 1979 a recruitment drive took place, resurrecting the club. During the early 1980s, membership grew dramatically from twenty-two members in 1980 to seventy-two members in 1984. In 1982, the first foreign trip took place to the Glénan Isles in France. During 1984/85, the club had ambitious plans in purchasing a 65-ft wooden trawler, the *Resolution*. During this period, the club undertook an underwater swim from Holyhead to Dublin, completing the endeavour in under twenty-four hours. In 1992, the first rigid inflatable boat (RIB) was purchased, and quickly upgraded to a 5.6m Osprey with a 90-hp engine. Throughout the 1990s and 2000s membership of the club remained strong. On 24 April 2001, the club officially opened its purpose-built boathouse at Westmanstown built on land provided by the committee of the Garda Club and Westmanstown Sports and Conference Centre.

The Garda Sub-Aqua Club is affiliated to the Irish Underwater Council/ Comhairle Fó-Thuinn (CFT), the national governing body for recreational underwater sports in Ireland. Currently, the club has sixty-five insured members with CFT. Under the auspices of CFT, the club runs internationally recognised scuba diving courses, commencing each year in November. Pool training takes place over a sixteen-week period in the National Aquatic Centre. In February/March each year, all members partake in sea snorkelling at Sandycove Harbour. The club also makes a number of trips around Ireland every year, visiting remote harbours from where the best diving in northwest Europe is to be found. In addition, the club offers diving in Dublin Bay every Thursday evening and Sunday morning during the summer.

Foreign trips are regularly organised and the club in recent years visited Mexico, Cuba, Egypt and Croatia. Wreck diving is also popular with regular trips to wrecks off Dublin Bay, including the SS *Guide Me II*, the RMS *Leinster*, the *Marley* and the RMS *Tayleur*, in addition to the local wrecks on trips away. The club currently

Above: **Garda Sub-Aqua Club at a boat dedication in honour of founding members**

Above: **Garda Sub-Aqua Club at a pre-dive brief in Killary Harbour**

owns a fleet of three RIBs and one inflatable. Superb four-stroke marine engines ranging in size from 80 to 130 hp power all the RIBs, which are equipped with GPS units, depth sounders, wreck finders and VHF radios. The club now has two portable compressors for trips away and a permanent compressor located at the boathouse. Ultramodern oxygen equipment is also available.

There is ample opportunity for advancement in the club, and courses are run right up to examiner/instructor grade. Members can undertake other courses as well, such as Rescue Diver, Diver First Responder, and Powerboat Coxswains. The club is also active in charitable and other events. For example, it has assisted with the Special Olympics Torch Run, provided boat cover for the Garda Swimming Club and Triathlon Club, held fundraising swims for the RNLI, and annually supports a local youth initiative in Bray.

Liam Geraghty, John Doherty and Kate Curtin

Below: Garda Sub-Aqua Club member underwater at Clare Island, County Mayo

The Engine Room

Club Officers and Committee Members

Teamwork divides the task and multiplies the success.

Chapter

9

Chapter 9
The Engine Room

SINCE the establishment of the Garda Recreation Club, the officers and the district representatives who formed the various committees down through the years were an important feature in the growth of the club and all its various pursuits. Though many received due recognition among their peers, others were unsung heroes who hid their lights under a bushel. The Garda Recreation Club truly owes these men and women an enormous debt of gratitude for their unstinting commitment and dedication. Those who spring to mind include Ned Garvey, Tom Ryan, Jim Daly, Charlie Gaffney, Brian Prendergast, Jim Murphy, Ray McEneaney, John O'Malley, Cyril Doyle and Bosco Muldoon, to name but a few. Those carying the torch today include Mick Feehan, Derek Byrne, Dave Dowling, Dick McDonnell, Fergus Healy, Enda McCabe and Tony Twomey.

The representatives elected at district level were renowned for their hours of work on behalf of the members and for the achievement of effective teamwork. There was no magic wand waved to make everything happen. Hours upon hours of meetings took place with bankers, architects, solicitors, planning departments, local authorities and numerous others. Time and effort was freely given by these dedicated representatives without fuss or thirst for recognition. The hours of personal time given by the committee bore much fruit that can be witnessed today by one and all. Indeed, the success of these projects is an example to all groups coming together and striving to make life and conditions easier for their fellow man.

Club records and minutes show that certain personnel on the governing body were there for many years, having been annually elected to their positions, which underscores their dedication, duty of care and ability to work together. It was surely a huge task to undertake, but the mandate for all was given on the floor of the AGMs time and time again. This trust was not misguided. From the engine room of Harrington Street, guided by fearless and brave captains, sprang Stackstown and Westmanstown. And what a legacy! Under the stewardship of dedicated chairmen, change, innovation and adaptation continues to be the hallmark of the Garda Club.

Garda Club Officers 1961–2011

Year	Chairman	Vice Chairman	Honorary Secretary	Assistant Secretary	Treasurer
1961	EP Garvey		Jim Daly	Tom Ryan	Charlie Gaffney
1962	EP Garvey		Jim Daly	Tom Ryan	Charlie Gaffney
1963	EP Garvey		Jim Daly	Tom Ryan	Charlie Gaffney
1964	EP Garvey		Jim Daly	Tom Ryan	Charlie Gaffney
1965	EP Garvey		Jim Daly	Tom Ryan	Charlie Gaffney
1966	EP Garvey		Jim Daly	Tom Ryan	Charlie Gaffney
1967	EP Garvey		Jim Daly	Tom Ryan	Charlie Gaffney
1968	EP Garvey		Jim Daly	Tom Ryan	Charlie Gaffney
1969	EP Garvey		Jim Daly	Tom Ryan	Charlie Gaffney
1970	EP Garvey		Jim Daly	Tom Ryan	Charlie Gaffney
1971	EP Garvey		Jim Daly	Tom Ryan	Charlie Gaffney
1972	EP Garvey		Jim Daly	Tom Ryan	Charlie Gaffney
1973	EP Garvey		Jim Daly	Tom Ryan	Charlie Gaffney
1974	EP Garvey		Jim Daly	Tom Ryan	Charlie Gaffney
1975	EP Garvey		Jim Daly	Tom Ryan	Charlie Gaffney
1976	EP Garvey		John Murphy	Tom Ryan	Charlie Gaffney
1977	EP Garvey		John Murphy	Tom Ryan	John O'Gara
1978	Denis Devine		Brian Prendergast	Ann Glennon	Dan Corcoran
1979	Denis Devine		Brian Prendergast	Ann Glennon	Dan Corcoran
1980	Denis Devine		Brian Prendergast	Ann Glennon	Dan Corcoran
1981	Denis Devine	Noel McDermott	John O'Malley	Ann Glennon	Dan Seery
1982	Noel McDermott	Jim Murphy	Cyril Doyle	J Seymour	John O'Malley
1983	Noel McDermott	Jim Murphy	Cyril Doyle	T Flanagan	John O'Malley
1984	Brian Prendergast	Jim Murphy	Cyril Doyle	John O'Malley	Ray McEneaney
1985	Brian Prendergast	Jim Murphy	Cyril Doyle	John O'Malley	Ray McEneaney
1986	Brian Prendergast	Jim Murphy	Cyril Doyle	John O'Malley	Ray McEneaney
1987	Jim Murphy	Bosco Muldoon	Cyril Doyle	John O'Malley	Ray McEneaney
1988	Jim Murphy	Bosco Muldoon	Cyril Doyle	John O'Malley	Ray McEneaney

Year	Chairman	Vice Chairman	Honorary Secretary	Assistant Secretary	Treasurer
1989	Jim Murphy	Bosco Muldoon	Cyril Doyle	PJ Browne	John O'Malley
1990	Jim Murphy	Bosco Muldoon	Cyril Doyle	PJ Browne	John O'Malley
1991	Jim Murphy	Bosco Muldoon	Christy McCarthy	PJ Browne	John O'Malley
1992	Jim Murphy	Bosco Muldoon	Christy McCarthy	John Leahy	Derek Byrne
1993	Jim Murphy	Bosco Muldoon	Christy McCarthy	John Leahy	Derek Byrne
1994	Jim Murphy	Bosco Muldoon	Christy McCarthy	John Leahy	Derek Byrne
1995	Jim Murphy	Bosco Muldoon	Christy McCarthy	Noel Vizzard	Derek Byrne
1996	Jim Murphy	Bosco Muldoon	Christy McCarthy	Ned Grace	Derek Byrne
1997	Jim Murphy	Bosco Muldoon	Christy McCarthy	Ned Grace	Derek Byrne
1998	Jim Murphy	Mick Feehan	Christy McCarthy	Ned Grace	Derek Byrne
1999	Jim Murphy	Mick Feehan	Christy McCarthy	Ned Grace	Derek Byrne
2000	Jim Murphy	Mick Feehan	Christy McCarthy	Seán Murphy	Derek Byrne
2001	Jim Murphy	Mick Feehan	Christy McCarthy	Seán Murphy	Derek Byrne
2002	Mick Feehan	Enda McCabe	Fergus Healy	Dave Dowling	Derek Byrne
2003	Mick Feehan	Dave Dowling	Fergus Healy	Tony Twomey	Derek Byrne
2004	Mick Feehan	Dave Dowling	Fergus Healy	Tony Twomey	Derek Byrne
2005	Mick Feehan	Dave Dowling	Fergus Healy	Tony Twomey	Derek Byrne
2006	Mick Feehan	Dave Dowling	Fergus Healy	Tony Twomey	Derek Byrne
2007	Mick Feehan	Dave Dowling	Fergus Healy	Tony Twomey	Derek Byrne
2008	Dave Dowling	Enda McCabe	Fergus Healy	Tony Twomey	Derek Byrne
2009	Dave Dowling	Enda McCabe	Fergus Healy	Tony Twomey	Derek Byrne
2010	Dave Dowling	Enda McCabe	Fergus Healy	Tony Twomey	Derek Byrne
2011	Dave Dowling	Enda McCabe	Fergus Healy	Tony Twomey	Derek Byrne

Year	Assistant Treasurer
2002	Dick McDonnell
2003	Dick McDonnell
2004	Dick McDonnell
2005	Dick McDonnell
2006	Dick McDonnell
2007	Dick McDonnell
2008	Dick McDonnell
2009	Dick McDonnell
2010	Dick McDonnell
2011	Dick McDonnell

Above: Garda Recreation Club officers 1988/89.
Left to right: Ray McEneaney (honorary treasurer),
Jim Murphy (chairman), Bosco Muldoon (vice chairman)
and Cyril Doyle (honorary secretary)

Above: Garda Recreation Club committee, 1988.
Back row, from left: K McHugh, S Flanagan, D Walshe, J Mitchell, N McDermott, C McCarthy. *Middle row, from left:* O Nugent, M Dunne, PJ Browne, P Brunton, G Trenier, P Murray, E O'Reilly.
Front row, from left: M Corcoran, B Muldoon, R McEneaney, J Murphy, C Doyle, M Leenane, J Maloney. *Inset:* John O'Malley

Above: **Garda Recreation Club committee, 1991.**
Back row, from left: **D Walshe, P O'Leary, J Tymond, N Brennan, D Byrne, M Dunne.** ***Middle row, from left:*** **N Grace, M O'Regan, G Trenier, N Vizzard, T Rock, E McDonnell, E O'Reilly, P Murray, P McInerney.** ***Front row, from left:*** **PJ Ruddy, B Muldoon, C McCarthy, J Murphy, J O'Malley, J Leahy, R Ryan**

Above: Garda Recreation Club committee, 1992. *Back row, left to right:* E Boland, J Leahy, P McInerney, PJ Ruddy, P Murray, P O'Leary, T Rock, N Vizzard, G Trenier, E McDonnell, E O'Reilly, M Corcoran. *Front row, left to right:* D Walshe, N Grace, J O'Malley, C McCarthy, J Murphy, B Muldoon, PJ Browne, M Dunne, J Tymond, J Byrne

Above: Garda Recreation Club committee, 1999. *Back row, left to right:* Brian Woods, T Shaw, W O'Connell, J Leahy, P McInerney, T Rock. *Middle row, left to right:* M Feehan, M Corcoran, D Power, P Kelly, G Trenier, D Dowling, E O'Reilly, E McDonnell. *Front row, left to right:* J Byrne, B McCarthy, C McCarthy, Assistant Commissioner A McHugh, J Murphy, D Byrne, B Muldoon, E Grace

Above: Garda Recreation Club committee, 1992/93. *Back row, from left:* P Murray, J Byrne, T Rock, R Ryan, M Dunne. *Middle row, from left:* N Vizzard, M Corcoran, G O'Gara, J Duggan, D Power, E Gallagher, G Trenier, PJ Ruddy.
Front row, from left: D Walshe, J Leahy, C McCarthy, J Murphy, B Muldoon, D Byrne, E McDonnell, P McInerney, E Grace

Above: Garda Recreation Club committee, 2000. *Back row, from left:* W Kilcullen, F Lavin, A Bailey, D Buckley, T Rock, E O'Reilly, J O'Donovan, John Schley. *Middle row, from left:* N Brennan, K Houlihan, G Trenier, S Murphy, W O'Connell, E McCabe, P McInerney. *Front row, from left:* D Power, D Byrne, C McCarthy, J Murphy, M Feehan, E Grace, D Waters

Above: **Garda Recreation Club committee, 2003.** ***Back row, from left:*** **P McInerney, P Kelly, D Levins, W O'Connell, T Rock, M Hiney, D Waters.**
Middle row, from left: **N Brennan, D Power, K Houlihan, J Twomey.**
Front row, from left: **D Dowling, C McCarthy, M Feehan, D Byrne, S Murphy**

Above: Garda Recreation Club committee, 2007/8. *Back row, from left:* N Doolin, K Harrington, T Twomey, W O'Connell, M Hiney, B Ryan, K Houlihan, J Twomey.
Front row, from left: B McCarthy, E McCabe, F Healy, M Feehan (chairman), D Byrne, D McDonnell, D Dowling, R Garvey

Epilogue

THE first fifty years in the history of the reconstituted Garda Recreation Club have been remarkable. Reading through the pages of this book what emerges is a story of great pride, energy and affection for 'the Club'. Oftentimes it was the sense of foresight, strength of character and unselfish devotion of its members that propelled them in furthering the aims of the club. From humble beginnings in Kevin Street in 1961 to the entertainment heydays of Harrington Street, stretching to the greens of Stackstown and the superb leisure, golf and conference facilities of Westmanstown, it is a story of which members can be proud.

The singular vision of Edmund Garvey in particular shines through. The club has also been blessed with such loyal officers and members as Tom Ryan, Jim Daly, Charlie Gaffney, Brian Prendergast, Jim Murphy, John O'Malley, Cyril Doyle and Bosco Muldoon, to name but a few. The legacy today is one of world-class sport and leisure facilities beyond measure and compare. That said, our achievement cannot be seen as a stand-alone endeavour but part of the great sporting and leisure traditions of An Garda Síochána since its establishment in 1922.

But there is no time to rest on our laurels. The world of 1961 is very different to 2011. We now enter a period of consolidation, where we aim to grow and expand the membership of the club. Cognisant of history, we must do all in our power to carry the torch to a new generation. We live in turbulent times. The recent downturn in our nation's economy presents challenges like never before but with that comes opportunities too. New ideas and ventures will prevail regardless of recession or boom.

Despite these straitened times, the commitment of the club officers and Divisional Committee is unwavering. Into the future, we are looking at the possibility of providing overnight accommodation at Westmanstown and extending our holdings should the opportunities arise. At heart also is to respond to the demands for extra sporting and leisure facilities from our members. Now more than ever, in times of recession and stress, sport and leisure is a welcome outlet. Our aim is to convert good ideas into deeds.

I along with club officers, Chairman Dave Dowling, Vice Chairman Enda McCabe, Honorary Secretary Fergus Healy, Assistant Secretary Tony Twomey and Assistant Treasurer Dick McDonnell, take this opportunity to thank our membersfor their loyal patronage and invite new members to join the ranks of our illustrious club. We trust the next fifty years will be equally as exciting.

Derek Byrne
Honorary Treasurer
Garda Recreation Club, 2011

Above: Westmanstown looking north

MMISSIONER

UP
STAINES

GARDA SIOTHCHAN

ANNUAL SPO

(Under N. A. &

CRO

ws) will be hel

PA

ULY

p.m.

Stackstown Golf Club
Proud of our 3 times Major Champion
Padraig Harrington

EVENTS.
p Invitation (Short Limit)
Confined to Army & Garda

GÁRDA SÍOĊĊÁNA
A Da
METROPOLE
FRIDAY, 18TH NOV
Dancing 9 p.m. to 2 a.m.
METROPOLE BAND under direction of
TICKETS
(Inc. S nd Ta
Eddie Keher